FUNDAMENTALS OF NETWORK GAME DEVELOPMENT

GUY W. LECKY-THOMPSON

Charles River Media

A part of Course Technology, Cengage Learning

COURSE TECHNOLOGY
CENGAGE Learning™

Australia, Brazil, Japan, Korea, Mexico, Singapore, Spain, United Kingdom, United States

COURSE TECHNOLOGY
CENGAGE Learning™

Fundamentals of Network Game Development

Guy W. Lecky-Thompson

Publisher and General Manager,
Course Technology PTR:
Stacy L. Hiquet

Associate Director of Marketing:
Sarah Panella

Content Project Manager:
Jessica McNavich

Marketing Manager: Jordan Casey

Senior Acquisitions Editor: Emi Smith

Project Editor: Kate Shoup

Technical Reviewer: Maneesh Sethi

CRM Editorial Services Coordinator:
Jen Blaney

Copy Editor: Kate Shoup

Interior Layout: Jill Flores

Cover Designer: Mike Tanamachi

Indexer: Broccoli Information
Management

Proofreader: Sybil Fetter

For product information and technology assistance, contact us at
Cengage Learning Customer & Sales Support, 1-800-354-9706

For permission to use material from this text or product,
submit all requests online at **cengage.com/permissions**
Further permissions questions can be emailed to
permissionrequest@cengage.com

All trademarks are the property of their respective owners.

Library of Congress Control Number: 2008929230

ISBN-13: 978-1-58450-557-0

ISBN-10: 1-58450-557-5

Course Technology
25 Thomson Place
Boston, MA 02210
USA

Cengage Learning is a leading provider of customized learning solutions with office locations around the globe, including Singapore, the United Kingdom, Australia, Mexico, Brazil, and Japan. Locate your local office at**: international. cengage.com/region**

Cengage Learning products are represented in Canada by Nelson Education, Ltd.

For your lifelong learning solutions, visit **courseptr.com**

Visit our corporate website at **cengage.com**

Printed in the United States of America
1 2 3 4 5 6 7 11 10 09

DEDICATION

This book is dedicated to Nicole, Emma, and William.

PREFACE

This is a book about fundamentals—that is, the underlying considerations that network game designers and developers need to bear in mind when building a game that uses network communication to connect the game with the players and the players with each other.

Networks come in many flavors—from the Internet to a local area network (LAN)—each with its own advantages and disadvantages. What is common to them all is that they need to be accessed by some form of client. Some game releases are geared toward a heterogeneous client platform, from cell phones to PCs to consoles to handheld computers. Other games are released on a single platform—an approach that also has its advantages and disadvantages.

Then there is the gaming model: real-time, or turn based? A Web platform or a binary client? Text or graphics? A hybrid? And what about in-game currency? Avatars? Customization? Questions come thick and fast when the designers get hold of an idea and shake all the possibilities out of it, and developers need to know how far they can go in pursuit of the perfect game. This book lays out the fundamentals of this process not only to help everyone involved get a proper handle on what those questions might lead to, but also to help those of you who are just getting started learn what questions to ask in the first place.

If you are just about to build your first turn-based RPG delivered via the Web, then you will find many useful techniques and strategies to create your game in this book. And as you progress, creating ever-more elaborate game environments, this book will grow along with you. After all, the more ambitious the scheme, the more important these fundamentals become. Understanding all these fundamentals is the only way to make sure that the result is a quality game.

Speaking of which: Many games are mentioned herein—some have even served as case studies to examine what their issues might have been and how they might have been solved—but not every networked game. For those who take offense, wanting to know why I haven't covered their personal favorite ("I cannot believe you didn't mention [game], it is a perfect illustration of [whatever]"), there are three possible answers:

- I haven't played it.
- There wasn't space in this book to cover it.
- There just wasn't time.

My objective was to pick games that helped illustrate the points I wanted to make. It's up to you to draw the parallels with the game that you want to create, using the examples to guide you in solving the problems that you come up against.

It's a fascinating subject, full of challenges. Good luck!

ACKNOWLEDGMENTS

Once again, I have been supported by a great team. In particular, Kate Shoup has done a tremendous job of turning my prose into a proper book, with correct formatting, a nice layout, and flowing text. Thanks also to the technical reviewer, Maneesh Sethi, for making sure I made sense, technically speaking. Also, thanks must go to the collection of managing editors, layout staff, and everyone else at Cengage who's helped me by managing the project and letting me get on with the writing.

As always, I beg forgiveness from my family for the occasional book-related rant, and the bouts of isolation as I hammered out the chapters, and thank them for sticking by me through yet another book project.

ABOUT THE AUTHOR

Guy W. Lecky-Thompson is an experienced author in the field of video-game design and software development whose articles have been published in various places including Gamasutra and the seminal *Game Programming Gems*. He is also the author of *Infinite Game Universe: Mathematical Techniques*; *Infinite Game Universe, Volume 2: Level Design, Terrain, and Sound*; *Video Game Design Revealed*; and *AI and Artificial Life in Video Games*.

CONTENTS

CHAPTER 3   **PUTTING GAME NETWORKING TECHNOLOGY TO WORK**   **55**

CHAPTER 4   **A COMPARISON OF NETWORK GAME TYPES**   **79**

INTRODUCTION

The intention of this book is to provide you with information about developing network games. It is broken down into three core areas:

- **Design.** Discussions of the initial stages of a game project and the decisions that need to be taken in order to produce an outline.
- **Design and development.** The creation process. How to choose the technologies and underlying infrastructure to implement the design.
- **Development.** The nuts and bolts of game creation. Practically a book in itself, this section looks at the basics of testing and programming network games.

The purpose of covering the topics in this way is simple: It guides you on a journey that covers *all* fundamental aspects of network game creation. At each step, there are examples of real games and solutions that have been developed to solve their various problems.

DESIGN

The design area looks at what sets network game development apart from single-player and multi-player offline game development. The chapters cover the material as completely as possible, and comprise:

Chapter 1: The Challenge of Game Networking

This first chapter describes the challenges that game developers seeking to unleash the power of network-enabled multi-player gaming might face. This includes a brief look at the types of networking and hardware available, as well as the platform considerations.

Chapter 2: Types of Network Games

The second chapter picks up where the first one leaves off, looking at the other side of the discussion: the game itself. While this will be, in many ways, constrained by the availability of networking technology on the chosen platform, you will still need a good understanding of the underlying styles of network games (from text-based multi-user dungeons to virtual worlds) before being able to choose the best technology for your game.

Chapter 3: Putting Game Networking Technology to Work

Every network game is built up of components in a layered fashion, from the front-end to the server. In between are layers that are consistent with the available technology and type of game chosen. The eventual implementation will depend on factors such as the user (player) platform, game environment update model, and type of networking used.

Chapter 4: A Comparison of Network Game Types

Having covered all the underlying design aspects, this chapter pulls them all together to compare the various possible game types to establish the differences and similarities between them. The general idea is to impress upon the reader the need for a best-fit approach to selecting the game type and supporting technology.

DESIGN AND DEVELOPMENT

The design and development section concentrates on ways that the design aspects and development aspects of game creation come together. The reason for grouping these two aspects is that they have to work together to produce the final result; design considerations have an impact on the development, and vice versa.

Chapter 5: Creating Turn-by-Turn Network Games

The first of the design-and-development chapters outlines the development tasks for turn-by-turn games—from e-mail-based to Web-based online games—highlighting the particular differences from other game models.

Of particular interest are discussions of the revenue models used to finance the game and a case study of *Project Rockstar*, a fairly successful Web-based online game.

Chapter 6: Creating Arcade and Massively Multi-Player Online Games (Real-Time)

As a contrast to the previous chapter, this chapter highlights the particular issues relating to real-time network game development and how the design can influence the success of the eventual implementation. Again, there are case studies, this time of two massively multi-player online role-playing games, that illustrate the various hurdles that must be overcome in designing and developing the game.

Chapter 7: Improving Network Communications

This chapter deals with the issues raised in Chapters 5 and 6, giving causes of, and solutions for, most of the major networking headaches that can plague online game development. As with other chapters in this key section, the solutions are part design and part development oriented, and can be implemented almost immediately.

Chapter 8: Removing the Cheating Elements

The more popular a game becomes, the more likely it will be that cheats will try to circumvent the game logic for their own ends. This chapter seeks to provide a reasonably complete analysis of where the possible cheats will occur (hardware and software hacks), as well as ways to plug the gaps in the game design and development that make cheating possible.

DEVELOPMENT

The last section of the book covers purely development topics—where the developers have a direct responsibility to see that the design is implemented correctly with respect to the various features that the final game should have.

Chapter 9: Testing Network Games

The penultimate chapter deals with testing the network, logic, and gameplay aspects of the game using various hardware and software solutions. Various advanced techniques are covered, showing how maximum test coverage can be obtained for minimum effort by reusing AI code, using prediction and test data sets, and using traditional testing techniques—all implemented in advanced solutions.

Chapter 10: Network Programming Primer

Finally, this last chapter of the book covers network programming, from TCP to datagrams to socket programming, as well as scheduling from both the client and server sides of the game. Attention is also paid to using off-the-shelf solutions to speed up development, whilst keeping security and scalability as high as possible. There are plenty of coded examples to illustrate the principles under discussion.

ON WITH THE SHOW!

Using all of the aforementioned knowledge, as well as traditional game-development skills, you will be well equipped to create a multi-player network game—be it a Web-based game, a turn-by-turn combat simulation, or a full-on first-person shooter with advanced networking support.

One thing to remember: Network game creation is not just about adding network support to an existing single-player game. Rather, it is about creating a network game from the ground up—hence the emphasis in this book on both design and development aspects. If this principle is followed, then the game stands a good chance of success, as long as it ticks all the relevant boxes. With that in mind, let the fun commence!

THE CHALLENGE OF GAME NETWORKING

In This Chapter

- Types of Networking
- Network-Gaming Models
- Data Exchange in Network Gaming
- Key Decisions

This first chapter sets the scene for the book, giving an overview of the decisions made in choosing networking technology for game design. In doing so, I refer to various existing game models, and even some specific games that take advantage of networking to add a new dimension to their basic gaming model.

In some cases the game would not even exist without networking, while in others the addition of networking technology opens new possibilities for multi-player gaming or extensions to the single-player experience.

Although the technologies and possibilities are very different, they share the same basic underlying networking philosophies, principles, and challenges that this book is designed to help the game designer meet. We concentrate on four essential areas:

- Dial-up and PPP networking
- The Internet and World Wide Web
- Wireless LAN
- Cellular technology

In addressing these four areas, we also look at related networking mechanisms such as local area network (LAN) gaming and simple text-based interfaces as well as graphical ones. Remember, however, that this is essentially a design book, not a programmer's guide; the technologies are always discussed for the various enhancements they make to the playing experience.

The guiding principles mentioned here are to help design a game that makes the best use of available networking technology. It is up to the programmers to realize that dream when the game is developed. On the other hand, designers need to be aware of what is possible and what is not before designing a game that is either impossible or impractical to create. Part of that is in understanding how the various technologies enable, or restrict, network gaming, and that is what this chapter seeks to achieve.

TYPES OF NETWORKING

The first thing that the designer needs to know is what types of networking technology are available to be used in games. They can then start to look at what network-gaming model might be most appropriate for the game in question.

The following is not an exhaustive list, but roughly follows the development of technology chronologically, from the very first network games to more recent enabling technologies. As always with game design, it is important to understand the early attempts at using the available technologies so that lessons can be learned.

The various types of networking are just tools, mechanisms by which the networking portion of a game is created. As such, they should not influence the gameplay or design, in the same way that the choice of platform does not influence the gameplay except to restrict or enhance where the platform has limitations or strengths, respectively.

Of course, the platform and networking technology available are probably going to be linked; this will have a direct effect on the kind of network game that can be created, but it should not be allowed to dictate the game design.

On the other hand, there are specific network-gaming models that can only exist because of some of the more modern network types and protocols. Without these protocols, certain games just wouldn't be possible. For example, the World Wide Web has made browser-based multi-player, multi-platform games possible where the server controls everything down to the presentation layer.

Arguably, this is an illustration of where the type of network technology available has influenced the design and development of specific games, and there are others. But, since most game networking will be *in addition* to existing non-networked gameplay rather than the core principle of a specific game, the principle that the type of networking chosen should not influence the core game design still holds.

This is an important distinction that will be frequently restated: Networking technology can either enhance a game that is essentially non-networked, or it can be the principal point of interaction with the game. In the latter case, there are some games (*Eve Online*, *Everquest*, and *Unreal Tournament*, to name a few) that simply would not work as non-networked products.

Dial-Up and PPP Networking

In the beginning, computers talked to each other over a modem connection, supported by the plain old telephone system (POTS). The term *modem* is short for modulator/demodulator and enables one computer to talk to another over a simple phone-line connection.

This works by taking the data (digital) and turning it into a sound-based signal (analog) that can be transmitted without loss over a standard copper telephone line. You might, for example, have heard a fax machine transmitting data to another fax machine using the same kind of protocol.

The whistles and crackles that represent the modulated data are created by the modem and transmitted as sound through the telephone system. They are then received at the other end by the modem of the receiving computer (or fax machine) and demodulated before being passed to the operating system for processing (or printed onto paper).

The data that is transmitted has to be standardized, and there is a certain amount of negotiation that happens between two modems (or fax machines), called the *handshake*, that allows them to settle on a specific mechanism for data exchange.

This basic model has remained with networking ever since. Data leaves the sending computer having been encoded by the operating system. The operating system (Windows, for example) then passes it to an external peripheral (the modem), whose sole function is to turn that data into something that can be transmitted over a network and make sure that it is done correctly.

For the most part, the mechanisms that can be used are transparent; that is, most development environments provide automatic protocol support, meaning that the developer has only to worry about the higher-level functions. So the work of actually performing the handshake, making sure that the data is received correctly and reporting that success correctly is usually handled by the device and operating system.

This basic premise of all networking technologies is shown in Figure 1.1, which illustrates the simplest approach—point-to-point networking.

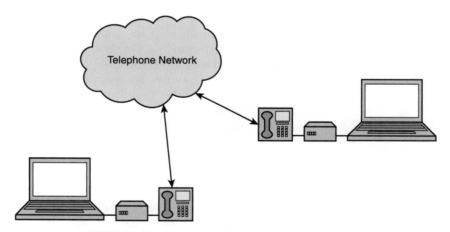

Telephone Network

FIGURE 1.1 Peer-to-peer modem networking schematic.

The term *dial-up* refers to the fact that the sending computer, depicted on the left side of Figure 1.1, dials a number to reach the other computer. This number is a regular phone number attached to the house (or office) where the computer on the right side of the diagram is located.

The computer forms a single connection over the phone network to a single point, and only that point. Each device can maintain only one connection at a time (think of a fax machine). This restriction is behind the meaning of the term Point-to-Point Protocol (PPP). Of course, from that point, other connections can be made to other computers, thereby connecting two networks by a single phone line. This internetworking is what gave rise to the Internet, and subsequently, the World Wide Web. However, we are getting ahead of ourselves slightly.

From a gaming perspective, despite the relative primitiveness of the hardware involved, PPP networking allowed some reasonably sophisticated gaming constructs. These were often made possible using bulletin board systems (BBS), which connected computers to a server capable of interacting and storing a persistent information state.

Initially, this information state was restricted to comments and communication via the BBS. People placed requests for software, which could be downloaded or just connected to share opinions, information, or chat. Over time, it became clear that the ability of the server to store persistent information and attach that information to a specific user, as well as allowing multiple simultaneous connections, could be used for multi-player online gaming. So, puzzle games like chess could be played in a two-player environment, with the server maintaining the game state and allowing for the conduit to be formed between the two players. Traditional single-player puzzle games could also be extended by storing the game levels on the server and allowing the player to play via his or her modem.

Play by e-mail also became possible thanks to the messaging systems—electronic mail—that made this exchange medium possible. Play by e-mail opened up some forms of complex social gaming (*Dungeons & Dragons*, for example) to wider audiences who would otherwise never have had the opportunity to play together.

There were, however, some limits on what could be achieved. For example, interactive single-player-versus-the-computer games were limited by the dial-up speed, which in turn limited the amount of data that could be exchanged in real time. In addition, the hardware limited the kinds of games that could be displayed; even if the computer were capable of graphics, early networked games could offer only a text interface.

Many games worked simply by the client computer displaying text-based graphics relayed back from the server. This was partly due to the fact that most of the systems involved were entirely dissimilar; the only common denominator was the fact that, because the computers connecting to the server could support BBS, the game developers could be sure that similar interactions were possible.

The obvious extension to this was to enable network support for *specific games*, allowing owners of these games to interact simultaneously, sharing game information directly (PPP) or through a server. Network gaming was born.

Local Area Networking

The local area network (LAN) is a step up from a PPP network; in a LAN, a collection of computers can be connected and can communicate with each other. *Local* means that the computers are connected directly together (usually by wires) and to a central server, but generally all within a very close distance.

The closer proximity of the LAN enables larger amounts of data to be exchanged, at higher speeds. The farther machines are apart, the more complex the actual data exchange becomes in order to maintain the same data integrity and throughput. This, in the early days of network gaming, understandably made LAN parties very popular.

A *LAN party* is essentially a game-playing extravaganza in which hundreds of gamers come together under one roof, connect their machines on a vast local area network, and play multi-player network games. These can be free events (sponsored) or events backed by an entry fee. Of course, LAN parties can also exist on a much more personal level, sometimes just between a small group of friends. Social gaming in this vein is growing in popularity with platforms that support both networking and non-networking components.

Contrary to what people might have predicted, LAN gaming has not been killed off by the rise of the Internet. For social reasons as much as anything else, LAN parties are still very popular amongst gamers.

The very first clutch of multi-player extensions to existing single-player games like *Quake* were played using a LAN. A LAN was the only way it was possible to allow large numbers of players to participate in such a complex game environment. The real-time nature, coupled with reasonably complex data sets, meant that the LAN was really the only solution.

Local area networking also provides the basic configuration for wide area networking. The protocol, TCP/IP (Transfer Control Protocol/Internet Protocol), that allows local networking also permits wide area networking with the addition of a modem. In the previous discussion of PPP, you saw how a server can provide this. The very first Internet service providers (ISPs) did exactly that—they provided a dial-in location, allowing users to connect to the server, and hence the wider worldwide network that was the fledgling Internet.

Once line speeds began to pick up, both at the dial-in level and the main networking backbone, Internet gaming—or at least multi-player network gaming over TCP/IP and wide area networks (WANs)—became a reality, opening the field to many more potentially *simultaneous* players than ever before.

The Internet and World Wide Web

I'm going to oversimplify this a little bit, since the underlying protocol is so similar. The Internet and World Wide Web (WWW) can be seen as an extension of LAN models, to connect multiple LANs together.

So, the extension of LAN gaming to include the Internet as a WAN is made possible by the fact that much of the same technology is used. LAN and Internet gaming can also co-exist, although it is clear that LAN users would have a theoretical performance advantage in any hybrid network model used for multi-player gaming.

This potential advantage might manifest itself through higher connection speeds leading to a reaction-time advantage, as well as advantages relating to the stability of the networking connection. The Internet is not renowned for being either particularly fast or reliable, although it is improving steadily.

Usually when we think of network gaming, it is with the real-time multi-player market in mind. We should not forget that there are many other potential gaming models made possible by network gaming. Some of these will take on a new impetus when the Internet and World Wide Web are brought into play.

The *Magic: The Gathering* card-based game is a good example of this. It can be played over a network and revolves around using cards wisely in a kind of statistics-oriented role-playing game (RPG). It really comes into its own, however, when the only method of communication with other players is through the game itself.

Although WWW and Internet networking technology can be looked at as just the LAN protocol TCP/IP writ large, it also comes with its own set of issues to resolve. These are various, but include unintentional disconnect and lag.

Unintentional disconnect occurs when the Internet backbone breaks down, forcing the connection between the client and server to be interrupted—sometimes for several minutes. The TCP/IP protocol is essentially connectionless. In other words, once the request is made and a response returned, the protocol goes into a dormant state.

This might work for Web pages, but is a little bit of a problem for fast-paced action games where a split-second delay can mean the difference between in-game life and death. The nature of the Internet protocol is that routes for the data are often decided dynamically, and so an alternative is usually found in time, but there are no guarantees.

Lag is a different, but connected, issue. It occurs less and less often, but is defined by the delay between the player requesting an in-game action and the action manifesting itself in the game environment. Quite often it is impossible to tell whether this is because the request has not reached the server or because the updated state of the game environment has not (yet) been received by the client.

Quite an issue for game designers.

There is another unique aspect of Internet gaming, and that is the fact that the user is largely on his or her own in the ether. Now, this aspect isn't unique because players are alone; single-player gamers were, after all, always on their own. It is unique because players are on their own and yet are *connected* to other players through an abstract game universe.

If players try to cheat or have a genuine problem, it is that much more difficult to interact with them. In single-player games this difficulty wouldn't matter much; it's only the player against the machine. But in multi-player games, this kind of issue has consequences *for other players*.

Of course, this issue is then compounded by the fact that there will be a potentially much larger collection of heterogeneous platforms to support than with other classical single–player gaming or LAN-gaming models. This is true not just from a machine-specification point of view, but from an ISP point of view also.

Different ISPs will have different configurations, allow different uses of their inter-network connections, and respond differently to technical problems—all of which is outside the control of the people running the game server and gives more margin for problems that will potentially affect sales of the game.

For example, connection speeds (bandwidth) vary between providers. Connections with a 2- to 3-megabit (Mb) bandwidth might be common for Internet access using broadband technology, but clearly the designer can't count on everyone having the best connection.

Ideally, the design needs to take into account the lowest common denominator. This might even be the humble 56Kbps modem over a plain old telephone line. The lowest common denominator will affect the gaming model; it will not matter for games that are played through the browser with text and minimal graphics, but it might restrict the gaming environment for a multi-player first-person shooting action extravaganza.

So, a design balance must be struck between complexity of the game and capability of the platform, *including*, for the purposes of this book, the network connection—over which, it is worth repeating, the designer has no control.

At the heterogeneous extreme, if a game designer wants to create games for the wider Internet market, then this will bring its own complications. Some people, for example, will be using cellular technology to access the Internet with a handset and not a computer. This will have an effect on bandwidth, platform technology, and so forth, which dictate the networking and game complexity. In effect, the more platforms, and the more diverse they are, the more the design of the game is going to be complicated. While we look only at the networking component in this book, it has a direct effect on the game design as a whole, and so we will be touching on most areas of traditional game design.

Wireless LAN

Wireless LAN (also known as *WiFi*) connects devices via radio technology, providing large-bandwidth, high-speed connectivity. Again, the protocol is basically TCP/IP, allowing any device with a driver to enable an application to use the technology.

Special hardware is used, which must be supported at the operating-system level—just like any other networking component. This insulates the designer and programmer from having to explicitly design for WiFi connectivity.

WiFi is not as fast as regular LAN, but public-access speeds of 1–2 Mbps are common at the time of this writing. It is worth pointing out that wired LANs typically offer 100Mb bandwidth, with gigabit (Gb) connectivity around the corner.

Over WiFi, machines can connect via a PPP to each other (and many others simultaneously) or they can connect to network points that provide services. These services include printing, file sharing, and Internet access. So, apart from the wireless aspect, WiFi is much the same as regular LAN.

Where WiFi is potentially special is in the fact that, given the right security access control protocol (proprietary to the game or using accepted security standards like WPA or WEP) and sharing of security information between trusted parties, anyone with wireless LAN can connect to anyone else with wireless LAN.

Since it is all based on open standards, special networking can be built into the game to allow these *peer-to-peer* relationships to take place. In this case, peer-to-peer means that one machine is connecting directly to another, for the purpose of information sharing. They could be ad-hoc relationships (discovered on the fly) or pre-arranged relationships. One obvious example is a temporary relationship with an Internet access point. Another might be the connection of two machines to play a game without a network being established to facilitate this communication.

Of course, there are also security concerns. For example, WiFi might be open to snooping technology because data goes out as radio waves. Partly because it might be poorly understood by the gamer, this could lead to possible security loopholes. In the worst-case scenario, this might extend to turning off security altogether.

This may or may not have an effect on the game design directly. However, the game is just another application that exists on the gaming platform, and as such provides a potential Trojan horse for malicious software to take over the player's system. It is the responsibility of the game developer to

- Make sure that his or her game has no loopholes.
- Educate the user such that he or she operates in a secure fashion.
- Build in as much security as possible and appropriate.

Clearly this list could be relevant to any kind of network gaming, but the nature of wireless networking means that the game developer and gamer both should be doubly careful. Since it is relatively difficult for the player to actually determine that an unexpected connection has taken place, it is a rich seam of hacking potential for those with malicious aims.

Along with WiFi networking, Bluetooth networking is also possible, but typically allows only for pairing with another device (be it temporarily) to share data. This means that the gaming model that will be most likely to make use of this technology will involve sharing of in-game artifacts (characters, prizes, etc.) for connectionless play. Bluetooth is a technology that uses low-power radio connectivity to replace cables between devices. WiFi differs from Bluetooth in both the speed of the connection and the fact that it is designed for true networking—i.e., replacing a LAN connection. In contrast, Bluetooth connections are point to point and typically, once a pairing has been created between a computer and device, that is the *only* pairing that can exist for that device. To use a different pair of devices, at least one of them will have to create a new relationship.

For example, a player might spend time in-game on his or her own machine (console or handheld, for example) building a character that can then be sent via Bluetooth to another device and interact with another player's character. The result can then be returned, again via Bluetooth, at some later moment in time. The time between the sharing of the character and the result could be measured in seconds, hours, or even days, depending on the gaming model.

Again, the technology used is wireless, but the lower range and pairing restriction tends to mitigate possible security threats. There are, obviously, security issues to bear in mind, but the closer physical proximity of possible threats reduces these considerably.

Wireless communication in general also limits its application in multiplayer network gaming, however, because of the fact that it is restricted by proximity. So, handheld consoles such as the Nintendo DS are therefore most likely to take immediate advantage of wireless gaming.

Naturally, as cell phones also become endowed with WiFi (most already have Bluetooth) or other wireless-networking and inter-networking capabilities, they will also become very capable network gaming devices.

Cellular Technology

More and more cell phones are being equipped with networking capabilities—from Bluetooth to WiFi and beyond. In addition, many can also access to the Internet via the cell phone operator at varying speeds. The standards involved are various—GSM, GPRS, UMTS, etc.—as are the capabilities of the phones themselves.

Despite the ubiquity of the cell phone as a life accessory, they remain heterogeneous in their implementation. There are many variables to contend with when considering using a cell phone as a network-enabled gaming device:

- Networking/access technology
- Handset capability
- Access speed
- Virtual machine type (Java, browser, etc.)

While not all of the above are unique to *network* gaming, they all have an effect on the kinds of network games that can be realistically implemented to achieve wide enough acceptance to be financially viable. Whether sales are from direct sources (off the shelf or virtual purchase) or indirect sources, it never makes sense to isolate any corner of the market. This is especially important for cell phones, as it is a very fast-moving, high-replacement market, with exceptionally high lifestyle penetration.

All the possible networking issues also come together in cellular networking technology—everything from varying protocols and access possibilities to screen size and memory capacity. This makes it one of the most difficult platforms for which to create network games. There is, however, middleware available to help target specific platforms and technologies, making the process easier.

The market is potentially so big that the trials and tribulations will be worthwhile if such a broad worldwide user base can be catered to. This can include everything from PPP gaming using temporary connections to full network Internet gaming.

There is also plenty of scope for hybrid models where cell-phone gamers and console gamers can live side by side, or where taking a Web-based PC game on the go by having a cell-phone client keep track of the game environment gives the same gamer two interfaces to the game.

NETWORK-GAMING MODELS

A network-gaming model, in this context, deals with the type, scope, and frequency of data exchange. It also deals with the interactive model that links the client and server, as well as the player and the game environment. Play by e-mail, for example, is one such model, and network multi-player team games like *Capture the Flag* (*CTF*) are another.

Indeed, there are as many potential network-gaming models as there types of networks. In addition, there are hybrid networking models to consider that might extend the possibilities even further.

As mentioned in the preceding section, a given game could feasibly operate on more than one network-gaming model based on the protocols and devices available or supported. The possibilities are limited only by the wishes of the designer and market, the richness of the game environment, and the capabilities of network devices.

Choosing the right model for the game style, genre, and playing mechanics will influence the network model used. This goes right to the core of the game-design process, and the networking component has to be given as high a priority as something like the in-game visual interface if it is to succeed as a gaming experience in its own right.

For example, as is generally the case, the aim of the networking component of the game design should be to provide such an experience as opposed to merely being a way to share in-game artifacts for no purpose other than self-promotion, or to try and add a networking component to an essentially non-network oriented game.

The other vital side to this is the way in which the network model is integrated with the game interface. Different genres will call for different integration mechanisms in order to retain the illusion of an alternative reality. For example, a World War II–style multi-player battleship game will have a different *presentation* of the network integration than does a space-age multi-player online game such as *Eve Online*. Taking communication between players (real or virtual) as an illustration, the presentation of the messaging interface might need to be adjusted accordingly.

On the one hand, a World War II battleship might rely on simulated Morse code exchanges, whereas a spacecraft can offer a more familiar e-mail–style interface. This might seem trivial, but it is simply not acceptable in my opinion to cross technologies and allow messaging in a World War II simulation that uses a computer.

The genre-based restrictions might also extend to the network model chosen, as will the way in which the network component has been designed. These two may or may not be related. For example, it could be

- The main emphasis of the game (e.g., *Eve Online*, *Second Life*, *Everquest*, etc.)
- An ad-hoc extension to a single-player game (e.g., a first-person shooter [FPS] game like *Quake*, adapted to multi-player over time)

(This list leaves aside those games that do not use networking as a gaming mechanism, but just as a multi-user communication mechanism.)

Somewhere between the two options is a gray area into which, in my opinion, many network-*enabled* games fall. Many games feel like they've not been designed with multi-player network gaming in mind, but market forces (and possibly the publisher) have dictated that networking capabilities be bolted on after the fact.

Then, as mentioned, there are the games that use networking not as part of the multi-player gaming model itself, but exist as a way to share information. They might also facilitate communication with other players.

So, taking all of the above into consideration, the following are the two playing models that this book principally concentrates on:

- Multi-player network gaming (be it in real time or not)
- The network as an information conduit for an otherwise single-player game

This last could just be a leaderboard/high-score table. It could be made accessible via all kinds of network- or Internet-connected devices from cell phones to PCs, as could other information-sharing paradigms. Into this last category we can also place those single-player games that allow sharing (and potential recovery) of in-game artifacts as a pseudo-multi-player extension to a single-player dynamic.

The second option (information sharing) is much less likely to have an effect on the networking model chosen. Unless, that is, there is some kind of ongoing dynamic behind it—for example, some kind of statistics battle in real time as a role playing game extension to the main game, where performance is fed back into the player's overall gaming experience (e.g., more wins in game = increase in statistics = more virtual wins online).

The Client/Server Model

The simplest kind of multi-player gaming model to appreciate, and the one that we are most familiar with, is called the *client/server model*. It is also the networking model used for static data sharing. It is called client/server because there is a one-to-many relationship between the client machines and the central point (server), which is the master of the data exchange. Figure 1.2 shows the client PCs, which can be on a LAN or connected via the Internet, all communicating via a central point: the server.

The role of the server is to run the game environment and manage all the in-game objects within it. This generally occurs at an abstract level; it is the role of the client systems to depict the unfolding state of the part of the game environment that each player can "see."

This realization of the abstract game state is based on data that comes to each connected gaming system from the server. Of course, player (or user) interaction is also relayed back to the server where it calculates the net effect of all the incoming data on the game universe.

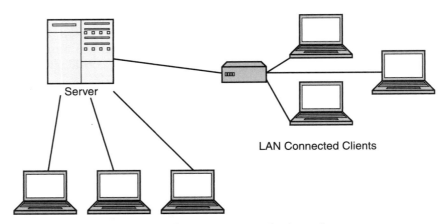

FIGURE 1.2 Client/server network schematic.

This can be seen as a kind of default networking model for most data-sharing paradigms over a network. We should not forget that online gaming, network gaming, and multi-player gaming in general, be it over a LAN, WiFi, Internet, or dial-up PPP connection, is often just an exercise in data sharing.

In browser-based Web gaming, a Web page is delivered to the browser using a client/server model. More precisely, a request and response (from client to server) mechanism is used—nothing happens unless the client is ready to receive data and actually requests it. This is an example of the most basic kind of multi-player network gaming, and one of the easiest to actually implement.

Other client/server mechanisms allow the client to indicate that it is ready to receive data (listening), which is then pushed to it. The data push happens when the server is ready to relay an update to the client, whether the client wants it or not. This model is entirely necessary in most online multi-player gaming models. The simple reason for this is that there is no way to predict what other players are going to do, nor how the game environment will react over time. Therefore, the server must inform the client of updates as they happen, in as close to real time as possible.

Of course, there will be some gaming logic in the client, too, but that will not necessarily allow it to predict with any certainty how the game environment will evolve over time. Most of the logic will just be there to maintain the illusion of the gaming environment and interface, as well as manage the connection and user interaction.

So, the data-push model is very important, as is the request/response model, depending on the kind of game the designer has in mind. The latter, for example, will mainly be used for games in which there is a turn-based mechanism at work.

In addition, there are all kinds of games (play by e-mail, browser-based games etc.) that make use of the client/server network model in a transparent fashion. In other words, the players do not necessarily use the same protocol, client, or software to access the game; the networking component is just another data-exchange service.

For these kinds of games, it is often not necessary to have any more than a very high-level view of how the underlying mechanisms work. However, for most network gaming, and especially real-time multi-player online action or simulation games, the designers need to appreciate what kind of underlying mechanisms are available at a reasonably low level.

To summarize this section, then, client/server is a network model in which there is a central repository of data and a centrally controlling entity. This entity is responsible for storing the game environment. It is a fundamental part of the vast majority of other network-gaming paradigms in the same way that TCP/IP is fundamental to network gaming in general.

Dynamic (Real-Time) Network Gaming

Many, if not the majority of, network games fall into this category, even if they are turn-based games and not real-time interactive gaming experiences. An example of a real-time multi-player Internet game might be *Eve Online*, or multi-player variants of *Quake*, which also supports LAN gaming.

Some games are not strictly real time in the sense that the action takes place as request and response, but where the game environment is still updated in real time. Subsequently, the consequences of decisions taken by players in the game are immediate.

The fact that, in this kind of model, the action unfolds at a less frenetic pace as in-game commands are carried out does not detract from the fact that they are still games that take place in a dynamic environment (hence the distinction between real time and dynamic). The game environment, objects in it, and other players evolve as the interactions take place in the virtual consciousness of the server.

Naturally, no multi-player network game is ever really static in nature; the game environment is, by default, fluid. There are, however, games where the environment remains in the same state for an extended period of time. This can be a period during which the users make their in-game decisions (covered in the next section "Connectionless Network Gaming,") and interact with the front-end interface of the system. This is a similar, yet different, model, and comes with its own set of issues, which is why it is dealt with separately.

The most basic example of a real-time multi-player network game is a multi-user dungeon (or MUD) game. These games have a text-mode interface and illustrate some of the key challenges of network gaming, being at once a real-time chat system and an online game.

One of the issues that rears its head in this particular model is the problem of network disconnects—both accidental and otherwise. An accidental disconnect is an irritation, both for the player, and the game designer. An intentional disconnect—often in an attempt to escape when things start to go wrong in the heat of battle—is really only an irritation for the designer. There is, as we shall see later on, a kind of balance to be struck between coming down hard on intentional disconnects and accepting that some kind of in-game mechanism is required to ensure continuity in case of genuine network problems.

This is all quite complex, and the connectionless network gaming model provides a slightly easier way to embrace multi-player network gaming for those just starting out.

Connectionless Network Gaming

As an example of a connectionless networking protocol, think of Hypertext Transfer Protocol (HTTP). This is the protocol that sits on top of TCP/IP and allows the programmer to request information (often Web pages or files) over the Internet. Once the response has been processed and all the data received, the connection is broken.

Unlike a dynamic or real-time dynamic network-gaming model, a connectionless network-gaming model allows the game universe to remain static for a given length of time during the play session. This might be brief or extended, depending on the way that the game is designed.

The purpose of this static period is to allow the players to make their moves—simultaneously, in some cases, before the environment is updated to take into account all the various requests of the players.

The game environment is updated periodically—overnight, for example—and the effects of all the players taken into account. Crucially, however, the interface between the player and the part of the game environment that they are responsible for (or interact with) can also be either dynamic or static.

A static relationship would mean that the player just sets up a series of commands (state changes, requests, etc.) and then logs off. When the player logs back on, provided that the environmental regeneration has taken place, his or her own little piece of the game environment will also have been updated.

The dynamic relationship at this level means that much of the impact of the player's own decisions is directly reflected in the player's own part of the game environment. The result of these changes drives the evolution of the game as a whole. The difference is that the player knows the *local* effect—the effect on his or her own part of the game environment—but not the emergent effect that this will have on the system as a whole.

For example, *Project Rockstar* is essentially a turn-based, daily-update gaming model. the basic premise being that the player can hire musicians and either let them loose as solo artists or create a band from them. Each musician has strengths, weaknesses, and other RPG-style attributes such as charisma.

Some attributes can be trained, and others cannot. It is the responsibility of the player to try to get a hit record by playing gigs, practicing, and recording music in virtual studios. Interestingly, although the result of the training, gigging, recording, and releasing of music is known only after each update, spending money is done using a dynamic model.

So, the player can hire a new musician and put that musician to work immediately, which is part of the dynamic aspect of the connectionless model. The result of the work, and the effect of that work on the wider game environment, is then part of the static aspect of the connectionless model. It is not known until after the static instance of the game environment has been generated.

Remember, however, that connectionless game models are not necessarily equal to turn-based gaming. *Project Rockstar*, for example is not turn based; players do not have to wait their turn before they can play. *Dungeons & Dragons (D&D)*, the RPG/board game, however, is. As such, it lends itself to connectionless gaming, provided that the correct model is established.

It is perfectly possible, for example, to have a *D&D* game in which players must take turns, in a given order, in a connectionless gaming environment with daily updates. A play-by-e-mail system with strict, order-based, turn-by-turn gameplay would be an example of an extreme application of this gaming model.

Such a model might prove laborious to some; a single game would take many days (even weeks/months/years) to unfold. However, play-by-e-mail and other connectionless gaming systems based on platforms like HTML have an advantage. Since they are played through the browser or a standard e-mail client, they have the advantage that any Internet-connected device can be used to play. This also makes them a good target for casual gamers, which is an interesting emerging market that can be tapped with a clever combination of game, platform, and community.

As a brief side note, we have discussed the play-by-e-mail turn-based connectionless model, but not the browser-based equivalent. In this kind of model, updates happen in real time; as players finish their moves, the environment is updated, and play moves to the next player in a round-robin fashion.

Note that with the move toward a dynamic real-time gaming model, we will again be confronted with the design issue that there is a possibility of disconnection, accidental or otherwise, which must be dealt with appropriately.

DATA EXCHANGE IN NETWORK GAMING

As we said in the previous section, all network-gaming mechanics can be reduced to a data-storage and exchange exercise. The challenge is to exchange data between the systems involved, whether it is in a peer-to-peer or client/server environment, as quickly and securely as possible. The designer must also take into account the constraints of the platform, networking technology, and model chosen.

Clearly, concessions are going to have to be made in the quantity and frequency of the information-exchange requirements. These concessions must be made at the design level in order to ensure that the network model is achievable in the development of the network-gaming portion of the game.

For example, the number of players that can be catered to in a single game session may be limited by a function of the servers' processing capacity. The network distance traveled and amount of data that needs to be exchanged between the client and server for each participant will also play into this equation.

There are ways to reduce this data flow such that the communication time (or lag) can be reduced. This can potentially be used to increase the amount of real data that can be exchanged during the play session.

One example might be to use compression. Techniques that require additional processing such as compression need to be weighed against the available processing resources of the clients. A cell phone will have less processing power to spend on compression than other, more powerful client systems.

Even in connectionless gaming models, this trade-off between data exchange and performance may have an impact on the design. It is likely to be less of an issue due to the non-real-time nature of such network-gaming models—another factor that makes them easier to design and implement.

Besides the data-exchange capacity and performance, there is also the security aspect to take care of. The security scheme chosen will also have an effect on the data exchange in terms of the resources needed to perform the exchange as well as the nature of the data that is exchanged (size, speed, etc.).

Security

One of the most important aspects to consider is the security of the data exchange—not so much because in-flight data can be intercepted and tampered with by unknown third parties, but because the players themselves might try to defraud the system in some way. The two most likely security threats are probably

- Denial-of-service attacks
- Player fraud for personal gain

The way that the information is used in game will have a severe effect on the amount of security that needs to be put in place. Primarily, we are concerned with adding security to prevent cheating. Other attacks might happen, but if we take steps to prevent active cheating, then we automatically reduce the dangers associated with attacks in general. In addition, there are non–game specific things we can do to reduce the chance of hacking attacks, denial of service or otherwise, which will not affect the game design so much as the way that the whole system is implemented and run.

However, it remains the responsibility of the game designer to make sure that the opportunities for foul play are eliminated. To the extent that it is possible, this should be done in the logic of the game itself, so that a technical solution is not required.

A technical solution in this case would likely be some kind of secure encryption algorithm, which will be computationally expensive for both client and server. Naturally, we would like to avoid any additional stress on either system, but if encryption proves necessary, it should be performed on as few pieces of data as possible.

The first key point, then, is this: In the design, try to minimize data exchange as much as you can. This has two advantages—the additional data-reduction effort also helps to sustain network performance, and not just improve the performance of any additional security measures.

The second point is to make any sensitive data non-obvious so that a casual interception (and eventual altering or augmentation) cannot yield any quick results. The aim is to make sure that only a concerted effort to monitor data exchanges over an extended period of time will yield any information at all, let alone useful data.

Finally, the third point is to make any data, as far as possible, non-consequential, reducing the gaming logic that the client system implements. This is a slightly different take on the data-security model that will need to be implemented. We assume, from the outset, that none (as far as is practical) of the data stored locally with respect to the client can be used to further the player's progress in the game without data exchange between client and server.

This is another balancing act of data exchange versus security versus gameplay. For example, it may seem to be a good split of the gaming workload (see the next section, "Split-Information Model") to allow clients some leeway in deciding how certain aspects of the game environment evolve during the play session. In other words, the client system helps the server out by providing some of the game environment update processing muscle.

Be it in a real-time gaming model or a connectionless one, this might seem like a good idea. After all, the less work the server has to do, the richer the environment can be, and the better the game will be—as well as being able to support more artifacts, more players, and more interaction.

The dangers in taking this approach should be obvious—namely, there is a transfer of control away from the one part of the system we can control (hopefully, completely): the server.

At one logical extreme (with only the absolute minimum data exchange), in a real-time gaming model, the client system is just an extension of the server. That is, it exists only to show the player what the current game environment looks like (and sounds like), and to capture any input from the player for eventual communication back to the server.

Thus, the data exchange that occurs is merely to send movement commands to the server and receive the current state of play (immediate vicinity only) from the server. The server maintains the state of the game environment and everything in it.

Furthermore, the server decides everything that it knows for each coded client, at each moment in time:

- Where they are in the game environment
- What each one is doing
- What they can see
- What can see them

This is the *only* information that the server passes on to the clients. Each client knows only what it has been told. It has no idea what else might be going on in the game environment and is not allowed to make any decisions based on the data that it receives whatsoever. Of course, it can decide how to render it and allow interaction, and so on, but the data that passes between the two is minimally useful.

Tampering with this kind of data should a) be difficult, and b) fail to yield any obvious benefits to the player. Even if players were inclined to do so, they would need to read and interpret the incoming information before acting upon it. This should require quite some programming skills—and it is the responsibility of the developer to make sure that it does.

This means that, at this logical extreme, the client is just a window on the game space. It cannot render (be it a real-time action game, rendering graphics in real time, or a text adventure) things that it is not told are explicitly within the player's sphere of influence within the game space.

The other side to this issue is straight hacking and cyber terrorist attacks. These are cases where third parties infiltrate the data layer and cause denial of service or disruption of the gaming model. Denial of service is usually nonpermanent, albeit irritating for the players concerned, as they are unable to get service from the overloaded server. Beyond the lack of revenue and loss of face, there should be no lasting damage. Disruption to the gaming model, however, might not be so benign. Parts of the gaming environment might become disturbed temporarily or, in the worst case, permanently. It is important, though, to note a difference here between hacking and exploitations of holes in the design that ought to have been plugged by the developer. Players cannot be faulted for these kinds of exploitations.

Split-Information Model

The example in the last section shows a data model that is biased toward the server. This might seem, at first glance, to be a sensible precaution, given that I've spent a good amount of time making you paranoid with respect to security and performance. On the other hand, it can also make good sense to store static data on the client and use a split-information model in which the client layers information that it receives on top of information received by the server.

In the split-information model, gameplay data is stored on the server, with some of the data required to render the game state stored on the client. The litmus test is that information can be held on the client as long as it does not include any data that directly influences the gameplay.

This litmus test is the safety net against the aforementioned security, but also introduces an added strength of the network-gaming model: downloadable content. In turn, designers wishing to build this into the game design need also to think about how best (and most securely and efficiently) to cater for these downloads.

A good example is a game model in which the game environment (without in-game artifacts or players) is stored on the client. Whether the client is a handheld gaming device with lower-end processing power, a top-end PC, or a console with Internet access, it will be responsible for rendering the immediate game environment.

Here is the crux of the matter: It may only render that which the game server tells it to. There should be very little logic, no decisions taken as to what the player might be able to see, and no data downloaded that is not part of the immediately visible game environment.

This model is something like the original *Unreal Tournament* network-game model. Players had to download a map to their PC (actually, the map is part of the game download) and then find a server to play it on. As long as the two were synchronized correctly, possibly through further downloads, everyone was happy. Players could then select from a variety of game modes (from *Capture the Flag* to all-out *Team Tag*–style warfare) and play over the Internet against other players, be they real or virtual (bots).

The point is that the game model that splits the information in an intelligent way—such that the downloadable client provides only the rendering—has the potential to expand the audience. Since only data that pertains to the environmental game session is ever actually communicated, security is maximized, and data transfer is minimized.

This is a popular model of information split, but it has some consequences. For example, the environment can only be expanded by downloading new portions of it upon demand (for games not based on single maps), which could cause issues relating to timing.

A dynamically unfolding environment must therefore be downloaded in layers of virtual zoom. If we take a space-based game like *Eve Online* as an analogy, this is the same as saying that we first download the abstraction of a galaxy (and all the stars within it), and then the system that the player chooses to visit (star + planets), and finally the exact planetary system in which the player finds himself or herself (planets + moons + game artifacts).

There is another technique that will be discussed in the book—procedural rendering of the game environment. This is an interesting and useful technique that splits the information exchange again. In short, the client downloads coded information, which allows it to create the game environment based on logic contained within the client and the local data it is shipped with. The key to this technique is that, if a new piece of the game environment is created, there is nothing downloaded beyond the codes required to create the new environment upon demand.

We should also dig down a little more deeply into the data split where *all* the information resides on the server. We have mentioned the model in which environmental information is downloaded inline, but there is also the possibility to take an extreme client/server approach whereby the actual *rendering* information is passed to the client, which is just drawing what it is told to. (Readers might remember the *X Windows* client/server model, or recent thin client computing, which achieves this. Also, the Microsoft Windows Remote Access Client works in this way.)

Of course, this creates a much higher processing workload on the server, produces very heavy Internet traffic per client, and is not an efficient information split for some game models. That said, simple text-based games (MUDs, for example) use this model very effectively, but do suffer from occasional lag (which is not as bad as it used to be, but can still be irritating).

It is highly unlikely to work well in an Internet gaming model, but there is potential for this kind of information split to work for LAN games. The closer proximity of the machines and the higher data-exchange rate means that it might be feasible. It also has the advantage that the client does not need to store any information about the game, and can therefore be adapted to multiple games by just changing servers.

Naturally, a hybrid approach is also possible, where game-world data can be downloaded and stored, to be used later on. This might suggest that additional security needs to be introduced to protect the downloaded data from prying eyes—an issue for an adventure or quest-oriented game, for example. For pure multi-player combat, however, where advance knowledge of the game map is not necessarily an advantage, this protection is not generally necessary. Due to the fact that play occurs against other players, at speed, and there are no hidden things to discover, the additional protection is not generally necessary. This last, simple model brings us full circle to the highest form of information split toward the client. That is, the map lives on the client system, and only positional and action information is relayed to the clients as the game unfolds.

Balancing Data Exchange

All the preceding discussion has been about extremes. But these are not binary decisions—it is not a matter of choosing one or the other. Each extreme in a decision process can, indeed must, be applied in a balanced fashion to try to design the most appropriate data-exchange model for the game, clients, and network protocol.

As we noted, data exchange is a balance between compression, security, and connection speed. The exchange of data between client and server needs also to be correctly balanced in order to yield a reasonable playing experience.

This is of course dictated in part by the split of the information model used—higher client content may imply lower data-exchange requirements, and higher server content may imply larger quantities of data flowing from the server to the client. The issues relating to compression and encryption (for example) are also applicable to the data that *is actually exchanged*, as well as *stored* on the client.

Depending on the capacity of the devices and networking protocols used (remembering that we have to cater to the lowest capacities being supported), the principles of size and security will come into play. Less-capable devices might not be able to (de)compress quickly enough or be able to decrypt or encrypt data at sufficiently high speeds to enable players to take part alongside others with more-powerful client machines.

Then again, data can flow in both directions. This naturally means that if there is any processing performed by the client beyond simple interaction with the user, the result of that processing needs to be passed up to the server. Typically, this *upstream* data has to follow the same principles of size and security as for downstream data; although the server will have higher processing capacities, it also needs to deal with more entities, so there is again a balance to be struck.

There is an additional point to make which may seem obvious, at first. If the client is doing any game-related processing (not advisable), then security comes into play. The data that results from client-side processing, and that must be sent to the server, must be secured adequately. If the data generated by the client and shared with the server is a result of an interaction in the game space, then it will have an impact in the game environment as a whole. This being the case, there is a risk that local security issues could lead to undesirable consequences and global security issues.

Now, this might feel a bit abstract, so let's look at a concrete example. Imagine that the server presents a puzzle (encrypted) to the client. This puzzle might represent a challenge that must be solved by the player, on the client machine, before the player can continue in the game. The actual updated position of the player's avatar in the game environment should be decided and monitored by the server. This is just an added safeguard against unintentional or intentional side effects. If the result of the puzzle solving is just a simple yes/no, the data needing to be exchanged is minimized. While this is good, it would allow the player to intercept the data and just send a "yes" answer rather than actually solving the puzzle. The player would then be permitted to proceed to the next stage of the game, which is clearly not desirable. What is needed is some way to package the network data and then encrypt it such that the player is not able to easily defraud the system.

Even worse, the result of the client-side processing might actually be something that is uploaded to the server and stored there. In a game revolving around city building, for example, this might call for the player to create a city using resources awarded by the server based on online performance. Then, the player could feasibly upload that city, which would then become part of the online gaming environment for interaction with other players (city builders, or some other gaming class supported by the system). If such a data exchange is not secured, then the data that is sent back to the server might well be tampered with to the detriment of the game for all players.

Getting the data exchange, network model, and information models lined up correctly in the game design, based on the networking platform (PPP, LAN, Internet, Web, etc.) is clearly very important. It is an integral part of designing a network game, or the networking portion of an otherwise stand-alone game, which we will uncover step by step through the rest of this book.

KEY DECISIONS

To design the network components of a game, it is necessary to evaluate the role of network gaming in the final product. Then the designer must decide on the network-gaming model and technologies to be used to deploy that model.

Console games, for example, will only ever be played on a console, and usually all the models of the console playing the multi-player network version of the game will be the same. The fact that the platform is homogenous works for the game designer. That said, while the network support is known, as are the capabilities, this can be restrictive as well as a key strong point in the game-design paradigm. Of course, it also narrows the decisions somewhat, and can feel restrictive as the design is created.

On the other hand, a game that revolves around the network as a central tenet—Web games, play by e-mail, etc.—can lead to many decisions that need to be taken with regard to the underlying game mechanic.

In developing the theme of the general challenge that has to be tackled, we have only really looked at games that are played through interaction with the network. There is also, however, the possibility of using network components as a way to distribute single-player games, but share high scores and achievements. Facilities such as those found on Xbox Live Arcade, and the equivalent PlayStation Network, are examples of this. We will cover this aspect as well, always bearing in mind the central questions that have been raised in this chapter.

The final question will be, Is network support integral to the game or bolted on? Even if the latter is the case, it should never feel like the addition of networking is an afterthought. It must always remain "in character" with the rest of the game.

TYPES OF NETWORK GAMES

In This Chapter

Having set the scene in Chapter 1, "The Challenge of Game Networking," this chapter details all the types of network game that have emerged with the introduction of networking technology. Both the client and server (as well as network) capabilities have expanded over the years, and this has helped shape the kinds of game that are available and popular. The basic types of network games considered in this chapter—and indeed, the rest of the book—are as follows:

 Although the emphasis here is on wide area networking, as can be seen in the list that follows, local network games (LAN games) share some of the same characteristics. They are dealt with where appropriate in the context of the other network models.

- **Multi-user dungeon.** One of the first kinds of multi-player network games, the multi-user dungeon, or MUD, was essentially a text-based environment through which people could interact, chat, and role-play. The textual interface was necessary due to the heterogeneous nature of the connected platforms, network, and machine performance.
- **Arcade.** With improvements in platform and networking technology, it became obvious that single-player games could be networked to allow players to play against (or even with) each other. Examples include allowing network gaming in *Quake* (especially in Capture the Flag mode).
- **Multi-player network games.** As the prevalence of the Internet increased, line speeds rose, and connectivity costs fell, the first wave of truly network-only multi-player games surfaced—one of the earliest being *Unreal Tournament* (*UT*). These games essentially had no single-player mode beyond simple robotic AI NPCs.
- **Web "through the browser" games.** While the computing power made games like *UT* possible, and despite the rapid adoption of networked consoles, the World Wide Web has still emerged as a gaming force, especially in niche and casual gaming markets. The low footprint of Web games also means that they can be played on a wide variety of platforms, from PCs to phones.
- **Alternate reality games.** Some games, such as *Perplex City*, mix real-world gaming devices, such as collector cards and locations, with virtual gaming via a Web interface that is little more than a glorified forum. The back story is all-important in these types of games, and the interplay between real and virtual can be more or less complex depending on the gaming interface chosen. This genre is in its infancy, and as a gaming community, we have yet to explore all the possibilities that handheld gaming devices such as cell phones and other wireless gaming devices might bring to the fore. One can envisage a time in the future when a player's very existence might become part of an evolving game played out over console, PC, and handheld

device, using technologies such as GPS and WiFi. Clearly the social aspects of such games will be vital to their success, as they already are in *Second Life* and other such pseudo-games.

- **Virtual worlds.** These are not necessarily classified as games per se. Rather, they are hyper-interactive pseudo-games that attempt to mirror reality to a certain extent within a stylized virtual environment that borrows from gaming technology. Virtual worlds can be seen as logical extensions of MUDs—replacing text with graphics, but retaining the powerful aspects of chat and location-based persistent environments, complete with rooms and objects that can be created, owned, and manipulated by the players who live within the virtual world.

For each of these game types, the challenges, technologies, and some historical background will be given. Coverage extends to issues such as hacking and other types of cheating, network performance, server-side issues, and the influence of the Internet and artificial players (bots).

MULTI-USER DUNGEON GAMES

The multi-user dungeon (MUD) genre covers a wide spectrum of games, ranging from basic talkers (*Foothills*, *Surfers*, etc.), where the underlying game mechanic is simply to customize and communicate, to more advanced hack- and slash-style adventure quest/player killing experiences. The latter have more in common with traditional role-playing games (RPGs) such as those influenced by paper-based real-world games like *Dungeons & Dragons*. Arguably, although these have split into other subgenres such as MUSH, MUCK, and MOO games, they still remain part of the MUD experience. (You'll learn more about MUSH, MUCK, and MOO games later in this chapter.)

Although the term "MUD" has become synonymous with the historical interface that has become part of gaming culture, it is feasible that it could be extended somewhat. (For those not familiar with this aspect of gaming subculture, the classical image of a MUD is a text-based Telnet client–oriented interface with lists of commands and short forms to enter via the keyboard.) But although it is arguably time to modernize MUDs, the premise of a MUD should remain the same: a simplistic gaming model allowing the user base to provide much of the content and intrigue.

Indeed, this idea has led to virtual worlds such as *Second Life*, providing a modern interface to what is, basically, a MUD. Despite the slicker interface and more game-oriented approach, *Second Life* shares much with the MUDs of old in terms of the various challenges and solutions used to facilitate the persistent game environment and player-to-player and player-to-room communication, and to overcome issues relating to the underlying network infrastructure.

Some of the key design/implementation features of the MUD system, then, are as follows:

- **Communication:** This includes local communication, remote communication, and player-to-player communication, also called "whispering."
- **Commands:** These include admin commands for superior users.
- **Emoting:** This involves presenting actions through words (e.g., <player> shrugs).
- **Interactivity:** This refers to the player's ability to use commands to modify the environment.

Even if the technology driving the architecture has advanced, the MUD gaming paradigm still lives on in one form or another, and is a cornerstone in network gaming history. To understand the impact of MUDs, and what you can learn from their implementation, it is necessary to start at the beginning, taking them apart layer by layer.

First Principles

I first came into contact with MUDs in the early 1990s, and these early experiences in large part shaped the way I think about multi-player gaming and how a game should be created. Key to the success of the MUD genre was the emphasis on communication and movement around a fixed and/or dynamic game environment. MUD gaming has always been about delivering a rich universe, with concentration on the multi-player aspect above all others. While single-player text-based adventure games also existed, a MUD just could not have worked as a single-player game; there would have been no point. This social aspect to gaming was lent more credence by the rich command set, enabling players to communicate directly through simulated speech and, indirectly, through thought bubbles and emoting.

Genres

More serious MUDs have embraced certain genres that reflect the manner in which players are expected to behave. There are as many genres of MUD as there are genres of gaming experiences:

- Science fiction
- Medieval
- Fantasy

The science-fiction genre, in particular, is very interesting, often based on science-fiction TV shows such as *Star Trek*. Other genres pull in descriptions, background stories, and even characters from other works of fiction that serve as an effective backdrop for the MUD and interactions within it.

Usually, within each genre, individual player characters can be created. The depth of character depends on the kind of interaction with the game and other players that the MUD authors require. Non-talker MUDs require a certain investment in this respect, as the emphasis is on playing a game and not just stopping by for a chat. If the MUD concentrates more on interaction than it does on gameplay *per se*, then the depth of character development might not matter so much, except as an interest point for discussion between online characters. At the other end of the spectrum, those MUDs that require players to complete quests (either as part of a team or individually), and that encompass a game rather than just a place to hang out require much more customization. More often than not, it is that customization that affects the progress of a character through the game.

Gaming Model

Although the MUD genre can mean different things to different people, all MUDs share a common gaming model—one that is based on a pure client/server infrastructure. Usually this requires that all the rendering information be passed from the server to the client—historically a Telnet client, which displays textual information received by the software application. Telnet is a specific protocol, like HTTP, for transferring data over the Internet. It allows the server and client to communicate in a standard way—although what the server sends, and what the client does with the data it receives, is entirely up to the game designers.

The server acts as a communication conduit and maintains the entire game universe, usually in a database. If the server or database system is slow, then communication is slow, and the game becomes generally slower. If the server goes down, then the game cannot be played, as no more communication will be possible. The server is administrated by people (usually also players) with special powers (like super-users in a Unix-based system), which extend to managing the other players and, usually, the system—although not necessarily at the operating-system level. It is the responsibility of these admin players to make sure that everything runs correctly.

Non-Interactive Environments

The dungeon itself (for want of a better term, the game environment) is created by the MUD administration and can be static or dynamic, fixed or interactive. A static non-interactive environment is often just like a chat room. There might be some basic descriptive text, allowing players to take a look at the environment but not interact with it. Although they may be able to move from room (location) to room, nothing can be changed.

Unless the admins decide that a specific room needs a change, once everything is set up, it tends to remain the same. Those players that become admins might take ownership of certain rooms and change their look now and again, but the underlying premise of the MUD is that it is a place for people to come and chat (talk).

A step up from this is a dynamic non-interactive environment. In these environments, the room descriptions (and possibly objects within the rooms) may be changed by anyone with sufficient privileges. This mechanism usually allows non-anonymous players (residents) to have their own rooms, which they can invite people to inspect or chat in— usually with the possibility to lock the room against unwanted access. The difference between a dynamic non-interactive environment and a static environment is the level of customization that is possible. There is still no interaction between the environment and individual players, and the game remains more of a chat room than anything more advanced.

Security concerns creep in at this point, as the server and database are opened up to players. If players find a way to insert a textual command in the descriptions of their rooms, and if that command is something subversive, then without specific safeguards, they could feasibly bring the system down.

Interactive Environments

A static interactive environment lifts the game to a status that enables the players to do more than just chat. The players might actually be able to interact with the game and game environment in a pre-programmed fashion. This opens the door for games involving quests or solving puzzles. In short, these types of environments open the way for "proper" gaming as opposed to just being glorified chat rooms. If players can interact with each other and the gaming environment in a way that allows the special "administrative players" to create games within the environment, then the possibilities for both fun—and security breaches—drastically increase.

It is the malleability of the environment, as delivered by the developers of the MUD platform, that allows gaming to take place. This is the purpose for which the original code was developed: to see what creative players would come up with, be it a sci-fi game inside the MUD or just a place to go to chat online.

At this point, in game-design terms, there are several decisions that have to be made. For example, what happens if you want to send two characters (or groups thereof) on the same quest? Is the entire game environment to be one big world in which this is not possible, or is the multi-player aspect selective, allowing groups to embark on quests at the same time in their own spawned alternative game worlds? Answering these questions is key to the game design—and will certainly complicate the game's development unless it is left to the MUD admins to decide how this will be implemented. The result is a game framework that can be customized by those responsible for the daily running of the game proper.

For example, admins might choose to have a system in which the rooms and objects required for a specific quest can be copied to a room set that can be accessed only by those who are going on the quest. Access to the quest, therefore would be via some kind of in-game portal, separating out those who are taking part in a quest from those who are not. This resolves, to a certain extent, any issues arising from multiple players wanting to go on the same quest.

These solutions, and the game design that spawns them, derive from the fact that the environment is interactive. So the key differences between the non-interactive and interactive environments are as follows:

- Players cannot affect the game world in a non-interactive environment.
- In an interactive environment, the mere fact of interaction leads to some consequences for the player—chiefly that players can often sustain damage and even be killed during a game session.

 Player deaths can be at the hands of the environment (or non-player characters, otherwise known as NPCs) or other players. So-called player killer or hack'n'slash MUDs allow players to kill each other, which is more usually reserved for NPCs. These possibilities are brought about by the introduction of game networking, which is more or less unique to multi-player network games, be they LAN- or WAN-based.

In contrast, a dynamic interactive environment enables players to add their own content—or, in MUD parlance, become *builders*. They might even be able to create quests. Whether their in-game creations are allowed to kill off other players is a decision usually left up to the admins.

OPEN SYSTEMS

Interestingly, the underlying technologies for non-interactive and interactive MUDs are so similar—in terms of the data-storage models and possibilities that must be opened up to the admins to customize the environment—that they are usually based on the same code. It is the customization that makes the game, not necessarily the engine that drives it.

MUD systems are usually open systems by design. In other words, most of the best known MUDs are based on one kind of kernel of code that arrives on the server as a download and is essentially empty. These days, that kernel can be officially open source, freely modifiable, using a language such as PHP and open-source database support with systems such as MySQL. This means that the behavior, as well as the interface and look of the MUD, can be freely modified and re-used.

This is important in another way: the MUD represents a set of solutions to network gaming problems that exist for even the most modern of network games. In other words, if the core can be built on, the game can evolve past a text-based adventure game into something else just by having the interface and game-environment representation tweaked.

It is these visual and representational aspects that set a MUD apart from *Second Life*. The under-the-hood code ought to be remarkably similar; whether the data transferred is a textual description of a room or a coded description for graphical display, the issues are the same.

Security

Clearly, security is high on the list of issues that need to be considered. Luckily, a MUD is fairly easy to secure because the only place a hacker could have any influence at all is on the server. As long as that is secure, then the worst that could happen is a denial-of-service (DoS) attack (also called "spoofing")—which easy to spot and not inherently damaging.

 We mentioned the possibility that players might introduce database (SQL) statements into their room descriptions, thereby potentially enabling Trojan-style attacks. These so-called SQL injections are also easy to spot and remove, but attention needs to be paid to them on the level at which the SQL statements are executed, as this may be performed by an account with system-level access to the database.

It is worth taking a moment to look at the potential weak spot that is the DoS attack because it applies to any gaming system. It has, in the past, also been the Achilles heel of MUD and other network-gaming systems with which one can easily interface using external systems.

MUDs are usually text based, accessed through an open protocol (Telnet) using plain-text commands enveloped within the protocol. This means that an automated system (bot) can be placed behind the client or in place of the Telnet client. This bot can even carry out automated tasks such as signing up for an account. Moreover, these days, multiple processes can run on a single computer, so multiple bots could be set up on the same machine. The amount of time required to crack most systems would therefore be drastically reduced—and the mere act of running multiple bots all trying to sign up for accounts might even cause the DoS to succeed.

Unfortunately, there are no "CAPTCHA" mechanisms possible to prevent such a scenario, as MUDs work over a pure text-based interface. Any challenge-response security mechanisms would have to be based on questions that only a human can answer, and this would prove to be difficult to implement. And although placing the server machines behind a firewall, thereby restricting access by IP address, would ostracize bots, so, too, would it ostracize legitimate players on LANs connected to the Internet. For these reasons, the MUD can be seen to be relatively unsecure.

In summary, although the benefits, in gaming terms, of the MUD system are that information exchange is minimized (it's plain text) and a wide platform base is addressed (even cell phones ought to be able to handle Telnet), it does have a key weakness: The client is not specialized enough to guard against spoofing. There should be automatic systems in place to guard against such attacks, which are covered in Chapter 8, "Removing the Cheating Elements." If no steps are taken to prevent DoS attacks, all someone would have to do is set up a series of bots to log in and spam the system with random text in a private room; this would slow down the system, crippling it for everyone else. Clearly, resolving this issue is key to understanding multi-player security in general.

Social Gaming

The principle driver for MUDs is arguably the social aspect. Long before the arrival of Xbox LIVE, headsets, and in-game communication, people were cooperatively gaming on MUDs. They were able to chat to each other (either privately or to the room at large), decide strategy, and interact with each other and the environment. This is referred to as "social gaming." The MUD was, and arguably still is, an enabling conduit for social gaming, as well as an innovative way to play games together.

Another aspect to social gaming is that it can be done using a combination of a MUD and interaction with the real world. For example, two MUD gamers can each get a chessboard and then play against each other or a bot—either in public or private. This has led to implementations of chess games within MUDs, as well as other games such as *Paper Scissors Stone* and *Battleship* clones.

Text-Based MUDs

Part of the challenge of text-based MUD (not to mention MUCK, MUSH, and MOO, all variants on the original MUD) design and implementation is that the interface is, well, text only, which requires a text interface for communicating with the system. The system is then responsible for interpreting the commands, carrying out the actions that they embody, and then relaying the result to the other players.

MUCK, MUSH, AND MOO

MUCKs, MUSHes, and MOOs are three types of games that are descended from MUDs. Depending on whom you ask, the name "MUCK" is either an acronym for multi-user created kingdom or a play on words from the term MUD, from which the concept of a MUCK is descended. The MUCK environment is shipped empty, but is extended through the addition of room descriptions. MUCKs are programmed in their own language, MUFR (multi-user forth).

MUSH—short for multi-user shared hack (or possibly habitat or hallucination)—games involve role playing. MUSH, too, has its own programming language with a syntax similar (some say) to Lisp. MUSHes are managed by wizards—that is, special users with advanced skills in programming and maintaining the MUSH universe. There are several flavors of MUSH, each with peculiarities and extensions of their own, which can be used to run a MUSH server.

MOO—short for MUD object oriented—games are also descended from MUDs, providing yet another online, user-oriented environment. These differ from other MUD variants in that their interfaces are developed using an objected-oriented approach. Everything is stored in a persistent object database, set up when the MOO is installed and the basic environment created. This makes it more advanced and flexible than some of the other MUD variants. Extensions occur via a proprietary programming language, although MOO server owners may extend that with their own genre-dependent verbs to provide in-game actions for players that are in keeping with the general theme of the MOO being hosted. MOO is arguably the most popular MUD descendent still in operation today—as proven by *LambdaMOO*, an incarnation started with the original MOO project.

As a result, the commands themselves need to be fairly self-explanatory and easy to type; but they also need to be short, because they have to travel over a network—usually the Internet, which is not known for its speed and reliability in data transfer. (This was a reasonably big issue in the early days, but not so much now, as data speeds and reliability increase.) Historically, sensible limits were placed on such things as room descriptions (often limiting them to as few as 255 characters), and a paging mechanism was often necessary to display multi-page text. These practices helped to ensure that the widest platform compatibility was maintained, with few extensions for more advanced terminals.

One early extension beyond plain text was support for ANSI screen control—allowing colors and reasonable layout control. Due to the multi-player, multi-platform nature, however, it became important that appropriate measures were taken to ensure that other display types were catered to. That's why, in the early days of MUDs, users (players) had to choose their terminal type at the start of the gaming session—vt100, for example, being a standard text-only non-ANSI terminal. This mechanism, of course, assumed that the players were well acquainted with their hardware and could make the appropriate choices. Fortunately, although the clients were fairly dumb, these early users, typically computer-science majors, had above-average knowledge of computers in general, and client/server computing in particular. In the intervening decades, networked multi-player games have moved more mainstream.

MUD clients now exist that can emulate the screen (terminal) types and automate the interactive portions of the game interface by automatically inserting text. Rather than having to type commands, the player can now just click a button and have the appropriate command inserted. Furthermore, for certain games, interfaces exist whereby the player can be substituted by a macro—a kind of program—that can insert commands into the stream and analyze the results. In other words, it is one step away from automatic playing. This automatic playing is at the core of most problems associated with hacking. The ability to insert commands into the stream in this manner also highlights the lack of security once a player account has been created. There are no checks to make sure that the player, and not some automated script, is playing. The text-based model makes this easy: Everything is text, and a generic client can be used to play the game.

The basic text-based MUD game model centers on a server that contains data for all the places that can be visited. Also on the server is the logic for passing from one to the other and a communications layer that allows players to chat with each other. All the logic that relays the state of the game environment to all the clients and governs their interactivity is also part of the text MUD engine. Nothing is farmed out to the client beyond simple display chores; even the logic that dictates how the game environment is to be displayed is contained on the server, which must then provide exactly the text to be rendered (and any control codes) to the client. This is partly due to the use of the Telnet protocol for data transfer, which is largely text based, and relies on a client that is fairly dumb.

Possibilities Beyond Text

The basic MUD model can be tweaked and extended in many ways. For example, the Telnet clients can be replaced by smarter, custom-built clients capable of displaying better graphics, playing sounds, and even implementing some of the game logic. (As you will see in Chapter 8, this last extension is not always a good thing, as it is opens the door to cheating by proxy.) Some of the tweaks have been made to improve the text-based nature of the MUD itself; others allow for the creation of entirely new gaming experiences. Such tweaks involve changing the nature of the data exchanged, as well as changing what happens on the client side when it is received.

The preceding section had one example of this: dropping in an alternative front-end to provide the interface for the player. Other examples include richer graphics (rather than text) and may necessitate either streaming the data inline (as in the Google Earth approach) or synchronizing with locally held data that describes the immediate environment. The World Wide Web provides an additional layer for the distribution of a front-end, with two added advantages. The first is that the player doesn't need to download anything. Secondly, the front-end can be properly adjusted to match the capabilities of the game on offer. An embedded front-end could be an appropriate middle ground between classic text MUD gaming and full-blown distributed client gaming systems. This approach could also feasibly culminate in an entirely proprietary interface that can even be used to extend the basic MUD in a proprietary fashion.

Graphics and Sound

At its core, a MUD is just a place where people can go to chat and occasionally embark on other activities. Even other flavors that add interactivity, objects, and role playing are just variations on that core theme. It is only natural, however, to seek ways to update this basic model to bring the appearance of the game up to modern standards. Because the core server-side processing will never be seen except through the client interface, it doesn't need a lot of modernization. Adding the ability to move through the game environment in 3D or 2D, however, would be a good starting point for an extension. It would allow players to be more creative with their in-game persona (or avatar), as well as allowing fast recognition between classes of player (or even friend and foe).

You've seen how a move from text to graphics has occurred as processing capabilities and networking technologies have improved. As a consequence, however, the server must farm out some of its responsibilities to client systems. The first place that this happens is in the graphics and sound that present the game environment to the players.

One approach might be to extend the GUI itself away from the basic text-based interface of the classic MUD, and on to a more typical modern-day RPG interface. Although this would make the game more accessible, it would still be a MUD; in fact, all that has occurred is a change the front-end. Since the gamer can get status information via the text interface provided by a typical Telnet MUD, it is easy to produce a front-end that can do the same, but display the results differently.

Taken to its logical conclusion, under this model, different players could have different visualizations, even if the underlying game was essentially the same—meaning that with very few logic changes to the underlying system, two players could cooperatively embark on games of different genres. This is an extreme case that probably doesn't have any practical use, but it does illustrate the power and flexibility of the MUD model—provided, of course, that the rendering tasks are farmed out to the client. The server just sends a command to tell the client what to play (or display); the client is responsible for the rest.

This also presumes some kind of synchronization of assets or inline streaming; if streaming is chosen, then the flexibility of the MUD is compromised slightly. If asset synchronization is chosen (the more common option), then there are a few other things to take care of, covered later in this chapter in the "Arcade Games" section.

Sound can also be introduced into a MUD, adding even more flavor to the gaming environment. Although sound was completely missing (beyond the odd beep) from the classic MUD architecture, it could be introduced/triggered as part of the extensions discussed here. In essence, the same arguments and implementation path can be used for sound as for graphics, with the additional possibility of allowing the player to introduce his or her own soundtrack via the computer's CD player (for the PC platform, at least). The underlying interactivity model for MUDs can be used to trigger changes in environmental artifacts (things switching on, or other background sounds, for example) based on the location of the player in the game environment; adding sound simply involves slightly extending the core to identify a sound rather than some kind of descriptive display.

All of the above relies on the server being able to identify the client, or the client being able to interpret the result from the server in a certain way—displaying graphics rather than a textual description. This is, however, required only where text and graphics (plus sound) must exist in the same game space. If this is not required, then identification may not be necessary.

Security

Some form of security is necessary for custom, open, homogeneous, and heterogeneous architectures alike. Traditionally, however, MUDs have been weak in this regard. This was because the Telnet model relied on a very simple underlying architecture: a connection-based architecture. If the connection was lost, then the security layer was ditched, and the player would have to re–log on. Moreover, the sign-up process itself was fraught with issues relating to platform restrictions. In short, it was very easy to sign up with a bogus user name and password, initiate a session, spout rubbish or just lurk in the background, whilst the automated client did the same with another account. It didn't take long for the server to become overloaded—the so-called denial-of-service attack having succeeded.

What can you do to prevent this? For a start, you can add a Web interface for the sign-up process, improving security and preventing DoS attacks by introducing CAPTCHA mechanisms. A CAPTCHA mechanism presents the user with a graphic of a word, suitably obscured to reduce the possibility that an automated process could identify the word in question. The user must then type the characters appearing in the graphic in the field provided. For example, Figure 2.1 shows a simple CAPTCHA containing the phrase "pure genius" with a pixelization filter applied. A human can more or less work out what the phrase is, but a computer would have a much tougher time. This is one simple way to keep the game universe clean—removing someone's ability to sign up using an automated process. In addition, it puts the onus on a sign-up mechanism that is separate from the MUD itself, thus retaining the underlying simplicity of the system.

FIGURE 2.1 Simple pixelated CAPTCHA.

Of course you don't necessarily want to prevent people from creating bots that try to interact in a way that is sensible. Some MUDs allow players to spawn robots that can be instructed to move independently of the player. These bots can even be made to emote and chat as if doing so independently, not just as a result of the human player manipulating them. (Typically, these are called *puppets*.) Such activities could also be used as a programming challenge or even a serious scientific experiment in machine-language learning and natural-language processing—not to mention a way to test the system in an automated fashion or enable others to help you test it from geographically remote locations. Indeed, much good can come out of such research projects, perhaps even helping future gaming and game security in spotting patterns of undesirable language elements. All this is to say that some automated gameplay is actively encouraged, and that too much security can be counter-productive in MUD gaming.

On the other hand, you don't want to open the system to attacks, either. Fortunately, moving away from a text-based MUD and the Telnet protocol to, for example, a lightweight Java client will help to increase security whilst adding the benefits of a richer game interface—perhaps even a full-featured virtual world.

Virtual Worlds

Virtual worlds have become very popular in the press. They revolve around chatting, ownership, and mirroring the real world in the virtual. Of course, they're not a *true* reflection, but they do allow the player to project his or her personality in a way that the basic MUD did not. Virtual worlds are not games *per se*, but are the modern equivalent of the old talker MUDs such as *Foothills*, *Surfers*, and so on.

A few examples of these virtual worlds are the 3D chat system *IMVU*, *Google Lively*, and, of course, *Second Life*. They graphically build on the social aspects of the MUD, allowing customization of the avatar and the things that the player can own (objects, locations, and other items of virtual property) that extend the basic model. Arguably the most popular of these virtual worlds, *Second Life* boasts an economy, complete with free and paid options, inline advertising, and shopping. The look and feel is, it seems, inspired in part by *SimCity* and the *Sims* games. It's all very familiar—except that every avatar is exceptionally good looking.

These virtual worlds remain, at heart, MUDs—albeit very sophisticated ones. They are dynamic interactive environments, being entirely fluid and allowing players to interact with each other and the game environment. Objects can be owned and stored, and land can be bought, built upon, locked up, and partied in—the *Second Life* equivalent of private rooms in the basic text-based MUD environment. Indeed, there are echoes of every underlying MUD feature in virtual worlds; these virtual worlds don't really (technologically) add anything beyond the representation of the environment and everything in it. Sure, there may be some unique object representations under the hood, but even these have their equivalents in scripted objects in the various incarnations of text-based MUDs from the early era of virtual worlds.

Beyond the massive scale (of objects, players, locations, and flexibility) on the server side, there is no difference between *Second Life* and a plain-old 1990s-era text-based MUD. It follows the same model, and the server has the same responsibilities, actions, chores, and so forth. On the client side, things are not much different either. Apart from the GUI, the game-environment rendering, and player options (objects, display), there are still the same basic commands.

As a player, you can examine another player and get a description of him or her, but that description is immediate and visual rather than a text-based query. The same goes for the environment and objects. Interaction involves pointing and clicking rather than using a text interface. The whole thing is somehow more accessible, but at its heart, it's still a MUD.

ARCADE GAMES

The term "arcade-style games," in this context, refers to everything from first-person shooters (FPSes) such as *DOOM, Quake, Half-Life,* and so on, to fighting games like *Street Fighter IV* and driving games like *Burnout Dominator.* For the sake of simplicity, I've lumped massively multi-player online RPGs (MMORPGs) in with these games, because they pull techniques from both the arcade and RPG genres. (I am aware that this constitutes a genre *faux pas,* but as this is a book about network game design and not just regular game design, this kind of categorization is a necessary evil.)

With the addition of headsets and Xbox LIVE, the arcade model also now includes cooperative multi-player gaming based on FPS and MMORPG models, all of which combine to make networked gaming more accessible and profitable than ever before.

The arcade-oriented network gaming model arguably began with the linking together of games that were essentially single player in nature without extending the gameplay itself beyond the existing platform. The gamer could play the game by himself or herself, or against other players over the Internet. For example, *Unreal Tournament* performs perfectly well as a single-player game, with the gamer playing against NPCs. It is, in fact, indistinguishable from the same game played against real human players—except for the fact that the behaviors might be different (and human players tend to send messages to each other). It is also possible to substitute real players for scripted NPCs—either by choice (to make up numbers) or for more devious reasons (for example, to build up a weak character by engaging in automated play or simply to disrupt the game by behaving in a way that runs against the accepted rules of play). All this is to say that the social aspects are what differentiate the multi-player from the single-player versions. In terms of look, feel, and capability of the opposition, the two are indistinguishable.

There is also, again, the question of asset synchronization. I remember having to download multi-player maps from *Unreal Tournament* servers in order to be able to participate, as well as needing to patch the client software and add bits and pieces to bring my system in line with everyone else's. This kind of activity still goes on—although it's less of a hassle thanks to higher network speeds, which makes it possible to stream a lot of the content in-line, as in games such as *Second Life* or Google's *Lively*. Nonetheless, if several players want to play on the same level map in an FPS, they all need to have retail copies of the game and the map in question. Despite all the advances, this aspect of networking multiplayer gaming hasn't changed that much.

Gaming Model

Whatever else gets added to the mix—be it a *Burnout Dominator*–style interface, which requires players to select game types by driving around, or new cooperative gaming modes—the basic model for arcade games remains the same: a client/server, pure connection–based, real-time gaming environment. In other words, it's like a MUD, but with extreme performance, reliability, and data consistency.

Those extreme conditions extend to the amount of data that needs to be evaluated by the server (including physics, for example) in order to relay the correct in-game status to the client machines. This, combined with the number of players that can play on a given map and the number of maps available, means that the server is required to do an awful lot of processing just to keep everything moving along at an appropriate speed.

For each layer of complexity that is added to an arcade game beyond the basic MUD model, support requirements will grow exponentially. For example, adding graphics introduces a multitude of issues to be solved—from addressing performance problems to keeping all the clients current. One strategy is to stream assets inline using a Google Earth–style model, but the data-transfer requirements will potentially be huge. Adding multiple downloadable maps results in a similar problem—with the added complication that if they change, the server must have some way of determining whether all the clients have the same map. If they do not, then the map needs to be downloaded inline either before the game can begin or whilst the game is in session—which is itself a kind of asset streaming. This last option, streaming map updates inline, is unlikely, however, and potentially dangerous—after all, what do you do about dropped connections? The arcade model has no immediate answer beyond the usual: ending the playing session and disconnecting the player until such a time as his or her environment can be brought up to the appropriate level. All this is to say that the arcade model has a lot more to contend with than the MUD model, simply because it is more time critical. In fact, this is the key aspect that sets the two apart: a MUD is much less reliant on time-critical data exchange—and exchanges much less data, less quickly—than an arcade game.

Complicating matters is the fact that competition in the arcade-gaming market is fierce—indeed, this sector includes almost every genre, and is the most prolific of all models of the modern era. Because of this, game developers must work hard to be better than their competition. This competition drives the success of the market, but also means that the success of an individual game is much more vulnerable in the marketplace if any aspect of it is perceived as negative. This reality is observed by Greg Costikyan in his report "The Future of Online Gaming," where he states:

> *"An online game's success or failure is largely determined by how the players are treated. In other words, the customer experience—in this case, the player experience—is the key driver of online success."*

That means anything that removes from the experience—be it cheating or network unreliability—will attack the success of the game. In game terms, the reliability of the connection is a matter of life and death. In other words, if the gaming system cannot combat the worst excesses of network lag, latency, and jitter (see Chapter 7, "Improving Network Communications," for more information about these glitches), it is quickly rendered unplayable. Moreover, the gaming client—which must be proprietary, capable of displaying complex graphics, and capable of playing complex sounds—must also be capable of communicating with multiple versions of servers. Getting all aspects of the model right is a good starting point, even before the implementation of the game proper begins.

Security

As in a virtual world (e.g., *Second Life*), discussed in "Virtual Worlds" earlier in this chapter, security in an arcade-style network game can both be made easier and be bolstered by the move to a proprietary client/server model. By introducing this measure of control at the protocol and encoding level, security can be enhanced at various stages:

- Data exchange
- Communication
- Authentication

Unlike in a virtual world, however, security breaches in arcade-style network games can have severe and lasting in-game consequences for players. This is because a player's own progress in the game (think of an online game like *Quake* or an online RPG) relies on the game's security remaining intact and on those with malicious intent being kept at bay. Admittedly, a security issue in *Second Life* might render some of the game environment permanently (or temporarily) unusable, but like graffiti in the real world, it can be cleaned up. It is much harder to "clean up," however, if a player has been wiped off a game map and lost all his or her hard-earned in-game artifacts, be they experience points, in-game cash, weaponry, or what have you. For this reason, security must be foremost in the designer's mind, because an inevitable side-effect of a game's success is that it will become a target.

The problem is that it sometimes impossible to detect when a player or game has been subject to foul play, as the player will probably have been destroyed in a game-legal fashion—that is, by using the rules that determine the game logic against the game environment in a devious fashion. For example, suppose there is an exploit that enables a client to see the location of all other players on the map. In that case, a player could create a bot designed to seek and destroy other players. Such exploits *have* been found in games; these exploits involve sending data to the server that elicits a response containing more information than it should. In essence, the client spoofs the server into believing that the player is simultaneously present at all (or many) map positions at the same time. (Note that this is only possible in those games where movement is processed on the *client* and relayed to the *server* as status information.)

Data Exchange

Arcade-based network games must react quickly. As such, the data-exchange model—how information is exchanged between the client and server, as well as any compression or encryption required—needs to be carefully planned. If a network-enabled arcade game is to work, data exchange must be fast, compact, and, preferably, obfuscated.

With respect to speed, LAN gaming benefits from the close proximity of the users involved in that data volume can be increased—meaning that there can potentially be more players on each map, larger maps, and more going on generally. In contrast, while Internet gaming benefits from a wider audience reach, there are considerable drawbacks, including slow network-reaction times, intermittent network connectivity, and the various security issues noted in Chapter 1. Because increasing the data volume is not an option, the game designer should instead attempt to construct the game such that less data (or more compact data) need be exchanged.

Let's further consider the issue of obfuscation—that is, obscuring the data that passes from server to client and back in such a way to prevent cheating and other types of exploitation. For example, rather than sending data that looks like this:

```
move <player> from <x,y> to <x1,y1>
```

the game might alter it to look like this:

```
DE 7A 4B CF 54 9A B3 FC 80
```

The same goes for downloadable assets—maps, characters, weapons, and so on. Their representation, the game logic that governs how they are used, and the eventual effect of their use in the game must be obfuscated in some way.

The fact that the arcade-style model is based on a proprietary client makes data obfuscation—as well as general handling of the security layer—far easier. The game designer can dress up the data however he or she wishes because only clients for that particular game need to be able to understand it—although there might be client-side processing-power restrictions that make extreme encryption and compression unsustainable. Be aware, too, that the extreme performance requirements of the arcade genre and related network-gaming genres dictate that designers be creative in keeping the overhead as low as possible.

DISTRIBUTION OF THE CLIENT PLATFORM

One aspect of data exchange for the arcade-style network-game model involves the distribution of the client platform—that is, enabling clients to keep up to date by easily obtaining any necessary game downloads, patches and other fixes, and software that supports new platform capabilities. This helps both to prevent clients from falling behind, which could cut off the player from the game environment for some length of time, and to ensure that everyone enjoys the best and most consistent gaming experience possible.

The precise data-exchange model might differ from consoles to PCs. Whereas consoles tend to use read-only media for distribution, PCs—as well as cell phones and other download-based platforms—typically install to the hard drive (although a CD may occasionally be needed for verification purposes). The times are changing, however, with Xbox LIVE Arcade

continued

and Valve's Steam distribution channels allowing a purely electronic distribution. Most consoles also now have a hard drive and feature memory card–reading capabilities.

All this is to say that the download, patch, and play model might work for small updates. For example, the game could be loaded from CD/DVD/BluRay, a restore patch loaded from memory card or hard drive to active memory, and the modified code played in place of the distribution code. There's a drawback to this distribution model, however: By using this kind of approach, you enable others to patch—possibly altering the game for their own ends.

MASSIVELY MULTI-PLAYER ONLINE ROLE-PLAYING GAMES (MMORPGS)

The two principal network-gaming models are MUD, where everything happens on the server, and arcade-style, where only the status is tracked on the server. Interestingly, these two models can be combined to produce other types of games. For example, MMO games add RPG elements to the MUD and arcade (FPS) models and usually have the look and feel of an FPS (with the exception that, in certain games, combat and other interactions can be turn-based; the use of turn-based combat and interaction, however, is more a genre adaptation than a requirement imposed by any technological constraints).

Many would argue that the massively multi-player online role-playing game (MMORPG) is the pinnacle of this genre, combining the ownership, puzzle, and quest aspects of a MUD with the philosophy of an RPG and adding the front-end of an FPS. The result is true adventure gaming, with server-side status updates, client-side interactions, and data exchange via the server to mirror the actions of each player and ensure that everything is kept in synchronization. Examples of the genre include *World of WarCraft*, *Eve Online*, *EverQuest*, and so on. While each one has something unique about it, all hold to the same model—a distributed closed binary client, communicating with a central server (or servers), offering real-time action with location-based adventure gaming and objects.

One of the clues as to the reach of this type of game is in the genre title. As shown in Table 2.1, these games truly are *massively* multi-player.

Table 2.1 The Reach of Various MMORPGs

Game	Subscriptions	Peak Logins	Source
EverQuest	430,000	118,000	Sony via Wikipedia [EQ01]
Eve Online	200,000	37,481	Eve-Online Forums [EVE01]
World of Warcraft	10,000,000	n/a	Blizzard [BLIZZARD01]

This means that, when the servers are running an *Eve Online* session, they must simultaneously deal with nearly 40,000 individual players. Clearly, some techniques must be used to spread the load over multiple servers, whilst also keeping things synchronized. You'll learn about some of these techniques in Chapter 6, "Creating Arcade and Massively Multi-Player Online Games (Real-Time)."

Key points from the player's point of view include ownership (of objects or locations), leveling up (to improve capabilities), revenue model (advertising, upgrades, and so on), and in-game currency and economy. Unlike in a pure arcade-style gaming model, players are generally encouraged to empathize more with their character. Additionally, the relationship between player and character tends to be long term in nature, as is often the case in real-world RPGs. Part of this comes from the amount of time each player must invest at the outset to create his or her character.

With regard to revenue models, they, too, tend to be long term, ranging from requiring payment to keep a player's account in good standing to pushing players to buy expansion packs and client upgrades. These may or may not include some free playing time, but are usually used as a way to generate revenue or compensate for continuing development of the game.

SIMULATIONS AND GOD GAMES

There are a few multi-player sub-genres that are worth mentioning: simulations and god games. A simulation game is simply a rendering of a gaming environment that reflects a possible reality in which processes are simulated—less an action game and more an unfolding of events. Examples might be the popular artificial-life game *Creatures*.

God games, such as *Civilization*, allow the player to step up from managing a simulation to actually participating in it. Every aspect is open to be

continued

tweaked in game time, and each tweak has direct consequences for the outcome of the game. That's another difference between simulation games and god games: You don't play a simulation to win, but god games are usually more of a competitive experience.

Although these are not massively multi-player (usually because of a restriction of the game model rather than a technological constraint; for example, *Age of Empires* and *Civilization* games tend to limit the number of concurrently active participants in a game session), they do share many things in common with MMORPGs, such as the distributed client game logic. (In these games, a vast amount of the game logic is farmed out to the client, which leads to some of the aforementioned consequences.)

In fact, in a case study of client-based decision making revolving around Blizzard's *Age of Empire* games—revisited in Chapter 8—covers how the games' architecture is like a MUD in that it follows a client/server communication model with location- and object-based logic, but that the high degree of complexity makes client-side processing a must.

One would expect that the same would be true of a real online *SimCity* variant, but this has yet to be tried in the manner presented here. The more complex the logic required to evolve the game environment, the stronger the temptation to farm that logic processing out to the clients. Supporting a reasonable number of players any other way would probably require daily update processing, a turn-by-turn mechanism, or some other way to limit the processing requirement on the server. Otherwise, it becomes impossible to make the game pay its way.

WEB AND "THROUGH THE BROWSER" GAMES

With the advent of the World Wide Web and enhancements to browsers through various client-side technologies, more sophisticated multi-player Web games can be created. In some ways, they provide a very viable alternative to the model presented in the previous section. After all, as a technology, the Web is in many ways better than Telnet. You can also have Telnet clients through the Web (using Java applets, for example) that allow interfaces to servers directly rather than using some kind of Web page–based interface. Web and through-the-browser games can also allow the designer to get the same kind of reach in terms of the platforms supported without really having to design for each one. This allows developers to reach a much larger audience for much less investment.

Through-the-browser games are usually Web based, although recent advances in client-side capabilities have made it possible to develop games that are played locally, but through a Web browser. Other Web games might be played through a browser or customized client software, merely using the Web as an information-exchange medium. An example of this would be playing chess by e-mail.

There are a few gaming models to think about here, including the following:

- Text-based Web games
- Flash-based Web games
- Alternate-reality Web games

For example, Figure 2.2 shows the *Samurai Of Legend* online game, found at http://SamuraiOfLegend.com, where the interface is clearly identified as a series of links. There is also a status area in the top-right corner, and the occasional piece of in-line advertising. In contrast, Figure 2.3 shows WidgetBox.com, a Web site that provides Flash-based games, which can be embedded into other Web sites by their owners. This clearly shows the differences in technologies available, depending on the chosen platform. Alternate reality games tend to be a mixture of elements—both presented through the Web and forums and in real life.

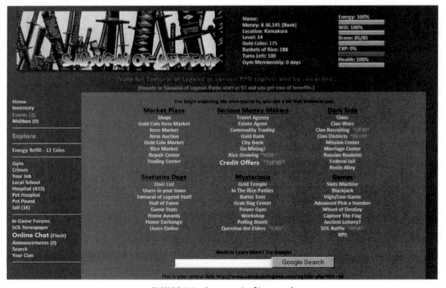

FIGURE 2.2 *Samurai of Legend.*

FIGURE 2.3 WidgetBox.com.

In addition to these are Java applet–based games, but these tend to fall into one of the previous categories—i.e., arcade-style or MMORPG. They simply use the browser as a vehicle to distribute and/or execute the proprietary client.

The Web-gaming delivery medium can also be made to fit some RPG gaming models, allowing quite rich environments to be built on the server and delivered through the Web browser. These include games such as *DragonFable,* for example, along with countless more. They have the advantage of being relatively easy to implement and will run any-where—at least from the player's point of view. Anybody with a Web browser and Internet connection can participate. That said, game interac-tion remains reasonably low due to the lack of action in the form of graphics, sound, animation, and so on. Web gaming also offers a great casual gaming model. It is attractive for its low initial investment both in monetary terms and in terms of time. The aim is to make it as accessible as possible, as easy to get into as possible, and as sticky as possible.

Text-Based Through-the-Browser Games

Text-based games are played in the browser as a collection of Web pages. Under the hood, this means they can be deployed using existing technologies such as open-source content-management systems (CMSes) customized for use in a gaming context. Games such as *Project Rockstar*, for example, use a basic CMS, overlaying forums, advertising, and other elements to provide an interactive interface. The fact that the game is also based around a turn-by-turn, overnight-update model is due in part to the fact that it uses technologies and services that are slightly more restrictive.

Some key concepts with respect to text-based through-the-browser games include the following:

- The network connectivity generally follows a model in which there is no persistent connection to a single server foreseen, such as one on the World Wide Web. This means that the connection with the server generally only lasts for as long as is required to transfer the data that it has been set up to exchange. (Note that leads to interesting points to do with session management; see Chapter 5, "Creating Turn-by-Turn Network Games," for more information.)
- The model used for the game itself is usually based on a fairly static environment, with a dynamic overnight refresh of that environment. This allows players to maintain a presence in the game, complete with varying parameters that define their in-game personae, but based on criteria that never change. In other words, the set of things that define the game environment are static, but their properties might change when the environment is refreshed.
- Due to the delivery medium, Web games may have limited graphics, but are not typically animated beyond simple animated GIFs or vaguely interactive roll-over graphics. The same is true of the game's sound.

Flash-Based Web Games

As mentioned, game interaction in text-based Web games is reasonably low. This can be combated, to a certain degree, by the use of Flash. Flash games use the Adobe Flash platform to deliver a richer multimedia experience that can include video, sound, clickable objects, and a keyboard interface. In short, arcade games, RPGs, front-ends, and navigation systems can all be created using Flash.

The model works using a downloadable-content-plus-streaming-asset approach. The game can be downloaded to the target platform, and additional data can be streamed in through a Web connection. The players' own statistics can then be fed back to the server and stored, just as with any other platform model.

The simplest Flash model is something I call the "cabinet model." In this, downloadable Flash games use the networking aspect purely for storing high scores. (Again, obviously, some care has to be taken to combat the adverse effects of cheating.) More elaborate games can then be created that make use of the client/server relationship in other ways, delivering the front-end via the Flash platform. These tend to follow other game-type models, and need no further explanation here.

The Flash model merely provides a way to deliver a better interface via the Web. It is not intended to be held up as some kind of vision of the future of network gaming, just an illustration of how such enabling technology, which is discussed further in the next chapter, can be used to build a workable game model relatively easily.

Alternate-Reality Web Games

An up-and-coming game-type category that I call "alternate reality games" typically combines the Web—used to provide game-related clues—with the real, physical world, resulting in a hybrid of armchair and physical playing. Other forms of this game type can combine GPS location data with person-to-person interaction, and augment the real world with a virtual storyline and eventual goal. Purchase of materials such as game cards to be used within the game or in the real-world extension of the game provide interest, collectability, and revenue. Examples of such games include *Perplex City*, which, for the uninitiated, attaches a real-world prize to Web-based multi-player interactivity, real-world locations, and game cards. The combination is magical—when it works; whether they produce economically viable game models remains to be seen.

As the market for these games matures, the games will almost certainly begin drawing on other technologies such as cell-phone text messaging, e-mail, and even face-to-face human interaction.

FROM THEORY TO DEVELOPMENT

This chapter should have given you a keen appreciation of the various types of network games, and helped you begin to see how you can best design your game using the network game models discussed in Chapter 1.

Usually, the first question involves choosing the right platform and networking technology to match up with your perceived audience and your available resources. You might even opt to create a proof of concept Web game before rolling out the full package as a retail product.

There is also the question of experience. That is, if the development team has had little exposure to network-game development, then it might be best to test game mechanics and audience by building up the final game through different models. For example, if you wanted to create a space-trading MMORPG like *Eve Online*, there could be various stages from the inception through to the final product. The game could start life as a plain old text interface Web game, enabling you to test the mechanics of certain static aspects of the game environment. The result would be a space-trading game without elaborate, real-time combat, for example. The rest of the game could then be built up, with new functionality added after the basic game mechanics were in place. This might include a specific client, interactive portions, or even new game logic. If the team wanted to build an online cooperative FPS, a similar approach could be taken—with a few differences. For example, the starting game model is quite likely to be some form of FPS laced with AI bots in the vein of *Unreal Tournament*. The trick is to layer up the design and try to keep it simple at each stage. Games are hard enough to create, and networked games hard enough to build and balance, that anything that helps simplify the process is a good thing.

By following a gradual process, keeping networking at the heart of the game design, and using the various types of games mentioned in this chapter, you can keep the project on track.

REFERENCES

[COSTIKYAN01] "The Future of Online Gaming," http://www.costik.com

[EVE01] http://myeve.eve-online.com/ingameboard.asp?a=topic&thread ID=638055

[EQ01] http://en.wikipedia.org/wiki/Everquest#Subscription_history

[BLIZZARD01] http://www.blizzard.com/us/press/080122.html

PUTTING GAME NETWORKING TECHNOLOGY TO WORK

In This Chapter

- Components of Network Gaming
- The Platform
- Complete System Architecture

S electing the platform for your network involves a complex decision process that takes the following into account:

- The kind of game being developed
- The target market
- The planned network infrastructure
- Funds available for development
- The size of the development team
- The life span of console/market

You might think that this list is not terribly different from one you would generate when selecting the platform for a single player, non-networked game—and you'd be right. This list is not unique; the same concerns must be addressed when developing other kinds of games.

That said, building a networked game is not just a case of adding networking support to a single-user, play-at-home title—although most, if not all, games for personal computers and many console games include networking support, usually just for a multi-player variant of the single-player experience (with some being better than others). The mix is more subtle than that. The key is in the blend of technology that comes together to make the game a much more enjoyable experience (and, let's face it, it is more or less a given that a multi-player networked game is more enjoyable than a single-player game).

To obtain just the right blend, you must first consider what players will expect from the networked portions of your game versus a non-networked equivalent, including how they will want to interact with the game and each other. Next, you must determine what technology—components, platforms, and so on—and networking models are available to help create a game that meets these expectations. The game doesn't choose the technology, nor does the technology choose the game. Rather, the developer must make the proposed features of the networked game work using the technology available—and make it fun.

Complicating things is the desire to combine technologies that players have at their disposal—i.e., a single player might have a console as well as a personal computer and a cell phone—to create games that enable different levels of involvement. For example, the game might be designed to support the use of the console for real-time, online play; a personal computer with e-mail for turn-based, non–real-time, low-involvement extensions to the game; and a cell phone to receive updates and send small messages representing possible game moves. A game could feasibly use the same back-end to serve all three needs—hard-core, casual, and occasional gamer—which would also leave the door open to attract gamers existing in just one of those pigeon holes.

COMPONENTS OF NETWORK GAMING

When deciding which bits of available network gaming technology are appropriate for use in your game, you must first decide how the network itself fits into your design and development. Some pieces of the overall game networking paradigm will have a direct effect on the playability of the game, while others will be relevant only in the way in which the player interacts with it.

In this chapter, I have broken up everything that could be termed a network gaming component (be it hardware or software) into two areas:

- **Communication.** The way the player and his or her system communicate with other players' systems and the game server
- **Interaction.** How players interact with each other and the underlying gaming environment at a higher (i.e., logic) level

So, the first is about *how* the bits that make up the game environment—players, machines, servers, and so on—talk to each other, while the second is about *why* there is this need for communication in the first place and how that interaction fits into the available technologies.

Players have certain expectations in both areas that must be met to prevent the game from seeming like a single-player game that had networking added to it as an afterthought. For example, just as people expect to be able to communicate in real time in the real world, so, too, will they likely expect to communicate in real time in the game space. If a multiplayer networked game does not enable players to communicate with each other in real time, then it will feel as if they are disconnected from each other. Now, in certain genres, this might be the desired effect—but generally speaking, the purpose of networking a collection of players in the same in-game space and asking them to cooperate on a given task is to have them do so in a manner that mimics real life. The more players can do this, the more immersive—and successful—the game will be.

Communication

Communication in a non-networked game is very simple: there isn't any beyond that which has been pre-programmed. With the addition of networking technology, however, players can:

- Talk to each other
- Talk to the server

There are two distinct models of in-game communication:

- **Real-time communication.** Examples of real-time communication systems include instant messaging and voice communication using a special headset—both of which have been widely implemented in action-based network games both in wide area network–based (WAN-based) and local area network–based (LAN-based) games. The communication path might be peer-to-peer or it might pass through a central server. Obviously each of these design choices has implications for the implementation on the chosen platform, which we shall see later on. Generally speaking, communication with the server—for action-based networked games, at least—will also occur real time, as will the effects of this communication and the relaying of those effects to other players.

- **Delayed communication.** Delayed communication is an option for Web-based strategy games, play-by-e-mail puzzle games, and games in which real-time communication is not vital to the design. Play-by-e-mail *Dungeons & Dragons*, for example, relies on a delayed communication model. Delayed communications are rather simpler to implement from a technical standpoint, but this model raises challenges in terms of game design in that some gamers just don't find it appealing.

 It is possible to mix these two kinds of communication. A fast-paced action game with an in-game forum for trading weapons, for example, embraces both real-time and delayed communication models.

The communication model you choose is based in part on whether you intend to create a multi-player or single-player networked game, as well as whether the game will be played on a WAN or a LAN.

Communication in Multi-Player Network Games

As you've learned, communication in multi-player network games is very important. If players are to be pitted against each other or cooperate on a team, they will expect to be able to ridicule, taunt, aid, and abet each other either vocally or using short text messages. If the game is a LAN game, the players' close proximity to each other likely enables them to shout to other players. WAN games, then, must replace some of the communication available in a LAN environment with a technological solution.

That solution can come in multiple forms. For example, platforms supporting keyboards (i.e., personal computers, cell phones, and mobile communication devices) can enable players to communicate via short text messages. Platforms without keyboards (i.e., consoles, handheld gaming units, and arcade systems) must usually make do with preset mood indicators (smiley faces, for example) or allow voice messaging.

As you might imagine, however, sending voice messages over a WAN connection is not a trivial matter; it uses up valuable bandwidth, and if it experiences glitches, the effect is spoiled. Moreover, not all gamers have access to the hardware that allows them to communicate in this manner. That means that games that rely on an external peripheral to facilitate in-game multi-player communication should be available in two packages: with it and without it.

Communication in Single-Player Network Games

One might assume that a single-player network game wouldn't require support for any communication at all. After all, the player plays in a vacuum, does he not? Well—yes and no. A single player *non*-network game is played in isolation. That is, the player is pitted against the machine and nobody can witness his or her progress. Likewise, a single-player *network* game enables players to conduct their play sessions on their own, against the machine— but also offers the possibility for players to share their results. Even if an online game revolves around solving puzzles in a single-player environment, the networking element makes it possible to add multi-player features such as leader boards, informal top-score competitions, and so forth.

Moreover, some games that might seem at first glimpse to be single player in nature may in fact be multi-player competitive environments. For example, suppose a game revolves around shared central resources (e.g., planets in a space-trading simulation, in-game characters, etc.); even if players are just playing against the system, it is inevitable that there will be competition for those resources. Communication between players and the system, as well as between the players themselves, will facilitate this competition. Allowing communication in real time or non–real-time using methods such as forum posting will introduce value-added benefits to the game.

Interaction

Communication is important in a game, facilitating two key types of interaction:

- **Player-to-player interaction.** This is the type of interaction involved when players hurl abuse at each other through the ether. Put simply, if a player can see other players in the game environment, he or she will expect to be able to interact with those other players—and this interaction goes well beyond the communication discussed in the previous section. Allowing players to do so, however, raises some technological issues, which are also intertwined with the game's logic. Many questions must be answered, primarily revolving around the exact amount of interaction that the game will allow between players and the nature of that interaction. For example, the game might allow simple 40-character messages to be exchanged, or it might support person-to-person voice communication. Physical interaction might be allowed, too, but with restrictions on how one player can affect the others.

- **Game-universe interaction.** Players must also be able to interact with the game environment both to tell the system in control of the game what they are doing and to move bits of game environment around—for example, various artifacts that exist within the game environment. Again, whatever the player can see, he or she will want to interact with. Some of these interactions might be persistent (taking an object from one place to another); the technology used to run the game environment will need to take this into account.

As with communication, there is real-time interaction and delayed interaction, plus a third category: real-time grouped interaction:

- **Real-time interaction.** In a network game, most interaction will need to take place in real time. Indeed, the ability of the game to support real-time interaction is even more important to the design of the game than its ability to support real-time communication; interaction is the game. We can accept that, in a real-time action game, the occasional voice communication between players might not quite come off—but the interaction must be handled *perfectly*.
- **Delayed interaction.** Delayed interaction is primarily reserved for non–real-time action games, where the interaction between players and other players and between players and the game system can be performed on a command-response basis. This command-response exchange can take several hours—or even days—to unfold. Clearly, the vast majority of Web-based games fall into this category, as do play-by-e-mail games and certain others. Of utmost importance here is that the players of these games do not expect anything more, and are perhaps less likely to be put off if the system is occasionally slow to respond or slightly uneven in its ability to process commands.
- **Real-time grouped interaction.** This model is used in cases where it is useful to group sets of commands (actions) that may take some time to carry out. The commands themselves allow the action to unfold in real time from the observers' point of view. They can even be interrupted, in some cases, provided that this does not disturb the flow of the action. The real-time grouped interaction model is an example of a delayed interaction model, but also very useful in games where lots of things are happening at the same time in different locations. It is handy to be able to queue up some commands, and then move to a different area to concentrate on some other aspect of the game environment under your control. Some strategy games and RPGs use this method to mix the real-time action model that delivers graphical and aural supremacy over a Web game with the core *Dungeons & Dragons*–style RPG model. Obviously, this approach can be implemented for Web games as well (discussed further in Chapter 5, "Creating Turn-by-Turn Network Games"), but it is most effective in

MMORPGs, where it can help compensate for underperforming network layer implementations.

THE PLATFORM

Having established what the player expects from a network game with respect to communication and interaction, you are ready to take a look at what hardware game developers have at their disposal to help realize those expectations.

Traditionally, there are four key gaming platforms:

- **Personal computer.** PC, Linux, or Apple
- **Console.** Home entertainment unit
- **Handheld device.** Mobile console
- **Multi-platform.** Usually several flavors of personal computer/console

Each of these has different capabilities and possibilities that stem from the platform's ergonomics and technical implementation of the network layer.

Personal Computer

Personal computers come in three flavors—those based on Windows, those based on Linux, and those based on Mac OS (i.e., Apple Macintosh). Each has its own particular capabilities, but they all generally support networking—natively and through the operating system. All personal computers, for example, have network connections that are usually offered via the operating system TCP/IP drivers. This means that usually, the application programming interface (API) that is supplied with the operating system's development tools also provides the libraries to interact with the network layer.

Personal computers are an easy platform to develop for because the tool support is quite mature, and there are many people who know about personal computers. The issue with targeting personal computers is the high amount of customer-support calls that the developer is likely to have to field. This is for two reasons:

- First, the actual performance of a personal computer is a function of its available memory, the graphics memory, the processor speed, and complexity of the algorithms driving the game (as opposed to the audiovisual aspects of it)—and each of these can vary widely. In choosing the personal computer as a platform, the developer must be very aware of the actual capabilities—and variance of capabilities—in the marketplace. To create an even game experience for all clients, the developer must account for every possible home-computer setup (within reason)—or else ensure that the minimum specifications provide access to the largest possible market—or risk the market being terribly restricted. In particular, the graphics need to be down-scalable—either automatically or by the end user—to keep the game playable.

- Second, it is difficult to know what a player will be using in terms of supported technology. The mix of processor, graphics card, hard drive, memory, screen, input devices (mouse, joystick, etc.), and the rest might not be known ahead of time, and must therefore be catered to by careful programming and testing.

Of course, the alternative is to *prescribe* the system specifications in such a way that the target market is limited to only those players whose system configuration conforms to a very precise model. This is undesirable in many cases, but can be used as a way to make sure that each player receives the same level of play.

Console

One of the real benefits of using consoles as a platform—and this is not exclusive to network game development—is that they represent a very even playing field. All units of a given console are created equal. As a result, a game can be written once for a particular console, and will work in an identical fashion, out of the box, in every other console of the same type. In turn, this means that you can factor out the hardware performance and networking interface from the estimates of bottlenecks and uneven performance criteria.

 For this discussion, consoles refers to home entertainment units such as the Sony PS2 and PS3, Microsoft Xbox/360, Nintendo Wii, and so on, as well as to some portable units that support networking, such as the Sony PSP and Nintendo DS.

Some consoles have wired networking support built-in, and some have it as an optional extra. These tend to be the home entertainment units rather than the mobile ones—meaning there is no point trying to create a game that is designed to be used on the move for a console that doesn't have the capability to be mobile. On the other hand, some portable consoles support wireless networking, which is great for close-proximity multi-player gaming, as well as for connecting to the Internet for true multi-player online action. These could be targeted with either kind of game, and could even be mixed in with other clients.

Of course, consoles don't have keyboards, so the data entry interface becomes a concern—especially with respect to the network configuration. Luckily, however, most of that should be standardized by the console manufacturer.

Typically, the manufacturers of a console have a certification and test procedure that all game developers must follow. This is designed to guarantee a certain level of conformance across the entire market—but it does come at a price. Certification for Nintendo, for example, is notoriously expensive. On the other hand, support is good, and the development kits come with all kinds of useful information and access to documentation that makes the transition from the development platform (e.g., the PC) to the target that much more bearable.

Except for the Microsoft platforms, however, development licenses for consoles are very difficult to obtain. Most smaller developers—and nearly all individuals—will be unable to obtain a development license. This barrier to entry is meant to weed out lesser-quality developers or those without the necessary resources to successfully carry through an incredibly complex development process. But if you follow the guidelines laid out by the console manufacturer and demonstrate real dedication with the development process, you stand a better chance. For first projects, though, it is usually better to choose a less-restrictive platform.

Handheld Device

In a nutshell, if you want to reach the largest potential target market, make your game to go by designing it for a handheld device. This book defines the true handheld as mobile phones (cell phones) and multifunction devices that aren't game consoles per se, but that are targeted by developers because of their wide reach. Everyone has a mobile phone, and their capabilities are being extended every single day. Moreover, the handheld device is probably one of the most versatile platforms in terms of networking technology.

That said, developing for this platform does involve multiple challenges:

- As with personal computers, different handheld devices employ different platforms—and there are many different types of devices on the market. That means that as a game developer you may feel as though you are creating a game for several platforms at once (and, indeed, you may be).

Enabling technologies such as Java, XML, HTML, and so on will help if the developer is creating casual games that don't require special graphical capabilities.

- The hardware components on handheld devices may differ by model. For example, although handheld units generally have a smaller screen, the exact size of the screen varies for different models—meaning that, depending on your game's design, you may need to contend with a scaling issue.

- Handheld devices run off battery power—which should not result in lost data or in-game penalties when the client disconnects.
- Handhelds may not have permanent networking, or they may rely on connectivity that is restricted in real-time power, such as SMS (text messaging). Note, however, that many devices do support wireless, so all the comments about close proximity multi-player gaming made in the previous section apply here.

A turn-based model might be the best of all worlds for the handheld platform. If combined with wireless networking, handhelds could be used in a kind of casual game that involves playing against other people in the real world (or at least in close proximity). The scores on the server, or even the progress of the players through the game, could be conveyed by the posting of special SMS messages or by a low-bandwidth data connection.

Multi-Platform

Developing for cross-platform network gaming can be very rewarding, as it maximizes reach within the same core game design. In this book, however, I take a slightly different approach to the "same game, different platforms" philosophy that is the norm. As far as I am concerned, the same game on a different platform is the same game.

Now, it is possible to create games for multiple platforms taking into account different game goals per platform, depending on the expected role of the player in the game environment. In addition, players might even change their role as they change platforms. But even so, it is the same game database at the back-end, with the same game rules in force. The platform selection simply specifies how the game environment is interpreted and what the players are able to do inside that game environment.

This approach enables the developer to address hard-core and casual gamers alike with the same product, simply by virtue of the platform selection. For example, the same game could be accessed through a Web interface, with only certain simple role-playing, turn-based aspects, but then turn into a fully interactive, real-time action RPG if a proprietary client is used. Different platforms offer different possibilities, and the developer may need to adapt the game model depending on the target platform, but the opportunities for crossover are clear.

COMPLETE SYSTEM ARCHITECTURE

While much of this chapter has concentrated on the game platform as a piece of machinery on which the player plays the game, there is much more to the technology behind the development of a networked game than just the client. True, for many games, a lot of energy is devoted to building the client, whereas for others, the database and server environment are the most important. But each game is an entire system, which is built on common foundations—be they the networking protocol, the operating system, or the backbone of the Internet itself.

Generally speaking, for certain simple LAN-based games, each client can also be the server, which has its own specific list of related issues. In contrast, where there is a central server that controls the flow, there is also usually some kind of middleware that helps everything hang together, as well as a database that keeps all the persistent (and not-so-persistent) data stored safely somewhere in the back. It is this, the most common architecture, that is shown in Figure 3.1.

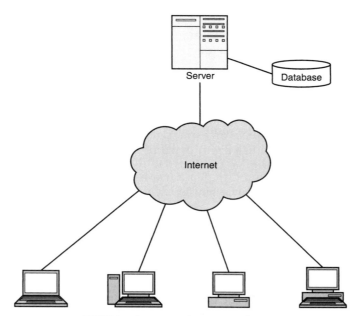

FIGURE 3.1 System architecture schematic.

At the other end of the scale—and not shown in Figure 3.1—there is the *front-end*, used by the player to interact with the game environment that is represented by the other clients and the server and database shown in Figure 3.1. The front-end provides the control structures that the player needs to interact with the game.

It is on these three key areas—the front-end, middleware, and the back-end—as well as the network itself that this section focuses.

The Front-End Interface

Of utmost importance to a game's design is the virtual interface, often referred to as the "front-end," offered to the player. This interface can be a fully implemented game or some kind of stripped-down browser, depending on the developer's vision.

The easiest kind of front-end interface, or client, to create is usually based on someone else's technology. For example, there is still some call for developing games based on a plain-text interface, which doesn't require any special coding. Other types of front-ends include the following:

- Decorated text
- Dynamic decorated text
- Applets
- Custom game interface
- Full game

Plain Text

In the past, many multi-player online games (MOGs) were played over the text-only Telnet protocol, using a standard Telnet client. Descriptions of the game environment and all the actions and reactions of the players within it were transmitted using this very simple technology. Purely as a technology, plain text is attractive—but limited.

For example, while the 255 characters of the ASCII character set might seem expansive, they are not sufficient for drawing anything but the most rudimentary graphics—and even those are hard to create, seeing as how the interface is usually limited to an 80×25 page of text. Most plain-text games will therefore be limited to textual descriptions or basic map-style character graphics. They are easy to create, but limited in scope, and not guaranteed to please players.

This technology offers one big advantage: It can be played on almost any platform, as long as the platform includes support for text entry. That support needn't be sophisticated; a game can be put together that requires only a very limited number of key presses. (That said, the lack of a keyboard will be an issue if players wish to communicate with each other.) Additionally, the plain-text interface is lightweight—that is, it doesn't take a lot of system power to display, and it can be rendered quickly and easily.

In a plain-text game, the server is where the game session unfolds in the environment. In other words, the server is in charge, and sends updates to the clients to tell them what is going on. So it is a good thing that the plain-text interface is lightweight, because the server will have enough to do maintaining the game environment. On the other hand, this type of front-end is relatively light on network traffic—as long as the descriptions of rooms and so on are not overly verbose.

Decorated Text

As with plain text, decorated text (HTML for example) is usually rendered using a third-party software application that is, in essence, borrowed technology. This makes it very attractive because you can augment the text with images and hyperlinks, whilst displaying the actions and reactions of other players.

Web-based games are great fun. Based on one of the most accessible technologies available, it is perfect for developing casual games—and even for testing more advanced gaming concepts. The great thing about Web gaming is that it all fits together with off-the-shelf, freely available, often open-source technology. In fact, it is possible to hire (rent or lease) the technology at a very reasonable rate, paying only a premium for high data transfer (bandwidth). The Web server serves up a dynamic environment, probably based on a database back-end, and communication occurs through Web forms and other easily accessible, easy-to-develop-for interfaces. The only drawback is that the game will look so good, even the casual player will want to interact with the game environment and might be disappointed when they find that they can't—which makes the case for using dynamic decorated text.

What makes it all possible is the flexibility of HTML (and other pseudo languages used for text decoration), which is used to deliver Web pages. Text can be colored, images added (even small icons can make a big difference), and various levels of formatting applied, including bold text, italics, and underlining.

 To avoid paying a premium, network communication must be bandwidth efficient—which will also serve to speed up reaction times. This is a worthwhile goal in itself, and so it all plays into the technology in a useful way.

So, we have the speed and ease of working with plain text, leaving the client software (i.e. the browser, for Web games) to worry about how it should be rendered. Decorated text is efficient, easy to program, and results in some pleasing effects, which can be augmented beyond simply clicking your way around by making it dynamic.

Dynamic Decorated Text

Dynamic decorated text is simply a fancy way to deploy technology that makes the playing interface come alive. This goes beyond simple drop-down menus into offering real windows on the game environment that probably don't extend to real-time action, but might extend to real-time strategy.

Again, employing dynamic decorated text delivers the game through the use of someone else's technology; even the application software—i.e., the browser—is not our own. The key enabling technologies in this category are

- Style sheets
- JavaScript
- XML

The technical term for leveraging all of this is dynamic HTML (DHTML). With it, we can do some remarkable things, such as creating a canvas onto which simple shapes can be placed and moved around. In addition, colors and images can be used to accentuate the game environment. For example, consider simple two-player networked games such as *Battleships*, *Reversi*, chess, and renditions of popular four-in-a-row games. Because the game state for these games is stored on the server, and there are no issues relating to hacking, you can feel free to adorn the interface with DHTML.

One tool that allows this is Asynchronous JavaScript And XML (AJAX), which is a technology for data exchange. Sadly, it is not very economical, as many XML schema tend to be bloated with respect to the kind of game data that they can transport. It is, however, a standard technology, and using it will reduce time to market—which is useful even if the developer will eventually replace it with something more efficient, as it allows you to test ideas before an expensive implementation is started (see Chapter 4, "A Comparison of Network Game Types").

There are, however, some dangers associated with implementing features on a client using this kind of technology, many relating to the visibility of the source code. In essence, all the code that makes up the front-end is visible to the player. If it contains game logic, the player can dig into it, work out how the game is put together, and perhaps use that information to cheat. That cheating might be anything from trying to create an interface that plays by itself to attempting to pass off bogus updates to the server. Again, the onus is on the server to manage this, as well as maintain the connections (part of the Web server technology), data storage, and congruence between all the game clients and the NPCs that inhabit the game space.

Applets

An applet is a small application designed to be delivered online. Although the first applets were extremely lightweight, they have become more and more complex as the processing capability of computers and the available bandwidth has increased. To reduce the burden on the game server, game developers sometimes use applets to implement game logic in the client;

because applets are generally more complex than dynamic decorated text, it is more difficult for players to reverse-engineer the source code in order to cheat.

Usually, applets are used to deliver games that are played in the browser, but they can also be standalone packages run in the operating system using a virtual machine (VM). As long as the VM is available for a platform—be it a personal computer or a cell phone—it can run the applet. Of course, this doesn't help the fact that a personal computer and a cell phone have different screen resolutions, but it will help on the networking side. The use of a VM to run the game client does, however, have performance implications, meaning that some of the more-advanced algorithms for managing the connection (discussed in Chapter 7, "Improving Network Communications") cannot be used with an advanced client because the workload might be too high.

Key technologies for applet-based client front-ends include the following:

- Adobe Flash
- Java Applets
- AIR

 AIR, an up-and-coming alternative, is more of an XML interpretation framework than anything else, although it does have some great API functionality, and the result is also interpreted via a VM.

These technologies are great at networking, but their networking capabilities are built in and managed entirely by the underlying infrastructure rather than the game developer. As a result, the server must be more robust because it will bear all the responsibility for managing the network infrastructure—although this might not matter, as some of the logic can be farmed out to the clients. In order to regain some of the network-level control, as well as increase the performance, the developer might instead consider using the custom game interface.

Custom Game Interface

A custom game interface is simply a window into the server with some capability to perform game-logic decisions. It is very similar to a decorated text interface, except that the display is much more sophisticated. Examples include a *Second Life*– or Google *Lively*–style interface, which is more sophisticated than a MUD but offers roughly the same kind of experience. The technology is very (relatively speaking) simple—an application in its own right, with some added functionality:

- Game-environment rendering (2D/3D/isometric 2.5D depending on the design)
- Network-management logic (to help smooth the connectivity)
- Game logic and control logic in real time

The extent of the last might vary depending on whether the game follows the true real-time or real time–strategy (RTS) model. For those games that follow the RTS model, the client must be more than just a game-world browser; for real time action games, however, it will have enough to do to render the environment and control the logic.

Custom game interfaces are not standalone games. As such, they are protected to a certain extent from casual hacking and cheating. And because they are compiled for a specific platform, they have the following added advantages:

- **Execution speed.** These game interfaces can be more heavily optimized.
- **Data/code hiding.** They are inherently more secure.
- **Ability to take advantage of the platform.** The feature set will be more or less known.

There is also a commercial side to it: The perceived value of a packaged (real or virtual) application for a specific platform is much higher than for a downloadable applet or play-in-the-browser interface. As such:

- It can be sold in a box.
- For a console, it can ship with a logo.
- It will be easier to get through the manufacturer's quality control than a full game.

This comes at a cost, however. Although an RTS–style custom game interface offers pretty much the same functionality as an applet or dynamic Web page, it is potentially more complex to develop and test than these other examples. It is up to the developer to gauge whether the perceived value and reach of a commercial product outweighs this cost. After all, if it is aimed at the console market, chances are it will have to go through the manufacturer's quality control anyway for those that do not support Web downloads.

Full Game

At this stage, you might be considering taking the plunge into a standalone game, with network (possibly massively multi-player) support built in. Akin to creating a full game, this approach is the most complex undertaking possible—and adding network and/or multi-player support adds exponentially to that complexity. That said, this approach enables the developer to do pretty much exactly what he or she wants with the hardware and software—meaning the platform can be targeted to get the most out of it.

The level of detail in the product also means that it has to stand on its own, including the game logic and the manipulation and rendering of the game environment. The upside is that the server needs only send minimal information on game-world action and reaction, which helps use less bandwidth, making it more efficient. In return, the client needs only provide the result of processing the server-supplied action and reaction data because the client knows that all the other clients have the same base code as it does. Therefore, this model fits into a robust distributed processing paradigm, albeit with a single point of failure in the central server.

THE BOLTED-ON PARADIGM

Often, a full game can be played by itself in single-player mode, sometimes with bots playing the part of the other players. Action games can be delivered using this technological approach: single-player games with networking possibilities. Many RTS games have also been delivered this way in the past. It has also been said, however, that modern games require some kind of networking component just to justify their price in the marketplace.

Putting the two together—creating a game with networking that has been bolted on in such a way that the bots are just replaced by real players—is a valid development paradigm. In my opinion, however, it's not sufficiently good to create a game that stands out *because* of its networking component. It simply offers networked play because the market expects it.

As you will see in later chapters, when you use this approach to game-client delivery, security becomes a big risk, predominantly because hackers will have all the tools they need to open the game and make changes to benefit cheaters. They will also have access to the raw network data, opening up further possibilities for unsportsmanlike behavior. For this reason, part of the technology that delivers this solution must also contain adequate protection against this threat—a provision that arguably starts with middleware.

The Middleware

The next layer up from the front-end, or client, is arguably the server side. In this case, it's a kind of virtual server as opposed to a physical machine. It might well be running on a server machine, but the reason we use the term "middleware" rather than "game server" to refer to it is because the responsibilities of the server portion could well be farmed out to the clients.

In a LAN-based environment, this initially meant that one of the player consoles had responsibility to synchronize the networked parties or that there was a central repository used for that purpose. Since then, however, things have moved on a little; any networked game now available is truly client/server, with a server used to actually process game logic as well as provide online storage.

Most of these games are now available for play over the Internet, so the server plays a large part in connecting very disparate clients with each other. This happens using one of two possible technological approaches:

- **A Web server.** The advantage of this technology is that it can be hosted virtually and relatively cheaply, and it uses off-the-shelf technology as a proving ground.
- **A custom game server.** The advantage of this technology is that it is entirely customizable, which means it can be made to be as efficient as necessary and is probably more extensible than a Web-server solution.

Web Server

Some application infrastructures for online development, such as the one used on social-networking sites like Facebook, are becoming attractive as technologies to enable online gaming because of their API for multi-user Internet communication. With these, the only thing the developer must do is host the application before it is rolled out through the social network. That means it will potentially end up in front of many people very quickly, giving the developer the chance to experiment with different game logic. So as a test-bed as well as a production-level technology, there are many advantages to using a social network such as Facebook.

Web servers are also available as open-source solutions, and can contain content-management systems (CMSes) that can be used as game platforms. These are usually a bit more flexible than ready-to-run APIs provided by a third party. Extending an open source CMS is as easy as adding modules that can be executed in a specific way. For example, it is relatively easy to modify a standard CMS to deliver gaming technology, as it is based on PHP, a standard open programming language. In addition, they provide an API for security and session management, can deliver HTML and dynamic HTML, and can deliver other client-side technologies such as Flash and Java applets.

CONTENT-MANAGEMENT SYSTEMS

Content-management systems (CMSes) are pieces of software designed to render an interface to a system that displays content. A simple example might be a CMS that displays three columns: a menu, some kind of text content, and contextual options or advertising.

In your gaming environment, you might want to display a menu on the left that enables players to select parts of the gaming environment, while the options on the right might include actions that the player can perform in the game environment. The central content panel might then display the current gaming context.

The CMS doesn't care that this is what you've chosen to do with it. As long as it can find content to display, and as long as there are sufficient customizations in the menu options that fool it into thinking that it is still delivering content, it will continue to do so.

The wonderful thing about this is that the CMS also has a strict user hierarchy, probably has its own built-in forum software, and has lots of automatic features that make writing a network-enabled game much easier than if you had to do it from scratch. After all, all a Web game does is deliver dynamic content in a certain user-oriented context—exactly what a CMS was designed to do in the first place.

For Web technology, then, a Web server is a good way to go, as it provides a low-cost infrastructure. Even for some games in which end-user delivery is through another medium, a Web-server solution might be appropriate for its connectivity. After all, the messaging interface is open and standard, so it ought to be fairly simple to connect, for example, a console front-end to a Web server–based game server. This might work for games with a low processing overhead and could prove to be scalable (just look at the size of Facebook, MySpace, or LinkedIn, for example).

Custom Game Server

Although a Web server–based solution works in some cases, for most games, a custom game server will be needed. A custom game server is a piece of software that is developed for the game to manage multiple users connected by a network of some description. Regardless of the networking platform (LAN, WAN, etc.), all game servers have to deal with the following:

- Networking
- Client communication
- Game logic and interaction
- Security

The split of processing responsibility between the client and the server is important enough that the decision on what kind of server solution to use must be made early in the design process. It is not enough to build a single-player game, decide to offer networked play, and *then* look at server solutions before deciding on a custom game server. If anything, the decision process should be the other way around—given the size of the target market, and the expected market share, how much processing can the server perform, and how much needs to be farmed out? Of course, the game model will weigh into that decision, as RTS games typically process locally for a number of reasons (related to complexity)—which means that the game server is a less-complex proposition, requiring only anti-cheat mechanisms and communication management. At the other end of the processing scale, MMORPGs such as *World of WarCraft* that have an action component as well as a persistent state environment require a good-quality, well-thought-out custom game server.

The Back-End

The term "back-end" refers to everything that supports the game server. Typically, for networked games, this is limited to persistent storage and security or session management. These are things that could be termed as "housekeeping" and are not part of the game-logic processing done by the server.

This section looks at two kinds of persistent storage technologies:

- Files
- Databases

While both have their advantages and disadvantages, it is worth pointing out that it is not an all-or-nothing decision. It is quite possible to choose appropriate technology for a given application and end up with a mix of files and databases.

Files

File storage has the key advantage of being native. In other words, it is easy to deploy and very efficient for small amounts of data because the underlying processing technology is provided by the operating system. This approach is very useful, for example, for storing level files that must be distributed to clients or for other resources such as images and sounds.

In a server environment, it is also possible to use files to store a persistent game environment.

Because they are natively supported, they store data reasonably efficiently, there being no management overhead. The management overhead is all in the code that is used to access them. That said, they do not scale very well in terms of multi-user access. The logic required to ensure that data is not overwritten—and the introduction of file-level security, user-level security, and other mechanisms for the preservation and use of data—puts a strain on development resources. The end result is that, although files are good for small, infrequently accessed pieces of data such as session and security information, they are not very efficient for large-scale, multi-user data storage such as would be required for an MOG environment.

Databases

Where complex relationships exist in the data, and where a standard query language like SQL is needed for development convenience, power, and flexibility, a database must be used. It is possible to get some benefit by using a third-party software extension like SQLite to deliver relational database–style performance through a file-based system. Its not being a real database, however, means there are drawbacks relating to management overhead and to the fact that the pseudo-database runs in line with the game server.

Using a fully independent relational database—such as the open-source MySQL or Postgres or commercial packages such as Oracle—means that the data storage, retrieval, and processing can be farmed out to an external processing asset—that is, another machine that does only the database side of things. That means you can split the functionality across machines, making it scalable. Moreover, with some clever design, the technology can even be made to process the data in zones or across clustered servers. Again, it makes it scalable in terms of game environment and number of users. In addition, it is possible to do database processing using SQL stored procedures, which are now available on open-source platforms. A stored procedure runs on the database as a mini application and farms out yet more of the logic to another platform.

The benefits of using databases are also in security and accessibility. Databases are highly protected against attacks from the outside, and the organization of the data inside tends to be much more logical than a simple file. All this makes it much easier to work with a database than a flat file—but there is a penalty in performance. Although they are very high performance systems, to scale properly they will require, over time, rehosting on their own server infrastructures once the game becomes popular.

The Network

Between the client side and the server side is the network itself, the core of the technology that makes networked gaming possible. For our purposes, I have split the technology that drives networked gaming into three parts:

- Hardware
- Protocol
- Application support

Networking Hardware

Networking hardware is what enables two computers (client/client or client/server) to connect to each other, usually via a cable of some description. Some of the key enabling technologies include the following:

- **Local area network (LAN).** In this model, machines are connected via a network card (client/server), various cables, and miscellaneous equipment.
- **Dial-up.** This enables a machine to connect to a remote network via a modem, which can be connected via the network card (as in a LAN) or another port.
- **Broadband.** A faster version of the dial-up connection, broadband allows much greater bandwidth and data-exchange speed, again connecting through the network card or a USB port. What makes it a version of dial-up is that it is still usually a PPP connection.
- **Wireless.** This is essentially local area networking without wires, using localized high-frequency radio signals to communicate between machines in an ad-hoc (peer-to-peer) fashion or as a network.
- **Mobile telephony.** This is a radio version of the dial-up technology used in cell phones and other devices such as the PocketSurfer.

There are a few points to note. The first is that the two common client-to-network connectivity technologies are network card and wireless. These can connect to other devices that provide wide area network (WAN) connectivity. In contrast, devices like the PocketSurfer and cell phones can connect using radio communications directly to networks that provide them with Internet access. So, the available hardware enables almost every device on the market, one way or another, to connect to the Internet. LAN connections are also quite useful in game networking, as they can be used to connect locally for fast, secure, multi-player games, or as an enabling technology for wider network reach.

Networking Protocols

Networking hardware must be combined with a protocol. Without going into too much detail, information that travels over a network is broken into packets, which are identifiable units of data exchange. Protocols are used to disassemble this information into packets on the sending computer and reassemble the information on the receiving computer. This happens in a stream, with each packet in the stream containing a unit of information. The protocol, then, provides the conduit for this disassembling and reassembling of information.

The two major protocols are transmission control protocol (TCP) and user datagram protocol (UDP). The primary difference between them is in how they deal with these streams:

- **TCP.** As its name implies, transmission control protocol (TCP) provides for all the things that could possibly go wrong with the stream of data—i.e., lost packets, dropped connections, out-of-sequence packets, and so on—but with a performance penalty.
- **UDP.** Predictably, user datagram protocol (UDP) leaves flow control largely in the hands of the user—i.e., the programmer. In short, if a packet is lost, it stays lost. If the packets arrive out of sequence, then so be it. UDP leaves all the decisions as to what to do about it to the developer, but is relatively high performance.

Besides these, there are a couple of protocols for dealing with cell phone–style communication, over which TCP or UDP traffic can travel:

- **GSM.** Global system for mobile (GSM) (or *groupe spécial mobile*, from its French origins) communication uses identity management and complex algorithms for noise reduction and bit-rate–efficient protocols to transfer data effectively. Otherwise, it works in rather the same way as a modem.
- **GPRS/EDGE.** These technologies add better data-switching capabilities to the basic GSM technology, which increases data rates far enough to be able to support high-bandwidth applications such as watching TV or listening to music.

In fact, it is also possible to use a cell phone as a modem, in which case the technological model used is rather like the dial-up technology already covered. The protocol used is likely to be TCP for basic communications and UDP for streaming multimedia.

Networking Application Support

Networking hardware and networking protocols are just the tools that enable network communication. On top of this base, we need to build the support for the various networking tasks:

- Authentication
- Data transfer
- Synchronization

Without these, networking simply will not work.

Although there are several ways to implement support for networking at the programming level, they can be broken down into two camps: third-party solutions, and solutions you create yourself. Using third-party solutions cuts development time, enabling you to concentrate on the game logic and everything that goes into managing the game environment and balancing the rules. The downside is that if there is a performance bottleneck on the networking side, it is hard to fix. (The easiest way to address this may be to reduce the complexity of the game.)

If UDP is chosen as the transmission layer protocol, then the game will have to do a reasonable amount of work anyway, so it may be just as well to use a third-party solution for the real transmission and a custom solution for everything else—everything else, in this case, being encoding, compressing, packet synchronization and stream identification, and so on. The three main technologies, then, are as follows:

- **Application programming interface (API).** Usually provided by the operating-system manufacturer for network control.
- **Library.** A specific set of functions used to manipulate network traffic. Usually provided by a third party (for pay) or from open source equivalent, but sometimes bundled with the development environment.
- **Customized solutions.** Written by the developer expressly for the purpose of providing networking support for the game.

Obviously, customized solutions might also use the library or API code for low-level manipulation of data, addresses, and so on. Chapter 10, "Network Programming Primer," covers most of the approaches at the code level.

A COMPARISON OF NETWORK GAME TYPES

In This Chapter

- Categorizing Multi-Player Network Games
- Comparing Network Game Types
- Design Principles
- Choosing the Technology for Your Game
- References

No two games are created exactly the same. Different network game types might involve tackling different design issues. Moreover, it is not always entirely obvious which design issues are actually important. Put another way, it is easy to get bogged down in minutiae and overlook something that later becomes important.

This chapter rounds up some of the design issues posed by various game types. You'll determine which network technologies will best support the type of game you want to build and how your target market will affect design decisions. You'll also consider the ways in which your game might (or might not) take advantage of the Internet, as well as the pace of your game vis a vis update cycles. All of these factors feed into your hardware and software decisions as you build your game—which must be robust enough to support the choices you make.

The chapter begins by looking at some general categories of multi-player networked gaming models, as well as different network game types. The chapter then examines the principle design issues factoring into the creation of network games, taking into account the game type, technology, and available resources.

CATEGORIZING MULTI-PLAYER NETWORK GAMES

Obviously, you know you want to build a network game, or else you probably wouldn't be reading this. And you probably want it to be a multi-player game of some description. But of course, there is more to the equation than that.

This section looks at different kinds of game models that can be used for the network-game architecture. The aim is to cover the structure and styles of gameplay that can be built into the game at the design level—or, roughly speaking, the *types* of games you may want to build. This is important not just because it enables you to envision your game more clearly; it also helps you estimate what kinds of resources (i.e., hardware and software) will be needed to support the game after it is deployed.

First, I'll build some rough categories into which different game types can be placed. Naturally, in a constantly evolving market, categorizing games that already exist is no small task—and new ones keep being invented all the time. For example, before the genre now referred to as *"Grand Theft Auto* style" was defined, there had never been such an open-ended, free-roaming, detailed backdrop for a game. So rather than trying to cook up some industry-standard definitions, I'll simply put forth what is unique or different about various game types. Then I'll compare some common game structures so you can get a feel for the kinds of *design* decisions that must be made. (And these are design decisions, and not *implementation* decisions—even if they might at times feel like it.)

There are few things worse than a networked multi-player game that has evolved poorly from a single-player game. The design is important!

Pseudo Single-Player Online Games

This first rough category—pseudo single-player online games—is an interesting one. It is founded on the idea that the player competes against a relatively unseen playing population. That is, other players are abstract—indeed, they might as well be non-player characters (NPCs). There is literally no in-game interaction between players. Players know they are competing against other players, but only in a league table–based way.

This approach can be used to create all manner of economy-based games, where "winning" is determined by financial success relative to other players and progress is measured locally. In other words, the player's own progress is measured against himself or herself, with only the outcome of that progress communicated to the server. Games such as *Civilization*, for example, or Blizzard's excellent *Diablo*, are examples of this game mechanic, as is the upcoming *Cities XL*.

If it is simply a case of uploading a high score, then this kind of game needs very little server-side support—although if the data stored on the server is cheatable (e.g., high scores), then this has some implications with respect to security. That said, if you go one step further along this path, you'll see that you can build some logic into the server to extend the concept. For example, an online pseudo single-player online game might be designed such that the player progresses against himself or herself, but the actual gameplay takes place on the server.

One-on-One Games

A one-on-one network game might be a digital version of a board game, such as chess, or a game that falls into the action genre. Either way, a one-on-one game pits one player against another, usually against a fairly static backdrop. These will include fighting games, for example, where two players fight it out against each other in real time. The proposed network component in *Street Fighter IV*, when it eventually comes to the console platform, would be a good example of this.

As with pseudo single-player online games, one-on-one games make use of league tables as players progress through the game—but now each player's progress is measured against another player's progress rather than as a global struggle. This gives rise to all manner of competition taking place on game servers as players challenge one another.

Generally speaking, in these games, the server is a conduit for the game, but in some cases the networking is peer to peer, in which case it is basically a match-up service. There's an advantage to using a client/server setup for the communication, however, in that the server can act as referee—which means that the clients don't have to. Nonetheless, as you shall see, the peer-to-peer route is equally acceptable—indeed, it can even prove to be much more efficient, with higher performance, than games that go through a server in real time.

Team-Based Multi-Player Games

These games move away from the one-on-one approach, instead providing a meeting place of sorts for multiple players. For games in this category, a server is more or less obligatory—typically a client/server (one-to-many) relationship, giving the system the opportunity to synchronize all the clients and adjust communication rates based on the slowest participants.

Although the client/server model is typically used with these games, multicast and similar technology could, feasibly, be used to deliver the experience.

One type of game that can fall into this category is cooperative games. These see players divided into teams (a.k.a. "clans") and carrying out a variety of missions against other teams. The server's role is partly to maintain the state of the game environment (although clients ought to be able to do that themselves) and also to support communication. In other words, the server acts as a multi-way chat server as well as a pure game server—another reason to use a client/server model. That said, game-state synchronization should always take precedence over chat and communication that is incidental to the game at hand. Games such as *Unreal Tournament* illustrate the clan model, while other games in the war-zone genre sometimes offer player-to-player audio communication.

Map-Based Multi-Player Games

Of course, loose team play can occur in other kinds of multi-player networked games, like map-based multi-player games. Indeed, the map-based multi-player games category is arguably a sub-category of the team-based multi-player games category; certainly, these two categories overlap somewhat. Game types include capture the flag–style games with teams or single players competing against the game environment and NPCs or against each other, with the aim to capture the enemy's flag. The maps are local, sometimes part of a single-player (with bots) incarnation of the game in question, sometimes delivered through a server (having been designed separately from the game itself).

The reason I have separated this type of game out is in the title—that is, they are "map based" as opposed to "team-based." Put simply, the maps are more important than the teams. Indeed, there might not even be teams, as in *Unreal Tournament 2003*, where players could opt to play on maps where there were no clans, making it every player for himself or herself.

Most cooperative multi-player games, of course, fall into the category of team-based games because the team, rather than the map, is the important component. Even when the map is the same one for each game, the interaction of the teams makes for a different game each time.

Real Time–Strategy Games

Real time–strategy (RTS) games are different from the games discussed so far, which are real-time action in nature, in that they are almost turn-by-turn in execution. In fact, some of the more popular RTS games tend to be strictly turn based. That means each round consists of one move per player, with the game unable to progress until all players have made their move. This category is notable in that players tend to play locally, with other players represented as characters within the local game. Only the actions (or perhaps just the results of the actions) of each player are communicated, via the server, to the clients.

RTS games pose a number of problems, such as what to do if a player has disconnected, is not moving, experiences network problems, is cheating, and so on. These are dealt with in due course in Chapter 7, "Improving Network Communications," and Chapter 8, "Removing the Cheating Elements."

The issue with these games is that the game code is terribly complex, requiring a lot of processing—the majority of which simply cannot be handled by the server. An example of this complexity can be found in an online *Civilization* game. As a result, the advanced behavior must be distributed to the game clients. This leaves the game open to all kinds of cheating, such as "adjusting" the output of the game so that the other clients believe a player has advanced more than he or she really has (although it should be noted that as far as I am aware, *Civ* has not been subject to cheating—but the risk is there).

You might have realized that, aside from providing cheat detection and synchronization, the game server is not strictly required. You could play RTS games in a peer-to-peer environment. What is mandatory, for complex RTS games at least, is that the client must do some of the processing that would otherwise be done on the server. Otherwise, the server could not keep up. This is, conceptually, halfway between client-server and peer-to-peer gaming.

Massively Multi-Player Online (MMO) Games

The "massive" in "massively multi-player online game" simply means that there are a lot of players—tens or even hundreds of thousands—playing at the same time or that they play against a massive game environment with many locations, artifacts, and players, be they real or NPCs. *World of WarCraft*, for example, is an MMORPG in which things can get quite complex.

With MMO games, the game environment must be big enough to house all the players without seeming claustrophobic. Apart from that requirement, MMO game types can vary from RTS and action-style games to sports simulations and other genres—provided they appeal to, and have the capacity for, a large number of players.

Massively Multi-Player Online Role-Playing Games (MMORPGs)

Although you could argue that this is essentially a type of MMO, the RPG aspect of these games implies something a little different from a purely action game or even an RTS game. MMORPGs usually add a dimension to what might otherwise be a game involving little more than wandering around randomly shooting things. That is, with MMORPGs, there is a sense of travel and progression that is not necessarily prevalent in pure hack-and-slash adventure or combat games.

This dimension is generally a result of the role-play aspect of the game, in part because actions taken ex game are almost as important as those taken in game—including the choices the player makes when establishing his or her account, any customizations the player makes, and interactions that occur in the player forums—with the one having an effect on the other. For example, in a space-trading game, trading in illegal goods has an in-game effect of being chased by police, and an ex-game effect of getting a reputation. That reputation may in turn result in an icon displaying next to the player's name in the community as well as in-game effects—for example, making that player a target for other players who seek to score bounties.

COMPARING NETWORK GAME TYPES

Now that you have a handle on some of the key game types, it is time to compare the features of some common implementations of the core game types. It is important to realize that the differences have both positive and negative connotations for a project, and will affect the realization of the final product—including whether it is implemented at all. A good game idea can be ruined by the selection of an over-ambitious game type given the skill, experience, and resources available to the game developer.

Turn-by-Turn Games Versus Real-Time Action Games

Turn-by-turn gaming is a very specific implementation of a network multi-player game in which each player makes his or her move in sequence, after which all the moves are executed simultaneously by the game environment (be that at the client level or the server level).

In contrast, with real-time action games, all the action occurs simultaneously—although this does not preclude the possibility that moves can happen asynchronously. In fact, in a game where moves can take a certain length of time, moves could be queued up (an approach taken by some MMORPGs, such as *Age of Empires*, or *Starcraft*, to smooth the pace of action). There are also client-side differences, which extend to the interface as well as the way in which the client software interacts with the player.

There are some advantages of turn-by-turn play over real-time action from a design and implementation point of view, not least the fact that they can be implemented very easily on the server with most of the logic on the server or with the responsibility split between the clients and the server. The disadvantages are that the game must be updated on the server, and action is relatively slow. Even so, this model is great for casual games where players expect to play only for a very small period of time each day.

 One of the easiest turn-by-turn mechanisms to implement would be a daily update system to update the game environment. This gives players a long time to set up their moves, which are then evaluated at a specific time of the day.

In contrast, real-time action games, obviously, are updated continuously, which implicates the game server and database in a period of player-driven update cycles. This, in turn, has implications for performance, synchronization, and all kinds of issues relating to the efficiency with which the database can be updated. These problems generally do not exist with the turn-by-turn approach unless the game is an RTS game. RTS games tend to happen in pseudo real-time, but a timer mechanism is some-times used to make sure that the moves are taken within a certain period.

Multi-User Dungeon (MUD) Games Versus Real-Time Action Games

MUDs and real-time action games have quite a lot in common, even down to the information exchange. And like a real-time action game, a MUD game—part chat system, part adventure game (complete with exploration and triggered events), and part RPG—happens in real time. The difference is mainly in how information is interpreted—and that is the responsibility of the client software. This interpretation might include using the client software to display a text description in a text-based MUD, or to display graphics if a different client is used. It is entirely feasible to create a text-based MUD server that will generate graphical information that is only visible to a client that understands it, thus elevating the experience for the player to something resembling a real-time action game.

Interestingly, when you combine the MUD system with the real-time action system, you get a MMORPG—a modern rendering of an old-style MUD, but with much more emphasis on gameplay than casual chat. While the original text-based MUD format was very low tech—meaning much of the game logic sat on the server (in fact, the only client-level logic tended to be keyboard shortcuts and other aids to help with playing the game)—the modern MMORPG is high tech, which means that some of the logic must be shared. At the rendering level, the client still bears the responsibility, as well as bearing the responsibility for some in-game decision making. These decisions usually revolve around estimating the effects of various network-level issues, as well as estimating the outcome of combat where the fluidity of play is more important than keeping artificial synchronization. Of course, the role of the server is to maintain synchronization when, as will happen, the local copies of the game environment advance at different speeds. Games such as *World of WarCraft*, *Eve Online*, and *Second Life* all rely on multiple server clusters, client-side rendering, and inline decision making, just to keep the environment reactive. Without these, the whole façade would fall apart.

NPC Combat Games Versus Pure Multi-Player

NPC combat is one example of a game type in which the decision making has to be split between the server and the client. Specifically, the server has to control the NPCs, but the clients will play out their interaction locally, sending information about the interaction back to the server. So the server can choose commands to be sent in a batch, and the client can execute them. Pure multi-player games don't have this problem, because each in-game player is mirrored by a real-life player in front of a piece of client software. On the other hand, they share some of the same issues relating to the time required for players to decide what course of action to take and to subsequently take it. The solution is almost the same.

The trick is to make sure that the client receives updated instructions before the queue runs out. At the same time, it needs to relay the results of the interactions back to the server; if the interactions result in a "kill," the server must be informed, as must all the other clients. (This is not so different from an RTS-style interaction.)

The problem is, what does the server do with differing ideas of what the status of the NPCs should be? In other words, whom should the server and the other clients "believe"? (This issue is akin to the RTS problem mentioned previously.) To rectify this, checkpointing can be used to make sure that the "real" view, as held on the server, is relayed to the clients. This capability is not necessarily needed in other game types.

Player Combat Games Versus NPC Combat Games

Player combat is part of both MUD and real time action–style games. It can take place on the client with data relayed to the server. It has issues similar to those associated with NPC combat. The key difference between the two is that, if you allow player combat in a real sense as opposed to "us against the world" (and simulated friendly fire), then you open up a Pandora's box of issues relating to what to do with a dead player. Some games—*World of WarCraft* springs to mind—work around a premise of re-spawning the dead player in more or less the same state as he or she was when killed. Other games might choose a harsher option: lose everything and re-spawn in a "safe" area.

Note that "combat" doesn't imply warfare per se. Player combat might just as likely occur in a driving game as a shooting game. Either way, synchronization issues abound as the various clients play out their local scenarios and try to keep the environment more or less level for all the participants. Generally speaking, the faster the game, the more likely client-side decisions will be needed over and above the server side evaluation of the evolving game session. Additionally, fast-paced games will need more synchronization than slower ones.

PLAYER KILLING

Whether your game should allow for players to be killed is both a design decision and a cultural one. It boils down to this: Players don't mind dying if, say, they are playing a single-player game against the machine. Indeed, they expect it. If, however, the game is an MMORPG—where the continuity of the game environment inevitably means that players will become emotionally attached to their in-game personae—players will feel differently about the possibility of their dying in game. Somehow, the dying seems more real when it happens in an multi-player game environment that relies on the underlying collective consciousness.

There are several sides to the question:

- Do you want to allow for player killing in the game design? Or do you want to engineer a system whereby players can sink low but never to the point of destruction?

continued

- If you do allow for player killing, what happens when a player is killed? To what part of the game environment do they return? In what state do they respawn? Again, you might decide not to kill off players, just relocate them with fewer possessions.
- How will you combat cheaters who fake disconnections in order to avoid death in game? If you are going to allow player killing, and if that is going to include complete destruction of the player's in-game goods and status, then you must expect that they will want to avoid it.

Obviously, these are not issues that you need to consider when designing most games, but you should if the game you are designing is an MMORPG.

In-Browser Games Versus Standalone Client Games

All network games are generally based around one of two network architectures: client/server or peer to peer. Even a game that uses a browser as the interface will subscribe to one of them, most likely—in fact, almost exclusively—the client/server model. (The exception to this is if the server is acting as a conduit for a peer-to-peer game without actively participating. This, however, is rare.)

The client is the software that the player uses to interact with the game environment. The server stores the results of that interaction. The client and server might be the same physical machine. The client/server model discussed here relates more to responsibility than physical or logical entities.

Certain games *lend* themselves to a specific architecture. For example, two-player action games lend themselves to the peer-to-peer architecture, while MMORPGs can really only be handled by client/server setup, even when there are multiple servers.

The design of the client, and the way that it is implemented, is dictated mainly by the target platform and market. For example, it is unlikely that a developer would design a browser-based game for delivery on a modern console. Rather, these are more likely to involve the use of a standalone client, which is a piece of software that can be installed on the target platform. The advantages of using a standalone client are mainly speed, control of distribution, and the possibility of charging a fee for the pretty box.

In contrast, in-browser games use a variety of different technologies to deliver the client experience. They are played in a standard Web browser, which has the advantage of portability—that is, any platform that can support the Internet can support the game. On the other hand, charging for such games is difficult both psychologically as well as in practice.

The design of an in-browser client will vary greatly depending on the game type and the technology used to build the game: basic HTML (supported everywhere), dynamic HTML (using JavaScript), Adobe Flash (supported where there is support from Adobe—likely not to be consoles), and Java applets (supported by a virtual machine on many platforms, again excluding consoles). Basic action, RTS, and even MMORPGs with real-time action can be implemented using Flash or Java applets, while non–real-time action RTSes, MMORPGs, and everything in between (except real-time action) can be created using basic HTML. The interface only gets prettier and easier to use with dynamic HTML in the mix.

Opting for a browser-based game design has some implications with respect to hacking and automated play because everything the browser does is transparent. This applies to the communication layer as much as to the logic layer; since the protocol, HTTP, is fairly open, one can reasonably expect to be hacked at some point. That means if you opt for a low-security solution like JavaScript or HTML, the game logic should reside on the server rather than on the client. (Luckily, this is quite likely to be the case, as client-side processing is not common in such in browser game models.) On the other hand, the client can be made to do some quite impressive things using dynamic HTML—which is fine, except that it leaves the game vulnerable to automated play. Again, the traffic is transparent, and if any kind of encoding is used, a quick analysis of the JavaScript will yield the mechanism used to encode—which is less than helpful. Flash and Java don't have that problem, nor does a standalone client, as the code is hidden by virtue of the fact that it is compiled. (As you will see in Chapter 8, what can be compiled can also be decompiled and disassembled—a possible security concern. There are, however, ways to combat that.)

So, what are the implications for the game type? That's easily summed up: If you are creating a game with real-time action, distributed processing for the sake of smoothness of experience, and high client volumes, it is better to go for a custom-install client solution. If, however, you're just starting out and want to make an RTS or even a basic MMORPG without the bells and whistles, or you are just testing ideas, then an in-browser game is faster to develop, easier to correct, and will reach a far wider audience.

DESIGN PRINCIPLES

The aim of this section is to encourage best-fit design principles as opposed to attempting to bolt networking capabilities onto an existing design with no real thought as to which game model would be best. It first looks at

how a single-player game is different from a multi-player game, and then
a   t
how you can add network support to a game design. Next, it deals with
how multi-player support can be designed in as well as the different kinds
of multi-player support that a game might include. Finally, it looks at how
the design process can be used to test ideas using prototyping through
low-cost, low-technology infrastructures. This is often a good idea because
the balance of a multi-player networked game can only be decided once
the game has been experienced in a multi-player environment.

*In this case, the "balance" dictates how the various players and NPCs interact, and
what the possibilities are with respect to their capabilities. The balance of the game
is also dictated by the rules that govern the game and the interactions in it. All these
things must be tested before the game reaches beta testers.*

From Single Player to Multi-Player

I've said it before, but here it is again: *bolting on networking to a single-player
game rarely works.* These are just a few of the problems that can result
from this approach:

- Lousy gameplay
- Inappropriate security
- Exposure to reverse engineering
- Lack of testing

One of the biggest problems is that single-player games have logic
contained within them by necessity. Otherwise, the game just wouldn't
work. For a game like *Unreal Tournament*, this isn't a problem—except for
the possible proliferation of bots (automated players), proxies that offer
automatic aiming, and so on. But even these don't attack the actual gaming logic, and are reasonably easy to detect besides (as you will shall see in
Chapter 8). The *real* issue arises when a single-player RTS is turned into
multi-player RTS. Because the resulting game has logic embedded that is
part of the game, it is open to hackers. So, in a game like *Civilization* or *Age
of Empires*, for example, game interactions can be easily faked (see Matt
Pritchard's "How to Hurt the Hackers: The Scoop on Internet Cheating
and How You Can Combat It," Gamasutra.com, July 24, 2000). All this is
to say that the transition from single player to multi-player requires that
the very game engine be adapted to allow for the issues raised here. And
that means it is better to design a robust networked multi-player solution
from the outset—a task that starts with adding network support.

Adding Network Support

Suppose you want to design a single-player game to be played in a large online game environment, populated at the server side by NPCs (automated bots). There are many things within this framework that would need to be sorted out before you can even *think* about what happens when multiple players log onto it:

Rather than reinvent the wheel here, I have taken my cue from a paper entitled "On the Design of Multiplayer Online Video Game Systems" (Hsu et al) [HSU01].

- **Scalability.** Does the server scale with respect to the expected number of players (or at all)? This is not necessarily a linear relationship—some games, such as RTSes, will scale more easily, while others (*Multiwinia, Eve Online*) will need elaborate multi-server solutions.
- **Delay.** This is also known as the latency of the end-to-end connection (covered in Chapter 7). Different game types have different needs with respect to delay; an action game will require very low latency, while an RTS can usually get away with intermittently bad latency due to the way the game unfolds.
- **Robustness.** With respect to how robust the entire system is—both physically (machine drop-out) and logically—the question is likely to revolve around what happens to the other players when a client drops out, and how this is dealt with. It clearly has more impact in a two-player action game than in an MMORPG.
- **Consistency.** Is the game state consistent across all clients? How does one maintain synchronization on the Internet?
- **Cheat-proof.** Who's checking the actions of the players, and what actions are taken automatically or manually to resolve possible instances of cheating? Have you done enough to protect the system against cheating, including automated play?
- **Easy to charge.** How do you decide how much to charge the players, and how easy is it to allocate purchased units to players?

Hsu et al. note that "The first three factors favor the distributed architecture, while the last three favor the centralized architecture." Let us now examine the different architectures and how they change with the type of network game to address these six areas of concern.

Centralized Architecture: Client/Server

In a client/server architecture, multiple clients are connected to a central point. This allows for a central point of security, but also represents a weakness in the sense that there is a single point of failure. Figure 4.1 shows the topography, from a logical point of view, of the client/server architecture.

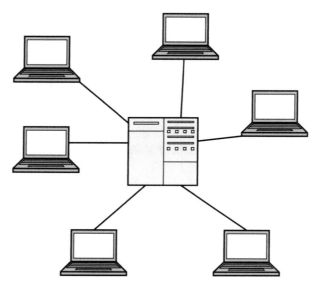

FIGURE 4.1 Client/server topography.

The communication layer at the server must allow for data to flow from each client, in and out, so all the connections are bidirectional. This is not unusual; it is the same as the request/response mechanism used on the World Wide Web. What is different is that the load is likely to be balanced roughly in each direction, whereas a normal client/server mechanism might be heavier on the download (to-client) side than the upload (to-server) side.

In the case of a game with a low load, multiple clients can connect to single server. If the load rises, however, this may need to be adjusted to a multiple-server system. A single server can cope with only so many clients; estimating this load is a function of the game type. This only becomes more complex when addressing the need to manage clients' logical existence with respect to the database. The database scheme, therefore, becomes very important, as does the location of the database with respect to the game server.

 Many game types can feature a client/server aspect, and the same constraints apply.

In terms of scalability, the client/server model is fairly poor. This is largely due to the use of multiple resources and databases for MMORPGs, the most common kind of game implemented under this topography. However, for RTSes and other games that do not require a large amount of server-side processing (i.e., simple Web-based games and those games in which the game logic is distributed), this may not matter. That's not to say that they scale well, just that it is unlikely that the developer will saturate a single server if all it's doing is serving Web pages—however dynamic the back end might be.

The delay, or latency, of these systems is also potentially quite poor. All traffic must pass through a central point, so the regular line latency is amplified by the system latency—a point that we cover in Chapter 7. This doesn't change by game type, either. Whether you're designing an RTS, action, or MMORPG, the best you can do is try to compensate for the latency by using clever programming.

Naturally, you could say that the client/server model is fairly robust across game types, at least from the point of view of client dropout. It is a design issue as to what you do in these circumstances, as noted previously. However, it was also noted that the single point of failure makes the system much less robust than other topographies. The consistency of the game environment, however, is likely to be very high, because the server holds absolute responsibility for making sure that it is so. This also helps to cheat-proof the system, because even if one of the clients does try to cheat, the cheating can be detected and corrected—almost without the cheater being aware of what has happened. This level of control also makes it easy to charge for game time, which is obviously desirable for those kinds of games based on a subscription model.

Distributed Architecture: Peer to Peer

The opposite to a centralized system is a distributed system; in game networking, that is known as a "peer-to-peer architecture." As the name implies, in a peer-to-peer network, each client is connected to every other client without the need for a central server *beyond that of setting up the connections*. In other words, there may be a matchmaking component offered by a central point to facilitate the actual setting up of the peer-to-peer network, but afterward, the server need play no other part. Examples of peer-to-peer networks are those used for wireless gaming, which is a very localized application, up to true Internet peer-to-peer gaming, where machines connect to each other using Internet technology. Figure 4.2 shows the classic peer-to-peer topography.

In this model, obviously, communication with the server is less important—but security is even more important than in other models, as there will be no cross-checking of the clients' behavior. Therefore, elaborate peer-to-peer security is likely to be required simply to stop people trying to get ahead. You can also can build AI techniques for cheat detection into the game client as well use the game design to try to limit cheating.

The wider game could be designed to make cheating less attractive, but that might just take the edge off the game, as the very reason for cheating is often that the player can get ahead in some way.

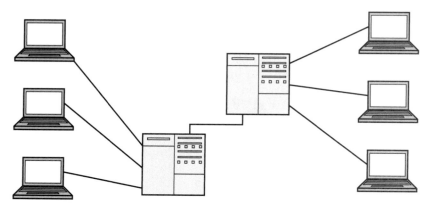

FIGURE 4.2 Peer-to-peer topography.

In terms of scalability, this model is potentially very strong—that is, as long as individual machines are not expected to connect to every other machine in the game simultaneously. So for RTS games in which player interaction is limited to, say, eight to 16 (or maybe 32) players, the model is scalable in that there can be as many games going on at the same time as there are client machines. The same holds for two-player action games; in fact, this topography favors such games. MMORPGs, however, are a different question. It would not be very practical to try to implement an MMORPG using a peer-to-peer network.

For those games that do lend themselves to the peer-to-peer topography, the latency is reasonable. At least, it depends only on the players involved, and there is no central point to factor into the latency estimations. The network is also quite robust, given that there is no central point of failure, and that one client dropping out is unlikely to affect the rest of the network. That said, the game design must take account of the client dropping out with respect to the ongoing game session. For some game types (such as RTSes), this will be easier to deal with than with one-on-one action games.

In terms of the consistency, there is a risk that the distributed peers will become desynchronized unless great care is taken to make sure that they are resynchronized. Part of this also has implications for the cheat-proofing of the game system. In fact, a distributed network game is not very cheat proof, as there is no central point to referee the clients. This leaves the door open for clients to lie to each other, giving false accounts of interactions that occurred during the game session.

Because the network is distributed, the game will play out as many times as there are clients. So, for an RTS with eight players, eight games will be occurring simultaneously. If one of the clients chooses to mislead the others, it can be hard to spot; designing in anti-cheat mechanisms is part of the whole development process.

A distributed network is not very easy to charge for. And once a player has bought the game, charging him or her afterward using some form of a subscription model is probably not possible. Then again, because the player is no longer actually consuming any of the developer's resources, charging may be inappropriate anyway (depending on the game model).

Mirrored Servers and Clustering

In addition to centralized and distributed architectures, there is a third option: mirrored servers and clusters. This offers a good approach to increasing reliability. Essentially, it means there are two or more servers that need to be synchronized, but not necessarily in real time, providing a moderately scalable platform. Figure 4.3 shows the mirrored topography.

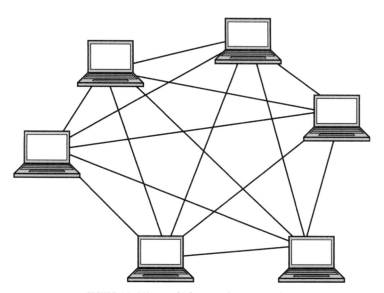

FIGURE 4.3 Mirrored/clustered topography.

In Figure 4.3, you can see that the game environment is likely to be designed in such a way that it can be divided into logical zones. This reduces the dependency on a single server and helps to split the load, but increases the complexity of the system.

Until a player moves from one server to the other, the other server does not need to know or care about them. When the player does actually move, then, it raises a synchronization issue. If the zones are divided by a physical or logical barrier (think teleport or doorways), then this becomes easier. Otherwise, there will be some common ground between the servers, and you need to design the game in such a way to make sure that this is dealt with properly. The overlapping virtual property runs the risk of being hard to deal with.

The main issue is that the latency will be high for these skirmishes, as there will be a high number of players in a restricted space existing on two servers. This means that an MMORPG could find itself suffering from different problems at the edges of zones. For example, if a robust approach is taken, entities on different sides of a zone wall might not be able to interact even though they can be seen. This can also manifest itself in exploits devised by canny players that can enable them to obtain an unfair advantage in certain circumstances. On the other hand, if a loose overlap is allowed, then the speed of gameplay at the edges of zones might be compromised as the servers do double-updates in order to a) stay in sync, and b) allow the game to be played out in real time with respect to their own clients. One other aspect to the multi-homed approach is that it also allows for multicast for local clients as info can be sent out in bulk at once to all clients. This can help to increase performance—at least in theory.

In terms of our criteria, the mirrored solution will perform reasonably well in all categories, whilst a clustered server may be the only way to obtain sufficient scaling for many large MMORPG projects. Because it is an almost centralized topography, it has all the advantages of the central server in terms of security, consistency, and being able to monitor and charge for game time, but with the added robustness of a semi-distributed platform. This architecture can be expensive to set up, however, as multiple server machines will be required—something that should feed into the decision process.

Adding Multi-Player Support to the Design

Having tackled the networking aspect, you can now look at the actual multi-player support types that you could select for the game. This is not as simple as it might at first seem, as there are a few points to address.

By definition, more than one player will play a multi-player game simultaneously—but there are, of course, different kinds of multi-player games. For example, players might be playing in a tight group (RTS), a wide group (MMORPG), or one on one (action). The kind of multi-player game helps dictate the network topography and game type or style. You can, for example, extend the concept of game servers for squad-based and map-based multi-player gaming, where different servers handle different aspects of the game.

One thing to remember is that more players equals more complexity—but it is not a straight-line correlation. In fact, it is actually a logarithmic relationship. If you add one more player, you more than double the complexity; but if you add 10, then the complexity increases only slightly. Add 1,000 or 10,000, however, and the complexity starts to increase drastically, again. Note, too, that the risk of hacking and cheating increases roughly in line with the popularity of the game and number of players in the game.

Location-Based Gaming

Location-based gaming describes the influence of the position of the player in the game environment on the architecture that is used to implement the game environment. This will have an effect on the way the game is set up in terms of data storage. Part of the decision with respect to architecture revolves around the correlation between the physical servers and the logical setup. For example, different kinds of games can be:

- Level based, in which a player plays on a level with other players, and he or she can move from one level to the next after achieving some goal.
- Map based, in which players play together on a map, never leaving that map until the end of the game (think cooperative combat and capture-the-flag gaming).
- Open free-roaming, in which players can go anywhere that their in-game status allows (like an MMORPG).
- Artificially constricted, in which players are restricted to a specific construction in the game, such as a racetrack.

The approach taken to the game-environment design will feed into the way the game infrastructure is designed. For example, maps might be distributed for a map-based action game with each client having a local copy—an approach that is clearly not possible for an MMORPG.

Location-based gaming, then, is an important part of the decision as to how the game is to be put together and an integral part of adding multi-player to the single-player game. One other aspect is being able to detect cheating and hacking.

Detecting Cheating and Hacking

If a player cheats while playing a single-player game, that player cheats himself or herself but does not damage the experience one iota for anyone else. Not so in a networked multi-player game. Indeed, cheating and hacking in a multi-player game is likely to be endemic if the game is popular.

For this reason, it is important to the longevity of game that cheating be able to be detected and dealt with at the client and server level, which is why I have devoted an entire chapter to this topic: Chapter 8. The methods for doing so must be ingrained into the game style and design, not bolted on afterwards. In addition, they must be tested properly.

Testing Through Design

This is partly an incidental discussion, but the design process—and the decisions taken to select the game type and infrastructure—can be tested using low-tech solutions as the game idea is developed. For example, you can use MUD or in-browser games, which have very low technical requirements, to test the game logic, rules, and balance before investment is made in a full client/server solution. It helps, when designing a complex system, to be able to prototype as soon as possible.

That means part of the design process could actually be a development process, because much of the existing infrastructure already exists. It might not look as pretty or be as versatile as the end result has to be, but it will work, and will give a good idea of how the end result will play. Even if you design a real-time game as a turn-based game by eliminating the action element, you can test and balance other important aspects that help to deliver the experience.

All this is to say there is nothing wrong with starting with a very modest type of game and then moving it up through the technological levels until it is as rich as you want it to be. Along the way, you will make excellent decisions as to how the game should be constructed and how the players will interact.

Choosing the Technology for Your Game

Here is a roundup of the decisions that need to be made before any further action can be taken. First, the developer needs to decide what kind of network technologies the game will use. Options include

- **LAN.** This is restricted to local play on a network of physically close machines, offering high security, high speed, and a low incidence of cheating.
- **The Internet.** This is a global wide area network (WAN) of geographically diverse machines, offering variable speeds (depending on client platform and quality of connection), low inherent security, and a potentially high incidence of cheating.
- **Wireless.** This is a close-proximity peer-to-peer approach or a method to enable Internet gaming. It offers low speed due to the WiFi protocol. Security depends on the device and settings, and there is a possible risk of cheating.

In addition, you need to choose a target market on which to concentrate. This might not be the *only* market at which the game will be aimed, but it should be the principal one. Examples might be:

- **Hard core.** People for whom gaming is a large proportion of their free time.
- **Casual.** People for whom gaming is a fun diversion, but who wouldn't necessarily invest a lot of time in maintaining a networked game presence.
- **Mobile.** This refers to gaming on the go, social gaming, and Internet gaming, predominantly in a casual way—although the actual gamer may classify himself or herself as hard core.

Another key decision is whether the online component is the game proper or just part of the supporting feature set that maintains the community of players. For example, resource-sharing games like *Little Big Planet* would fall into this second category. Some ideas to consider with regard to implementing the online component as part of the supporting feature set might be:

- **High scores.** Here, secure high scores are fed to a central server in Xbox LIVE fashion.
- **Community features.** These include forums, avatars, competitions, and so on—things that extend the game (whether it's played online or off) and make it more fun to play *because* of the networked component.
- **Message exchange.** In-game, or ex-game communication between players in a controlled environment is often a part of a healthy collection of community add-ons.

Next, having decided (we assume) that networking is going to be an integral part of the actual game logic and not just added on, you must decide on the pace of the game:

- **Real time.** Action happens in real time, and the player's actions are immediately apparent on the screen, as in a first-person shooter.
- **Turn-based real time.** The players queue up events, which are executed in a linear fashion as they take turns, as in a real time–strategy game.
- **Turn-based delayed action.** This is strictly turn based, where a player takes his or her turn and cannot move again until other players have moved. A turn-based delayed action game could be, for example, a daily update game, a two-player game like chess, or a play-by-e-mail game.

This choice of pace of play will influence also the update cycle—i.e., the rate at which the game environment is updated with respect to the playing out of the game logic that drives it. There are essentially two variations:

- **Real time.** The game environment, housed on the server, is updated as the action unfolds, with the changes being immediate and persistent.
- **Periodic.** The game environment is refreshed on a periodic basis, which could be daily or even hourly.

Updates are player driven in most models, except where a fixed update cycle exists. So players who do not move or otherwise interact may stall the system, as it will not update on its own (unless that update cycle is part of the design). This will be discussed further in the next chapter.

All of these factors feed into the hardware and software decisions that make up the platform. It must be robust enough to support the choices that are made; indeed, the realization of how much resources may be absorbed as a result of a particular decision may well lead to that decision being overturned.

REFERENCES

[HSU01] "On the Design of Multiplayer Online Video Game Systems," Chia-chun Hsu, Jim Ling, Qing Li and C.-C. Jay Kuo, Integrated Media Systems Center and Department of Electrical Engineering, University of Southern California, Los Angeles, CA 90089-2564, http://hsuchiachun.googlepages.com/SPIEitcom03.pdf

5

CREATING TURN-BY-TURN NETWORK GAMES

In This Chapter

- Turn by Turn Defined
- Case Study: *Project Rockstar*
- The Fictional *PlanetStar* RPG
- Revenue Model
- Commercializing a Turn-by-Turn Game
- References

This chapter is about creating games based on one or a combination of turn-based gaming models discussed in Chapter 1, "The Challenge of Game Networking, and Chapter 2, "Types of Network Games." With this premise in mind, we look at all aspects of the creative process from an abstract point of view—design principles as well as building in revenue streams. This last is important, as in many cases, the final product is not a shrink-wrapped game but an online service that has no direct revenue. Therefore, to sustain development (and operations), it can become necessary to build in additional revenue streams.

Generally speaking we also accept that turn-based network games will be multi-player in nature. Players will usually either be playing for themselves or as part of a team. If they are playing for themselves, it will have an impact on the way the game environment is deployed and managed since the effects of their individual moves should still be felt on other players. It is this dynamic that instills the appropriate level of competitiveness that keeps players coming back and provides the basis for revenue generation.

The turn-by-turn aspect lends itself to relatively straightforward implementation. This we shall see when we examine a possible implementation of a game based on the *Project Rockstar* model (a free game from Curb).

The *Project Rockstar* game itself is also picked apart as a good example of an online, Web interfaced, turn-by-turn game that works. It has a large following, generates revenue, and is fun to play.

The chapter closes by looking at possible revenue models for such ventures. As mentioned, these might be very different from the classic video-game revenue models used in most other implementations. The classic game-development paradigm derives its revenue streams from sales of a core product or service, but there is room to deviate from this and still turn a healthy profit.

Some readers will no doubt be wondering why *Project Rockstar* (*PR*) has been chosen over the plethora of RPGs and MMORPGs that are available, as well as over some of the "empire building" games that are playable through a Web interface. This is a valid question, but there are good reasons to study *PR* rather than something more inherently complex and finely balanced. I wanted to choose something with universal appeal, that any reader could understand. The game's premise had to be simple enough that any reader could appreciate the dynamics even without playing.

Above all, even if you couldn't implement it yourself as a side project, you should be able to imagine how it should be implemented. All the detail that *Project Rockstar* has aside, the model is easy enough to appreciate that you will understand the balance and premise.

Other games might be superior in terms of sophistication, interface, and interactivity, but they are simply too massive to contemplate for a fundamentals-oriented book like this. Indeed, there are whole books given over to the creation, development, and running of MMORPGs; it is a vast topic in its own right. Turn-by-turn Web games, however, are an excellent proving ground for intrepid network game designers, and it is worth taking a moment at the outset to discuss exactly what is meant in this context by the phrase "turn by turn."

Turn by Turn Defined

I use "turn by turn" to refer to a gaming system where players have a finite number of things that they can do per turn. The scope of a turn will vary from game to game, as will the kinds of actions that are possible within each turn.

The key is not what players can do, but the fact that once they have exhausted their turn they can do no more to influence the path of the game until their next turn. Players can take their turns simultaneously (which implies some form of central update cycle) or in a player-by-player manner (which implies that the bottleneck is the player whose turn it currently is).

Strict turn-based combat, for example, requires that players be forced into a sequential turn-by-turn playing model (as in *Dungeons & Dragons*, for example). This may or may not be appropriate for certain projects, depending on the mindsets of the people involved.

For example, in a closed playing group, there is less chance that play will be held up by a single player. In an open-access game, however, one unreliable link in the chain can cause a delay whilst players are given every chance to redeem themselves before they forfeit their move.

We look at two kinds of projects in this chapter, one where a strict sequential turn-by-turn model isn't used because it isn't appropriate, and one where it could be. We also cover lots of alternative solutions and approaches to solving the sequential versus simultaneous turn-by-turn playing models.

The other aspect to turn by turn is the overnight system update. This is implied in systems where all the players take their turns at the same time. Clearly, some aspects of the game environment need to be updated immediately (as they take resources out of the system), but the overall effect of their actions can only be known once all other players' actions are taken into account as well. An overnight update, which is used to calculate the net effect of all the limited moves taken by players and the effect that each has on the other, is one solution for daily play, and is a workable alternative to continuous update environments. It also happens to be the solution chosen by Curb for *Project Rockstar*.

Something else that *PR* implements is a sense of rounds. Other Web-based RPG-style games like *Miniconomy* also take this approach. Simply put, a *round* is denoted by a point at which the whole environment gets reset and everyone starts again from scratch. This gives some sense of end of game, and perhaps even a winner, with prizes. Without clearly defined rounds (quests, epochs, or what have you, depending on the game style) there is a tendency for the game to stagnate, with players losing interest due to a lack of urgency or closure. Rounds bring some of this back, give players an impetus to do better, and keep their interest level high.

The Game System

While the premise and background for the game is important—players can connect more easily with a well-rounded story or game that reflects real life—the design has to take into account some vital aspects of the mechanisms that drive the gaming environment. This will mean imposing some rules on the players in order to level the playing field.

Leveling the playing field is important for casual games, as we want to take away the hard-core aspect where dedication in terms of time can mean almost guaranteed success. We want people with 10 minutes per day to potentially be as successful as people with nothing else to do but play.

So, we bring in ways to limit moves, and the scope of moves. In a strict turn-based combat game, this is also important, as the balance of combat rests on the amount of damage that a single player can do inside one of his or her designated moves. Various limits can be used, such as availability of money (in-game) or time, or just a pre-defined number of steps (moves) after which the player can no longer perform any actions. The limits can also be linked to the strength/weakness (relative or otherwise) of the in-game entities. In such cases, we reward good playing style by giving players more opportunities to make the most of their time in-game.

There is, however, a balance to be struck to avoid unnecessary feed-forward loops, which see players getting more and more powerful. This happens when a player gains a certain capability, which then, in turn, means that they can do more per move. With the additional possibilities this offers, they are able to *again* increase their capabilities, which gives them even more scope per move; and this enables them to *further* increase their capabilities. Before long, they will be unassailable, and only rigorous play-testing will ensure that the balance is not skewed by attempting to reward players for their industriousness.

But, giving playrs the possibility to grow in this way is an important part of any in-game reward system. Therefore players have possibly several ways to increase what they can do per turn as they gain experience in the game. For non-casual games, this also gives motivation to dedicate more and more time to it, as well as rewarding that investment.

There is another side to this kind of model, in that it can provide a revenue stream as players try to increase their capabilities by buying expansions. This aspect is slightly controversial as it enables players to replace innate skill or dedication of time with real-world money. The threat is that players will buy skills rather than working through the game to develop them. The other side of this, however, is that it will, eventually, happen anyway. Games like *Eve Online* and *Everquest*, as well as some others such as *Second Life*, which all operate points-based systems (in the case of *Eve Online* and *Everquest*, skills-based combat) that dictate player capabilities, have all fallen prey to racketeering.

This occurs when players with a lot of time, skill, and devotion build up player accounts with vast sums of money, skills, or other measures of in-game success, for the sole purpose of selling the account details on an auction system like eBay. It is better to provide the possibility to trade up an account in the game system than try to prevent this kind of transaction taking place.

All of the above decisions feed into the way the game's rules are developed, and the result has an impact on the infrastructure used to support the game from the point of view of the interface and back-office systems.

The Game-System Infrastructure

The game infrastructure has to store the state of the game environment and all the entities in it, as well as provide an interface for the actual playing. Choosing the mix of back-end and front-end technology is another aspect of the game system that will feed into design and implementation decisions.

There are many different possibilities for the front end: it can be via HTML over the Web or it can be via a special custom software package, for example. They both have their own specific drawbacks and strengths. One obvious strength of an HTML interface, for example, is its portability. On the other hand, a custom interface package might provide a richer playing environment—although the gap between the two approaches is continually narrowing as machines become more capable.

To obtain the widest reach, portal style connections can be used. These make use of multiple and varied interfaces for different devices and different kinds of interaction. For example, updates can be received by e-mail, and limited access can be offered via a handset-specific Web portal, with the full richness of the interface only exposed via a dedicated Web page or specific software package.

The Playing Infrastructure

One of the key points of a multi-player game is that there is interactivity between players both within the game and outside it. We can look at two ends of the interactivity spectrum—low interaction between players and high interaction. Helping players communicate and interact is a key part of developing the game system as a whole.

Interaction between players will be different depending on how the game is implemented. Low interaction, for example, is typical for games where the player spends his or her entire in-game time creating something that only ever interacts with the rest of the game environment. For example, where the impact of the player on the game environment is known only after the daily update has taken place, there is often no *need* to communicate or interact with other players in order to play the game, and even succeed. However, this sense of operating in a vacuum can actually harm the longevity of the game.

Players like to interact with each other as well as the game. Curb, when designing *Project Rockstar*, for example, put a fake album cover competition in place, where players could vote for each other's (invented) album art, as well as read song lyrics.

On the other end of the scale are those games where players can't move unless another player has moved. These are highly interactive, and encourage players to communicate more; there is more of a sense that players are playing together. While interactivity is high for these games, they can also suffer from potential disconnect drawbacks, which can make them harder to play and can also restrict longevity. This becomes more of a danger the closer the game design moves toward the real-time game design described in Chapter 6, "Creating Arcade and Massively Multi-Player Online Games (Real-Time)."

Generally speaking, the games at this highly interactive end of the scale don't restrict players' moves beyond the natural restriction brought about by the various capabilities of their in-game representations. This is in contrast to the tight restrictions and guidelines that we examined in games with lower interactivity and longer update cycles. In order to keep the interest for these games at the lower end of the interactivity scale, a good community must be fostered. This eventually becomes part of the gaming system, and players often turn up as much for the social aspect as for the gaming side of it.

Player Customization

People like to feel that they own their games. Personalization helps them to achieve this, whilst also standing out from the crowd (visually or with profile descriptions). In addition, part of being customer (player) oriented in the game design is allowing players to customize their own game experience within the confines permitted by the game rules.

A cornerstone of any multi-player game, then, is the players' ability to customize their in-game representations and personalize their experience. Turn-based games benefit from this kind of approach probably even more than the other kinds of network games discussed in this book.

Part of that is because, whilst waiting to play again, there's not much else to do, and participating in ways other than just playing the game helps to keep interest high. There's also the sense of kudos that comes with a well crafted in-game persona, as well as a certain level of one-upmanship.

An essential part of the attraction of customization is in creating a persona that reflects the in-game personality that the player wants to project. That persona might be real or imagined, and the level of choice that the player has in deciding which way to skew his or her in-game representation should be carefully considered.

Games that have a high level of personalization options will probably be more sticky and keep the players coming back for more. This is especially true if the personalization is linked to the way the game is played, as well as the visual aspects.

A few of these mechanisms might be

- **Avatar:** The look and feel/accessories relating to the players' in-game persona (or personae)
- **Community:** Forums, communications, update notices, etc.
- **Competitions:** Increases in player interaction, and a way to reward them for diligent playing

These aspects of the game environment, which are not part of the game per se, can be approached in a variety of ways. They can be all-in-one, tightly integrated with the game interface, or they can be two steps away from the interface itself, as a separate service.

Integration with the game is often vital—keeping both the premise (i.e., scrolls in a fantasy environment and e-mail in a futuristic setting) and the look and feel of the game design. This can be mixed with the availability of services at the point of interaction to create a seamless experience.

For example, an all-in-one approach would mandate that all the community was supported through the game interface. From a visual aspect, this is made easier if HTML and Web technology are used to deliver the game to the player. On the other hand, if custom software is used (i.e., a standalone module), then it is possible that tight integration with the theme of the game will be easier.

The temptation is to use a two-step approach, delivering the game through a custom interface but the community aspect through standard Web interfaces. This eschews the tight integration that is the mark of a well–thought-out game design, but offers the best of both worlds in certain cases.

In the end, the two can be combined to use browser technology (skinning) through a customer front end. On the PC, this is relatively easy, but on other platforms it might be less so. There is also the issue of compatibility— gamers do not generally like to be told that they have to have Internet Explorer x.x installed in order to play the game, and this requirement may damage their perception of the game before they even try it out.

A good combination of open-source and closed-source techniques can often be found to support the desired delivery method. Care must be taken to use non-GPL components because otherwise-derived work (in certain cases) should also be open source in order to remain within the terms of the license, and the game creator might not actually want this.

 The GNU Public License—or GPL—stipulates amongst the various obligations of the licensor that derived works be made public as a way to establish sharable intellectual property rights that extend beyond basic copyright and licensing of technology. This forms the cornerstone of the open source community.

Avatar

This is the face of the player in the game, as presented to other players. Therefore, players might like to have some initial control over the avatar beyond just having a standard set of looks for different classes of in-game entities, which is a workable default.

The more the avatar can be made to represent the actual looks (or desired looks) of the real-life (or imagined) player, the more of a connection that player will feel with the game, and the more emotional investment he or she will make. This then translates into an investment in time, and subsequently provides one of the hooks that retains old players and entices new ones.

Where many turn-based games fall short is in this aspect of the interface. They would, on the whole, do well to borrow from techniques offered by real-time games such as *Second Life* and *World of Warcraft*. Granted, these games have been developed on a larger budget, but it is perhaps more important for smaller, less-complex games to over-deliver in this respect in order to bolster their offering.

At the very least, customization should include the following:

- Face shape and skin tone
- Hair color and style
- Body shape
- Facial features

There is an additional benefit: once the customization has been built in to the game, it can be exploited to generate characters later on as well as offer a randomization function to players to allow them to start from a semi-blank canvas. This can be taken one step farther in extending it into all parts of the game, at which point it becomes a part of the feature set, and even part of the game proper.

The chances are good that, on top of this, players will extend their time in the game environment by sharing screenshots of particularly bad-looking or good-looking in-game characters that they generate or come across. And, as we have pointed out, anything that extends the time that the player spends immersed in the system increases the success of the game by creating an emotional and time investment.

This effect can be further enhanced by the introduction of clothes and accessories that can be acquired with in-game currency, either earned or won. This can be extended also into areas of the pseudo game environment such as owning property (as in MUDs/*Second Life*/*World of Warcraft*/etc.).

While we call this the *pseudo game environment*, this customization might actually be part of the game itself. However, in a turn-based asynchronous environment, it is more likely to be just an extension of the original premise. For this reason, any extensions used to foster a community should remain in character for the genre of the game—for example, using an abstraction of scrolls in a medieval context or computer screens in a sci-fi context, etc. This will help to add to the authenticity—but, of course, will also be dictated by the level of abstraction used in the game itself.

Additional customization can be offered at the level of player profiles where their in-game statistics are shown. These collections of otherwise drab numbers can contain parts that should be customizable through a variety of mechanisms—graphical and otherwise—and this then becomes part of the community feel. For example, some players might, at the simplest level, be depicted in forums with a special symbol (or set of symbols) reflecting their relative success within the game. Or perhaps those who have proved specific skills can obtain badges that display alongside their avatar, or are even woven into their virtual in-game clothes. For the creation and delivery of avatars, it is probably better if the interface is somewhat customized. This adds another layer of complexity to the system, of which designers must be aware, but provides more flexibility than other techniques. There are plenty of precedents in real-time MMORPGs—from *Eve Online* to *Everquest* and *Second Life*—that prove that dynamic custom generation of characters both works and is capable of becoming a feature in its own right.

Services like Yahoo! manage quite well to allow creation of avatars using just HTML and CSS, and *Project Rockstar* also provides semi-custom graphics (they are actually static but can be recombined in interesting ways) that reflect the player's in-game choices. However, Curb may have missed a trick here. It seems that the in-game representation of bands does not directly reflect their make-up—i.e., it is perfectly possible to create a band with six members, where only four are required by the game, and then end up with a band photo containing only four. It would have given a far greater sense of immersion if each band member had been chosen with respect to the player's decision for hiring him or her—instrument, looks, style (genre), and so on—rather than presenting a stock graphic roughly representing the band. This might have added an extra layer of complexity, but it would also have given the game a little more depth that would have compensated for other visual flaws, if any became apparent.

The same error has been committed in the superficial customization options that *Project Rockstar* offers the player in terms of their in-game avatar, which, oddly, does not extend to the look, but only the textual description and name. The avatar is perhaps the most important part of a turn-based asynchronous game, and offering extended customization is practically a prerequisite in a non–real-time environment.

All of these tweaks add to the underlying turn-by-turn game and form the gaming community.

Community

The community in any game is important. In fact, I would argue that fostering a community in a rule-based, turn-by-turn game that is basically all about exploiting statistics for the benefit of the individual player (or, more rarely, a team) is even more important than for other kinds of network-gaming models.

This is partly because of the social aspect of these kinds of games, but also because the player can choose a level of participation that matches his or her available time. Other kinds of games are an all-or-nothing proposition. Turn-by-turn games run the risk of becoming boring if no community is available to extend the basic playing model.

Adding a community element to the game can be as simple as adding forums discussing various aspects of the game and the players' individual successes in the game environment, as well as sharing them visually. HTML gives a great way to do this using links, images, and dynamic content.

Games can take the community concept farther by allowing players to give gifts to each other or even hand out in-game money to their friends. In-game trading can then be either a part of the game mechanic itself (i.e., the design and model) or it can be conducted outside the game as a community feature.

Players also like to communicate with each other to discuss in-game strategy and possibly form alliances within the game; these can be either formal or informal arrangements. Many people prefer this form of communication over sharing their e-mail address with people who are otherwise strangers. The forum lets them stay in character whilst also preserving their privacy.

Some games also report that players use the forum to engage in semi-serious or serious competitions amongst themselves. These can be either instigated by the players themselves or by the game's administrators.

Competitions

Competitions can become a vital part of the community spirit. Gamers are naturally competitive, even when the competition is not strictly part of the game proper, and adding competitions outside the gaming system can be a great way to extend the turn-by-turn nature of the game and allow those players who want to, to become more involved.

So, competitions can be used as a way to reward players or just for the sake of one-upmanship. As with all other aspects of the multi-player environment, competition is just another way to use the background of the game to introduce ways to keep the community alive, and add stickiness to the game as a whole.

The reward can be a rare object, in-game currency, or special privileges. In the old days of MUD gaming, competitions based on knowledge about the game and its history were employed to choose users with administrative privileges, for example. More recently, *Project Rockstar* has used competitions to let players earn power-ups, which give their account benefits—usually by adding statistical points to one of their bands to make them either slightly or greatly improved in one of their key skill sets.

Stickiness

I have used this term a few times now, and it essentially means engendering the site with qualities that retain the attention of the player once his or her official game session has ended. It answers the question that the player is asking himself or herself, having just expended all in-game move capital: What else can I do?

It is also possible to derive revenue from advertising based on player participation and visibility of promotional material. The success of advertising as a revenue stream largely depends on stickiness (see the "Revenue Model" section at the end of this chapter). Put simply: The stickier the community, the more advertising revenue can be generated.

Part of the reason for choosing a turn-by-turn Web game, for example, may be that it is easy (relatively speaking) to implement, and the low investment in time makes it appealing to the casual market. This is the wide audience that will react well to a site that backs up the game by being sticky. If, however, it is just a pick-up-and-play game that nobody cares about, it will not make any money. The attempt to make it sophisticated and sticky may well end up costing the game developer more than just the time spent to create it in the first place.

So, there is a balance to be struck between the effort needed to entice players to stay awhile and the revenue that can be generated to cover those costs. All the other aspects of this first section of the chapter must be brought to bear on the issue, principally:

- Customization
- Community
- Competitions

If these three combine correctly, they will generate stickiness—and, more importantly, make the player *care* about his or her in-game representation and *desire* to do better.

CASE STUDY: *PROJECT ROCKSTAR*

I could have chosen any one of a collection of casual, browser-based, turn-by-turn games to use as a case study. There are many, ranging from text-based simulations of business and warfare to two-player games like chess, and multi-player online variants of classic board games such as *RISK*. *Project Rockstar*, however, illustrates two kinds of mechanics— a strict turn-based gaming model and an overnight refresh of the game environment. It also has its problems, and highlights areas where future games might improve upon the basic model—and these will be addressed as we come to them.

PR also cannot be adjusted to fit other gaming genres—for example, it doesn't illustrate the stricter kinds of turn-based combat, nor does the update model really permit this kind of structure. In such models, the principle is that nobody can move until the next player makes *his or her* move. Clearly, if the model is based on an overnight update, it is not a good idea to try to use it for this kind of combat.

There are some aspects of the game that work in this way, however, even if it's not at first evident. For example, the pool of possible band members is largely static. Moreover, bands can be disbanded (returning artists to the pool) and formed (thereby removing them) during the on-line play session, without waiting for an overnight update.

Every aspect of *PR* is played in HTML through the browser, with server-side scripting used to keep track of everything. There are intricacies to the model that we will gloss over in the interest of looking at how a clone might be built, and you are encouraged to take a look at the game (www.ProjectRockstar.com) and see if you agree with my conclusions.

It is important to remember that nothing that players do has an immediate effect on the game environment, only on their own in-game entities (apart, that is, from hiring and firing artists). The net effect of the choices that players make with respect to their own bands, their financials, and aspects like in-game charts is worked out overnight. So, it's only by waiting until the next update cycle that players know if their choices have paid off.

Another reason for choosing *PR*, as mentioned in this chapter's introduction, is that the premise is universally accessible.

The Premise

The premise of *Project Rockstar* is very simple: The player is responsible for forming a band. Each band can be formed from a selection of server-side entities (artists), each having specific statistics that govern its abilities and current status (tired, happy, bored, etc.), as well as intelligence, talent, and other facets. The more talent it has, the more expensive it is—but the better it will perform. Hopefully.

Each of these artists also has an affinity for specific instruments, or skills. New skills (dance, instruments, etc.) can be trained through practicing, but during this time the band will not be doing anything productive—like writing songs, gigging, recording, or promoting. Each band (by genre) needs to have a combination of specific skills, depending on the style. For example, a rock band needs to have bass guitar, drums, lead singer, lead and rhythm guitar—with a minimum of four band members. As mentioned, the skills with these instruments can be trained, so the competence of the band can be increased. As their skills increase, so does their success—and also their cost. And this cost plays a key part in the premise: Money drives everything.

The more expensive a band member is to buy in the first place, the higher his or her skills will be—and the bigger the cut of sales the member will take and the more it will cost to keep him or her employed. In other words, this means that anything that the band member doesn't do that makes money will cost the player.

The idea behind the game, then, is to make money by selling records, playing gigs and festivals, and eventually topping the charts. That is the aim. Along the way there is a ranking system for managers, an album art competition, a thriving community, and in-game competitions and decisions.

It works because it's very accessible—people understand it, can connect to it, and it has fostered a great online community. The addition of the album art competition, lyric competition, and forums also helped. These competitions are run on the basis of community voting, with the results displayed in the players' main screen. Each time the player revisits the main screen for one of his or her bands, there are sections that display the best album art of the moment, and selected news from other managers in the game.

So, it's an entire package working together—with people interacting, but also playing somewhat in a vacuum until the general game-environment update starts and the net effects are worked out for every player. What holds it together is the fact that you care about how well you do and about your in-game characters, and much of that is based around sharing them with the community.

Setup

There is a certain amount of setup that the player needs to embark on before playing the game, which fosters an increased sense of ownership. It doesn't require a huge investment in time to get started—the interface is easy to understand and the choices are limited at first. This makes it great for casual players, but the fact that the involvement increases over time also means that there are quite a number of hard-core *PR* player-fans. Much of this is linked to the level of customization that the setup stage of the game offers.

Leaving to one side the account customization, in which the player names himself or herself and creates some profile text, the first piece of customization in the game proper is setting up one or more bands. Given that the player starts with limited funds, this can be either a lengthy process of calculation and examination or a quick-pick approach where money is the only criterion used to decide whether or not to use a particular artist. The player has to choose from a list of band members, each of which has a made-up name and a collection of favorite instruments, favorite musical style, and associated skill points.

Having names helps the player to connect with the artists on offer. Of course, being able to name them yourself would add to that connection, but there are good reasons not to allow it. Chiefly, it would be out of kilter with the game's premise, which is based on selection from an available pool of talent.

Each band has to be formed within a given genre, and once chosen, this genre cannot be changed. In selecting a genre, the player has to make sure that certain limits are respected:

- The band must have a certain number of members.
- The band members must possess a certain mix of skills.

Each band member chosen has a rating for each of his or her skills, and a price that roughly equates to his or her talent. More expensive does not necessarily mean better, but an expensive artist will be more skilled than a cheaper one. These statistics can be checked before hiring. This means that, if a player really wants to find a skilled collection of individuals for a reasonable price, it ought to be possible given an initial investment in time. That said, those who prefer to make the investment *over* time rather than up front can pick and choose on the basis of cost, and then train the skills as required to make the band more adept—and hence, more successful. It's a salient lesson: Turn-by-turn games can be made much more appealing to a wide audience if players have the option of an initial large investment in time followed by quick evolution (toward success *or* failure), or a smaller initial time investment, taking a longer time for the game to unfold.

In the case of *PR*, once the band has been assembled, it's a set-and-forget operation—until one of them quits or their skills become honed. For many players, it will be worth the initial investment in time to get as good a band together as possible for the money available.

One way in which this sometimes painful process could have been improved would have been by the addition of AI to control a "create band for a certain price" approach. The player could then choose to let the AI loose on the artist database (with some restrictions) and put together a band semi-automatically. This would serve to reduce the initial investment in time that the player must make. With casual games such as this, although the game will have its fanatics, the less setup time required, the better in order to hook players in as quickly as possible.

The Game Environment

In the game environment itself, there is plenty of scope for allowing customization as well as the way in which the environment is presented to players. This starts with players providing simple textual descriptions of themselves, lyrics for any songs that their band writes, and other simple, gradual tweaks. The bands can be named (although not, as noted, the band members), and descriptive text attached to them. Also, a band's progress through the game is more or less public access, so anyone can examine the band and see what the player has created.

The color scheme can also be altered (with CSS). This requires that players wanting to adjust it have some knowledge of HTML, and also opens up the possibility that players can get involved creating, sharing, and helping others create by way of informal tutorials on the forum.

There are also standard options for players to receive e-mail updates, and all the usual housekeeping aspects, as well as a vacation setting.

Playing the Game

The actual playing cycles are easy to appreciate. Once a band has been set up, there are a limited number of actions that each manager can assign to his or her band. In addition, not all the actions are available at the same time; some are available only after an initial probationary period has passed, while most are merely limited by available funds.

Some actions are designed to help generate *more* funds, money being the center of the game (see the section "In-Game Currency" later in this chapter), as it so often is. Generally speaking, all similar games follow the same model—there are some actions that cost money, some that require money to set up but may earn money in return, and the default of doing nothing costs a fixed amount.

In the case of *PR*, doing nothing is always an option, but the band needs to be paid, and this will diminish funds. Other actions are

- **Practice.** To increase skills in a given area.
- **Write songs.** When enough songs have been written, an album can be released.
- **Record songs.** This occurs at a cost.
- **Play gigs.** This occurs at a cost, but also provides income.
- **Create/attend promotional events.** Again, this occurs at a cost.

So, each day that the band does nothing costs their minimum weekly wage. It is vital to start earning; otherwise the manager (player) will run out of money. It is also vital that the band practice to try to get better at their various skills, although this might start to affect their wages as they become more of a hot property.

Turn-by-turn games often revolve around the scarcity of some central property. In a fantasy setting, that might be hit points, experience points, special skills, or spells. In games like *Miniconomy* and *PR*, as well as the various fantasy-league soccer, football, baseball, and other sports-strategy games, the commodities are skill, talent, and money.

Money

Each player in *PR* starts with 30,000 units of in-game currency and is invited to create a band. The player must remember to set enough aside for five or six weeks (each week is a real-time day) of updates before the band starts to earn any money. This is typical of the general start-up process for any game based around strong characters, be it real-time action or turn by turn. Often, a certain fixed amount of points or cash is attached to the creation of in-game personae.

Again, looking toward other gaming styles, the player might be asked to create a team of characters and given a pool of points to assign to various in-game attributes such as strength, intelligence, charisma, and so on. Each of these aspects is likely to cost a certain number of points, and in *Project Rockstar*, those points equate to in-game money.

Getting the balance between a solid skill set based on available funds and the depletion of those funds (be they hit points or money) is part of the game's own balance. From a design point of view, this is also a vital area to work on to make sure that the balance is just right.

For the first real-time *PR* week, the band will also be on probation, which limits the amount of things that a player can do—i.e., no gigging. This concentrates the player on trying to build up a rapport with his or her virtual creation rather than wasting money without appreciating the nuances of the balance between money and power. It is like a tutorial mode, but can be irritating if it's the third or fourth time the player has set up an account. Unlike many other games that use true tutorial modes, it cannot be bypassed. However, it does give players the chance to see what the various skills and weaknesses of their new creation might be. Almost nothing that takes place in this first week will bring in any money; that can only be earned through releasing a record or playing a concert. Money is also used for trading between players and setting up labels, which can sign acts and share the profit—just like in the real world.

Allowing Interactivity

The game itself is a simple Web-based, point-and-click interface. There is nothing advanced about the way the game is presented. This makes it playable on almost every platform; I have tried it on all kinds of desktops, laptops, and even a portable media player, with excellent results. This is something of a bonus over those games that use a Java- or Flash-based user interface, often something that is badly supported over multiple platforms. As Java becomes even more prevalent, though, it may be a good candidate for Web-based games in the near future, although it will always require that the game front end is downloaded to the client platform. The beauty of a pure Web interface is that this is not necessary, and the game can be played wherever there is an Internet connection.

The Update Cycle

Turn-by-turn games have to have an update cycle of some form. This cycle can take a variety of different forms, from turn-based update triggers to continuous re-evaluation of the playing environment. They all have their advantages and disadvantages; usually it is a tradeoff between processing time and availability and the practicality of the platform.

For *PR*, Curb has chosen a daily update (an in-game week). This ties up the system while it evaluates the results of the in-game actions of all players. Obviously, the more players there are, the longer this will take.

It works because once the bands have been instructed to perform certain actions for a day (or several days), there is nothing else that the player can do. The player's turn—for that band, at least—is over, and he or she must wait for the daily update to see the results of his or her choices.

At the close of the day, whether or not the player has instructed his or her bands, the system updates itself and the decisions made (or not made, as the case may be) are played out. At the end of the update cycle, several things happen:

- The fictional charts (affecting the success of player's releases) are updated.
- Players are debited for any actions with associated costs.

- The effects of any band actions are evaluated.
- The moods of band members are adjusted accordingly.
- Players are credited with any earnings.
- Players are e-mailed with the result of the day's play.

There are a few other things, but this list reflects the core of the update cycle.

Some randomness is also built in, so players can find that their artists have been involved in scandals and the like, at which point the player has to decide what course of action to take. These random events are also combined with ongoing updates such as voting on album art and activities in the various forums and community platforms. There is also the risk of a band member leaving after a string of bad gigs that leaves him or her demoralized, at which point a replacement must be found. It is these little attentions to detail that add spice to the game, and all are part of the daily update cycle.

Balance

As noted, balance is important in any game. Forcing players to connect with their in-game representations by making some stark decisions as to the various skills that they assign to them is vital; that way, they know that they have only themselves to blame for failure.

This ownership helps retain players, which is tricky for a game that only updates periodically. Between updates, it is easy for a player to lose interest. In *PR*, the initial question of balance comes when the player is creating his or her band—it's a balance of available funds and anticipated earning potential and time-scale against risk:

- **Low.** Spend little, have funds left over.
- **Medium.** Spend half,/keep half.
- **High.** Spend everything, hope to get a good song the first time.

In a fantasy game where the setup is about assigning points from a limited pool to attributes of a character, the same kind of trade-offs exist, but it is unlikely that the player would need to have anything left over.

Once the player is up and running in *PR*, there is a continual balance of income against money spent, the traditional video-game–design conundrum of risk versus reward. This leads to certain rules, some implicit and some explicit. The latter are as much there to *help* players as to make the game more enjoyable.

One case in point: the requirement to have 30,000 in game currency units available before being able to start a new band. Besides adding to the initial set of band-creation constraints, this also protects players from doing something silly and running out of money, at which point they must start over. On the other hand, some rules are there to provide balance in the larger community such as the requirement that players only have one band in a specific genre (i.e., rock/indie) and no more than three in one main genre (i.e., pop). This restriction is purely for the good of the game, and simply adds a little spice to each player's decision-making process. In addition, it fosters a sense of repeatability—can the player repeat his or her success in another genre of music? (This is also bolstered by the fact that certain songs from certain genres must be recorded in studios of the same genre—revealed by their names—and that concert success is likely only in venues that appreciate the genre of the band playing there.)

All of these genre-based rules add to the immersion, and form a technique that ought to be repeatable across other genres of game.

Financial Balance

Besides the setup and genre rule balancing, there is the balance brought about by the investment/earning ratio. Each possible action—from hiring band members to playing gigs—has several levels of investment, which differ in cost. In some cases, these costs vary by several orders of magnitude.

Band members, for example, can range from 100 credits to 10,000. This presents the player with the choice to buy an expensive yet well-honed and experienced artist or buy raw talent (with a bit of luck) and hone it by training and gigging.

Clearly, players can afford more cheap bands. Perhaps in this case, it is best not to put all their eggs in one basket and spread the risk. Then again, there are more decisions to make, more investment in time, and more knowledge required of the game mechanics to be a success across the board.

These decisions have to be taken into account with respect to genres, too. With each recording studio being named according to the kind of music they specialize in (and that's the only clue), a player would be unwise to start recording heavy-metal tracks in the Bubblegum Studio, even if it is cheap.

Finally, there are gigs to play and promotional events to arrange to try to raise awareness of the band and hence increase sales. Each of these has to be considered in terms of the anticipated income against the cost of actually doing the gig or promotion.

If every choice is balanced appropriately, success will follow, from mild to moderate, and occasionally to super-stardom. There are also likely to be parallels across other gaming genres, and the designers just have to find the correct features of the gaming mechanics to balance in this way.

The result has to be that playing is never boring or tedious. Even waiting overnight to see the results of actions should not be irritating because of the sense of community that has been built up around the game.

That is yet another kind of balance that *Project Rockstar* has gotten right—the implementation of community support versus the game proper. In the end, this will be as much down to the fans as anything else, and it is up to the game designers to try to make sure that the fans are involved to the point that they want to contribute to that community because they care.

Maintenance

Clearly this aspect of running systems could be an issue. In the past, one of the weak points of *Project Rockstar* has been the manual nature of the update cycle. If the chief engineer goes on holiday and something breaks, the updates have been known to stutter on rare occasions until the engineer could access the system and make a fix.

For a game that rests so heavily on the daily update cycle (a process that takes several hours), this is unforgivable. At least with a game that operates on a continually updating environment (even if it is turn based), there is no possibility of the ship being left unmanned; plenty of engineers should be available to monitor events. In other words, the game design dictates the necessity of a staff monitoring the system around the clock. In exchanging the complexities of a real-time action system for a daily-update model, one hopes to recoup that saving elsewhere—spending more on design, for example. But it can backfire by having only one member of staff dedicated to maintenance tasks—be they scheduled or unscheduled.

The point to take away from this is that maintenance is a necessary evil. Outages will happen, and there will be problems that result in the system going down and requiring a restart. They shouldn't affect the game, however. At some point, turns still need to be calculated, even if it's a manual operation based on a backup procedure.

Most turn-by-turn games will be broken down into sessions lasting a set number of iterations—soccer and other sports games can be based around well-known seasons, for example. Abstract games that are based on a continually evolving game world such as *Project Rockstar* can be divided into arbitrary rounds. These natural breaks give the developers a chance to perform maintenance, as the system can be made less available for a limited length of time as the changes are rolled out.

Solutions to Possible Problems

Humans need maintenance too, and we call it "vacations." The fact that the whole gaming cycle plays out over an extended time span (read: months or years, in some cases) means that sometimes players will miss update cycles. There are, however, ways to make the game fit in with the players' lifestyles that also add to the complexity, enjoyment, and global appeal. If the solutions can be made to fit in with the game rules too, they become part of the infrastructure, and subsequently, add to the enjoyment factor even more.

Vacation Settings

This is the classic solution to player absenteeism. As long as the player remembers to set the vacation settings (like setting a vacation auto-responder on e-mail), then it is an elegant solution.

Most turn-by-turn games (and *PR* is no exception) have vacation settings, which allow players to set the system to an automated update while they are away from their machine. At the simplest possible implementation level, it puts their session (indeed, their entire account) into suspended animation.

This in itself presents a small problem: If the account is suspended, then the player will lose ground to other players in the system as he or she will not accrue in-game points—be they in the form of in-game currency, experience points, or any other measure of in-game success depending on the gaming model and premise. *Project Rockstar* addresses this by enabling some updates to take place—although no vital decisions will need to be made. Money can still be accrued, but the band will not disband by itself, nor will any other make-or-break decisions be made.

Ensuring that the game continues as normal for the player with respect to the mundane, business-as-usual, aspects of the play session, whilst protecting them from anything that they might have been able to prevent had they been actively playing, is a key part of developing a robust vacation mode. Having said that, it ought to be possible to enable players to take a gamble and allow some decisions to be made on their behalf—we will cover this a little later on. The game design can also come to our rescue in that there are some actions that will take more than one update cycle to complete, and so it might not even be necessary to provide for an explicit vacation setting for short-term absences.

More frequently, a turn-based game where the update is driven by player action, and where several players must move in strict round-robin fashion (i.e., sequentially), might lead to a natural situation where there can be weeks between moves. This will probably be the case for play-by-e-mail turn-based games, for example.

In addition, if the game is being played on a platform that allows players to set their own pace, they might even decide amongst themselves to take a break. As long as nobody moves during the unofficial vacation slot, the game will simply not progress until they all agree to resume. Again, though, this is restricted to gaming models based on turn-by-turn, player-driven update game implementations.

For any other centrally managed game-update system, if a player leaves his or her account executing a task that takes five days to complete, and something unexpected occurs in that period, it could spell disaster for that player's in-game persona. Subsequently, it is a good idea to offer some kind of extended safeguards in the guise of pre-programmed behavior.

Pre-Programmed Behavior

What makes the *PR* model easy to appreciate and implement is the fact that it appears, on the surface at least, to be a statistics-based game. The natural emergence that makes it challenging to play (and more fun) is simply the playing off of each player against the others. In other words, the behavior is preset, the rules and calculations that determine success are set in stone, and the only thing that players can do is schedule tasks and try to influence the statistics that govern their own in-game properties. By doing this, they hope to ensure that they at least do better than the others, and eventually win.

Many, if not most, turn-based games are themed around the management of statistics, hiding behind an immersive abstraction. If you think back to the classic *D&D* model, for example, the roll of dice determined your fate, and the skill was in making decisions that balanced risk against reward.

This is where real-time action games and turn-based strategy or simulation games differ, of course; the skill in the former is based on reactions and inventory management, while the latter requires a slower, more considered form of decision making. Puzzle games sit somewhere in the middle—fixed moves, highly strategic, but with a player-driven update system.

All turn-based games tend to share one thing in common: There is no way to change behavior or create new behavioral models for the in-game entities to follow. At the most extreme end, we could say that there is usually no player-available scripting language. (There are a number of reasons why this is not usually a good idea, but we can break it down a little farther so that the solution is not quite as extreme as letting players make their own scripted turn-playing mechanisms.)

The innovative twist to the predictable pre-programmed behaviors is the occasional make-or-break decision that can be implemented in a turn-based game. In *Project Rockstar*, for example, these range from finding money in the street and deciding whether to hand it in or not up to full-blown scandals in the press and invites to appear on TV shows. Sometimes, choosing options leads to additional record sales; sometimes it leads to a dip in record sales. There are parallel decisions possible in most genres; all that needs to be done is to tweak them slightly to fit the game genre and premise.

While on vacation, these events should not happen. During normal play, however, they do happen, and will cause problems if the player does not take steps to deal with them. The game design usually calls for a time limit to be placed on making these decisions, and the default (random) option is usually bad.

Before we look at how a turn-based game might be implemented that takes note of all the success points from our case study and adds some innovations of our own, we should note that there are a few alternative approaches to the *Project Rockstar* playing model.

Alternative Approaches

There are three principal areas in which alternatives to the *PR* model can be adopted:

- The update cycle
- In-game scripting to extend basic behaviors
- Alternatives to the standard vacation setting

Depending on the game genre and style, each of these can be adapted to fulfill the game model presented by the rules of the underlying game. For example, chess, as a two-player game, would not benefit from a daily update cycle, and should follow a turn-generated update cycle. Other board-game adaptations would also follow this model, as well as most combat- or exploration-based role-playing games (RPGs).

The turn-generated update cycle is an interesting alternative to the *Project Rockstar* daily update model. A strict turn-generated update cycle would refresh the game environment with every turn. This is quite acceptable if there are four or five player groupings that have an effect on each other, and play in a vacuum, as the time to update will be reasonably small.

Of course, the online/offline debate will weigh into this decision. A play-by-e-mail RPG, for example, can afford to use a pure turn-generated update model as long as the aforementioned conditions are respected. As soon as the moves taken by individuals begin to affect the entire game environment, however, it becomes necessary to make sure that the updates cater to this.

This leads to a continual update model. The time scales might be different for a play-by-e-mail game as opposed to a Web gaming approach, but the challenges are the same. Indeed, the more the game leans toward a continual update model, the more the influences in Chapter 6, where we look at true real-time gaming, will come to bear. (Part of this is isolating what changes to the environment need to be made with each move, and then scheduling the moves as they come in from disparate player groupings.)

I can also propose some middle ground, which I call the "activity threshold model." The basic premise is that a threshold amount of activity on behalf of the players causes the system to start refreshing itself and working out what happens to *all* the players.

This may well cause temporary, unplanned system unavailability (or at least suspension for an indefinite time) as the whole environment starts an update cycle. The trigger could be a simple weight of activity or a key player milestone or target event. Furthermore, the player who triggers it might be rewarded in some way via in-game currency or other mechanism. This would help to drive the desire to keep playing, as well as provide additional community talking points that could be interfaced to the community itself.

The next area, after the update model has been tinkered with, that can be tweaked is the availability of in-game actions that can be assigned to personae within the game environment. Again, there are extremes:

- Default action (fixed, little flexibility)
- Basket of actions (fixed, scheduled flexibility)
- Action-event chains (semi-fixed, challenge-response flexibility)
- Scripting (open, complete flexibility)

Obviously, *PR* falls into the first category. The only choice players can make is how long they let the band do a certain action, and how much they're willing to spend on it. And that's it.

Having a basket of actions from which players can choose, and letting them choose the order in which they are executed whilst keeping an eye on proceedings from a distance, is also quite attractive in certain game genres—for example, soccer simulations, where the manager might not want to intervene for every little detail but where several bad results can cause him or her to change the order of certain in-game actions.

It would be nice if the relationship between events and subsequent in-game actions could be linked together in some way, and that is the goal of using something I call "action-event chains." These are different in approach from opening up the game to full-blown scripting, as they only link specific events in the game to some kind of response. Some strategic games based around fighting, training, leveling up, and procuring resources work on this kind of model. They allow the player to program a response action to certain events, such as invasions by forces from other players. Because of the turn-driven nature of some games, this is vital unless, as in multi-player real-time action games, the player is expected to be connected all the time. The casual nature of the target audience for the games discussed here, however, means that this is unlikely; consequently, there needs to be some method whereby players can devolve some decision-making authority to their in-game virtual selves.

At the other end of the scale from simple pre-programmed response mechanisms is a full scripting environment. This would be some kind of human-computer language allowing the in-game entities to have their behavior altered. New behavior could then be introduced by players based on various models. For example, state machines could be implemented in a visual way, whereby the player would create simple state-driven programs along with appropriate actions causing state changes and thereby build behavior in a blocks approach.

Less visual alternatives include allowing budding programmer-players access to a richer text-based scripting language. Some real-time games have proven to be quite open to this approach, allowing for the creation of bots (multi-player *Quake*, for example), so it is a valid possibility.

This kind of openness can be dangerous, however. There are risks associated with quality control. The more open the environment, the more difficult it becomes to predict with any certainty what people will try to do with it, and hence it becomes impossible to test adequately (see Chapter 9, "Testing Network Games"). Therefore, we have to follow the same kinds of restrictions as for real-time game bot programming (see Chapter 6), but doing so is less dangerous in a sandboxed gaming environment, such as is provided by the kind of turn-by-turn games discussed here.

There are a number of reasons why. Chiefly, it becomes very complex for players to introduce some kind of automatic playing where they stand to gain from exploiting the system. In addition, they have a lot less to gain than in a real-time action game where speed of reaction is generally more important than being able to understand the game and the game mechanics intimately. This is covered in more detail in Chapter 8, "Removing the Cheating Elements," when we look at the various kinds of cheating that are prevalent in network games.

Finally, we can extend the interface to overcome the possibility that the play should continue even when a player is absent. For example, we might choose to allow play-by-e-mail (or even mobile-phone text message) extensions for vacationing players. For discrete decisions where the only possible answer is yes/no or a choice from several options, this might prove to be the perfect solution to the problem.

Time-elapse settings can also be exploited. For example, a player might set up an action that he or she knows will take three days to process. Perhaps the player will be away from a computer because it's a weekend or he or she is taking a short trip, but still wants to keep playing. If make-or-break decisions come up while the player is away from his or her main machine, the player can still be offered the possibility to make in-game decisions by e-mail or text message. Again, this relies on the choices being discrete (binary, ternary, *n*-ary) and on using a medium that adequately describes (albeit in text format) the nature of the decision and choices.

With these solutions in mind, we can now look at how all these lessons can be used to create an actual game design.

THE FICTIONAL *PLANETSTAR* RPG

At the time of writing, this game does not actually exist. However, the following should be complete enough for you to appreciate how it might work in practice and whether it would be fun to play, and even give you a fighting chance to implement something similar yourself.

The design is based on the preceding analysis of *Project Rockstar*, and we shall look at how a possible game might be built around the premise made famous by the space trading and combat game *Elite*. For those not familiar with *Elite*, the premise is very simple: Players embark on journeys between stars, trading goods at a profit in order to collect enough money to upgrade their ships, and occasionally engage in bouts of combat. There are several ways to play the game—all variations on the binary decision to follow a career of trading or bounty hunting.

The Game Environment

The principle of the environment is that it is open ended (or at least large enough to give the illusion of being open ended). This environment is divided into a network of stars, clustered into galaxies. This arrangement provides a good way to segment the database in the future, which becomes a requirement due to the expansion of the game.

Each star has its own basic configuration, which can be generated in advance or even during the game time. This is easily achieved using pseudo-random procedural content-generation techniques (see *The Infinite Game Universe: Mathematical Techniques*, by the author and published by Charles River Media).

By generating the star systems as they are "discovered," we can allow the whole environment to evolve with the players. We might decide, for example, that each star system has the following makeup:

- **Economy type:** agricultural, industrial, service
- **Wealth:** rich, average, poor
- **Population:** in billions

This allows many different configurations, and the attributes must be stored in a database even if the stars and their makeup are generated upon discovery. By doing this, we allow the very nature of the stars to evolve. Care must be taken to maintain the current topography of the environment if new attributes are added, however.

Each star system should also have a name; again, this can be procedurally generated, or generated in advance. Either way, to avoid duplicates, allocated names must be stored in a database.

These star systems also have goods for sale (to facilitate the trading aspect of the premise). The price of these goods is sensitive to the system configuration. For example, food will be cheaper on a poor agricultural system with fewer than 1 billion inhabitants than on a rich service system that has 10 billion or more inhabitants. (This relationship is a key part of the original *Elite* game, and works to offer clues to players as to which stars make good trading partners. There is, however, still an element of chance/unpredictability to the actual price that players will receive, and hence the profit that they will make.)

The same principle is also valid for ship equipment. We might decide to set up the algorithms such that industrial systems offer cheaper ship equipment (easily available processes and factories), but that service economies will have more choice because of the research that they do into hi-tech ship equipment.

Deciding how all of the various factors that make up a star will influence the price of goods and equipment is part of the balance of the game. You should be able to appreciate that the relationship between the complexity of the algorithms that give rise to this balance has a non-linear relationship with respect to the number of variables. In other words, keep the variables to a minimum, as the complexity will rise exponentially with each added star-system attribute or piece of equipment for sale.

Players will, in principle, spend their time going from place to place in their ship. Along the way they will choose either to trade with each star and remain more or less peaceful and defensive or turn toward piracy and buccaneering, taking a more offensive point of view.

Profile, Ship Design, and Customization

Deciding how much customization to allow is a fairly open-ended design decision. The principle is that the players must be made to feel like they own their ship. As such they need to be able to customize it—color, decals, imported graphics and photos, and so on. Of course, the same goes for their profile, too.

The statistics that make up the player's profile all need to be stored on the server too, and they will have an influence on the player's journey through the game. Experienced traders might be able to get better prices, and good pilots will use less fuel, whilst those with many kills under their belt might also fare better during combat.

Of course, different ships can be bought and sold, and each is slightly different. Some will be designed for combat and others for ferrying large quantities of people and/or goods around. This implies sets of ship-capability statistics that need to be incorporated into the game design.

The same rules with respect to complexity apply here too—the more capability factors are needed to build into battles, encounters, trading, and exploration and travel, the more complex the algorithms that work out the relative success of each action will be.

These possibilities also all need to take into account the in-game currency, which can be backed by real-world money, of course. Offering players the possibility to upgrade through payment rather than doggedly playing the game is one way to raise revenue (see the "Revenue Model" section later in the chapter), but also provides a realistic way for less-gifted players to get a head start.

With the scene set, it is time to look at the update-cycle model that should be used for this fictional game.

Update Cycles

For this fictional game, I have chosen to illustrate several kinds of update cycles by suggesting an effective approach to combining update-cycle models. The advantage of this is that the pace of the game should be more evenly matched to the player, whilst allowing many different playing styles (from casual to hard core) to be catered to.

The cycles that will be combined are as follows:

- Player-movement driven
- Turn by turn
- Daily environment update

The first of these, the player-movement update cycle, is the result of each turn causing knock-on effects in the game environment directly. For example, if the player chooses to purchase goods from a system where those goods are in short supply, then the available quantity might dip and the price slightly increase.

Next, there is the turn-by-turn interaction between several crafts (see the section "Pre-Programmed Combat" later in this chapter for more details), which causes each craft to be updated with reference to the others and possibly the game environment. These interactions might occur in a vacuum from the rest of the game, or they might have a direct effect (as in the turn-by-turn model) on the game environment.

Finally, there is the daily reset of the various variables that are behind the scenes—i.e., trading prices, production volumes, and so on. These will occur along with any daily updates that are sent out via e-mail to inform the player as to the status of his or her individual in-game entities.

The first updates are relatively easy to take account of—depending on the number of simultaneously connected players, that is. Currently, *Eve Online* holds the record, at around 35,000, so clearly high numbers can be catered to (source: *Guinness World Records, 2008, Gamers Edition*).

The second set of updates needs to follow specific rules (see the next section) that govern craft interaction. This method is chosen because this is supposed to be a turn-by-turn game, played anywhere, without real-time combat. To make the game easier to play, less reliant on split-second reactions, and more interesting strategically, pre-programmed combat and interaction has been selected. (We shall come to this in a moment.)

The third update cycle is just like the *PR* daily update. It is easily implemented, but might cause downtime, so it needs to be monitored. It also gives the programmers a chance to perform system updates or maintenance at the same time, behind the scenes.

Pre-Programmed Combat

Pre-programmed combat (and interaction) is a solution to the problem in a turn-based Web game of what happens when two ships meet in space. Clearly, there are many solutions, and I do not pretend that this is the most elegant or efficient. I do, however, believe that it offers a workable model that has many strengths.

There are several solutions that could be chosen:

- **Solution #1: arcade-style combat.** This suffers from being challenging to program. We'll see later on how to do it correctly, but in a game such as we are describing here, it might be inappropriate. It is also not easy to do in a heterogeneous Web environment where we do not control the hardware used to connect to the game.
- **Solution #2: traditional** *Dungeons & Dragons*-**style dice-roll combat.** Iain M. Banks has succinctly summed this up as "getting shafted by a dope with bigger guns" [BANKS01]. While it remains a reasonable way to solve tabletop gaming issues, in video games we have more scope to be creative with the solution. It is also, in my opinion, inelegant, as it is based purely on statistics and ship strength, which can be bought rather than earned. At the same time, it is very, very easy to implement since each encounter is just a function of the pilot's experience, strength of armor, and weapons, combined with kill history.
- **Solution #3: strictly turn-based combat.** In a turn-by-turn gaming model, this means that we have to wait for the other player to make his or her move before deciding what to do next. This is clearly an option, but in a disconnected gaming model like the Web, it might not work properly. We also have the issue as to what to do if someone disconnects, either accidentally or on purpose. Again, this is something that comes up quite a lot in network gaming. In the Web-based environment, it is relatively hard to combat. If the game takes place on a client/server closed binary system, however, then this gets easier to manage. If the choices are very restricted, then the overall effects of player disconnect become slightly easier to manage.
- **Solution #4: a mixture of the above.** In other words, pre-programmed moves scheduled by the player that result in a series of non-interactive scissors-paper-stone encounters. Clearly, there must be some AI in the system, as well as some possibility for the player to feel part of the process, but the guiding principle is a good combination of real-time action and a strategic game like chess, complete with gambits. Also, this solution lets us choose the update model—either turn by turn (triggered) or on the basis of a daily system update like *Project Rockstar*. So it offers flexibility in the final implementation, which the other approaches do not. In addition, this solution also has

quite a lot of flexibility. In fact, it has at least as much as the equipment types that can be introduced into the system. That said, it might be hard (albeit interesting) to maintain, depending on the complexity of the in-game environment. This is another reason to trim the variations of craft, weapon, and so on back as far as possible.

There's one last problem: what to do when several craft occupy the same area. Just because we have elected to use a rule-based system with some openness to player customization, combat need not be automatic. In fact, in many cases, it must be selective and allow several craft to attack each other at the same time. This will certainly liven things up a bit and encourage players to interact, either in a positive (helping each other) or negative (against each other) fashion.

This section should have given you a feel for the challenges that await anyone trying to implement Web turn-based games, as well as insight into the way that any kind of network multi-player game based on a turn-driven architecture might be developed. It is not meant to be a complete design and development guide, but the comparison between the different game types as well as a look at a real (*Project Rockstar*) and an imaginary game, which should hopefully provide food for thought.

REVENUE MODEL

Before any game can be developed, it is necessary to look at how it should be possible to make money from it. After all, without steady cash flow, the project will quickly cease to exist. We close this chapter by taking a look at the various revenue models available. They are inherently different from the "full game plus expansion pack sale" model used by almost every other networked game, based, as they are, around a service delivery model.

It is still possible to employ the retail model, but your ability to do so will depend on the strength of the game as an immersive universe and experience. This will, in turn, depend on the quality of the front end, support of the server-side gaming, and ingeniousness with which the game has been developed. For example, a browser-based game like *Project Rockstar*, aimed specifically at casual gamers or hard-core gamers looking for a quick diversion, would not be able to justify a for-pay model. In the past, gamers have been queried as to whether they would be willing to pay, and the response was cautiously negative. Perhaps this is simply because it does not measure up, in the gamers' mind, to something like *Eve Online*, which towers above it in terms of in-game graphics, depth of play, and gaming model (at least superficially).

This may seem to be an unfair comparison, but imagine *Eve Online* without the front-end system and combat, and played through the browser as a trading and ship-management simulation. The result would be rather like the imaginary space RPG presented in the last section. It would work as a game—it would even be fun to play—but ultimately, it is unlikely that players would pay a subscription fee to do so. Part of this is also due to the fact that the for-pay model would turn away the very market that it's aimed at—those who don't wish to pay for gaming and those who already invest 99% of their gaming time and money into another product.

The question is: Given that we cannot charge for the *game* per se, can we charge for part of the *experience*?

In-Game Currency

One way to raise money for the game developer is to introduce a system of in-game credits, which can be traded using real-world money. Those with the money can afford to have bigger guns and are more likely to win fights. The in-game money usually already exists: It is the nominal credit system used in *Project Rockstar*, or the ISK (in-game currency) used in *Eve Online*. It's also, usually, the underpinning factor that separates success from failure in many such games.

The advantage of allowing trade of real-world money against in-game currency is that it lets casual players remain casual whilst also giving hard-core gamers a choice between earning and buying currency in order to play the game. Casual players can just equip themselves by buying solutions, while those with a penchant for RPGs can do it the hard way.

Such a system needs to allow for the fact that a diligent player investing a substantial amount of time in earning in-game credits should not be able to be beaten by a casual player with a credit card. One way to do this is to allow elective leagues, or restrict purchases such that without *some* in-game experience, certain advanced weapons (equipment, spells, and so on) cannot be bought or, if they can, that they cannot be used as effectively as by someone with more experience points.

One thing is clear: The balance is important—not just for the playability of the game, but also in terms of the end experience and popularity of the game with the target market.

Upgrade Packs

This area is great for generating income. It works on the principle that, after a certain level of play, the player faces a humdrum existence. To face new challenges, the player can pay a fee to upgrade to the next level, which might include more places to go, more interesting people/things to go there with, or just an enhanced experience.

A humdrum existence might then repaid over time by an automatic upgrade. However, the impetus is on generating revenue from players' desire to continue (advance) quickly in the game. This is eventually coupled with peer pressure from players they have built up a relationship with in-game. Consequently, the drive to succeed and the kudos associated with it become a revenue opportunity.

This system could feasibly be coupled with a donation system whereby upgraded players could sponsor their peers to join them on the next level. It is a system that has been tried on the *Fark.com* Web site with some success. Although Fark is not a game (it classifies itself as "not news"), the upgrade system allowing paid members access to more entries than the general public generates healthy revenue for the site owner.

The other side to buying expertise, technological advances, and the like is limiting the capabilities of players with respect to their in-game prowess.

Time/Move Limitations

Besides specific upgrades, in turn-by-turn games it is also easy to implement limitations on movement and/or turns. These limitations could be a way to change the balance of the game where specific capabilities have been acquired, or used as a way to generate revenue.

For example, we can place limits on money required to do something as well as limits on the number of actions that can take place in a single play session. This is the approach that *Project Rockstar* takes, but there is no way to extend the limits.

Players reaching the end of their move limit for the session in other games might choose to buy a few extra movement credits in order to try to finish off their plan for the day. This is not available in the current *Project Rockstar* build, but it is a possible extension.

However, this should not upset the balance of the playing model. For example, in *Project Rockstar*, once a player has set one of his or her band members to a task (say, improving core instrument skills), then this task, logically, cannot finish until the requisite number of play sessions has elapsed.

The danger is that this mechanism would completely upset the gaming balance if players could buy additional time, allowing them to skip this limitation. So, offering players the possibility to buy themselves out of these limitations risks redressing the balance in a way that presents several drawbacks.

Drawbacks

The limitations of a gaming system are the very things that we use to manage the difficulty level and keep interest high. As noted in the last section, there is a danger of upsetting playing model if we start to play with the limitations that have been designed in order to present players with a challenge.

In addition, there is the possibility that any approach that can reduce the natural limitations or even the explicit limitations of a system can give rise to cheating. We look at this later on in Chapter 8; for now, you should be aware that the more popular a game is, the more prone it will be to people trying to circumvent its limitations for their own ends.

Linked to this are practices that are not cheating per se, but more like devious playing tactics. These often have the sole purpose to raise vast amounts of in-game cash or capabilities for the express purpose of building an account position of high value. Then, a natural cycle of buying in and selling on occurs, where players with money will buy into other players' positions, and those with time and money can build up a high-value in-game account very quickly and then sell it on. This would be fine, except where it becomes the norm, at which point it becomes loaded in favor of those with money—and the balance is, again, destroyed.

The final responsibility rests with the game developer: It is up to you to make sure that the in-game exploitation of rules and mechanisms does not detract from the game. Some games will build this around reset points, where the end of a round signals a loss of all in-game wealth and accumulated possessions. This has the desired effect, but can also be very frustrating for players who have invested time and money in building a strong presence. Clearly, if another solution can be found, as well as offering the possibility to raise revenue, then a compromise position is better than the black-and-white mechanism that total resets offer.

Advertising Networks

Anyone familiar with Web publishing will realize that a high-volume game (i.e., one with lots of visitors, regardless of player turnover) is an attractive place for advertisers. In the same way that real-world media attract advertising, so does the interactive virtual media of games.

The modern, Internet-based, advertising market has more or less stabilized into three areas:

- PPC (pay per click)
- Display (a.k.a. banner advertising)
- Sponsorship

Since advertisers don't have time to do deals with every possible advertising outlet, they have become organized into networks. These networks deal with one advertiser (or a set of advertisers) and many possible advertising platforms. Some are discretionary. In other words, the advertiser–content provider relationship is preserved and each one has the possibility to select or allow the relationship to supply advertising. Each publisher can choose *what* to advertise, and each advertiser can choose *where* to advertise.

Other networks are entirely non-discretionary. This means that it is the network that selects who will be advertised, and where. Google AdSense, for example, works on the basis that it selects locations to advertise contextually (based on the content) and therefore might not work well for a game.

Choosing the method and network for advertising will have a direct effect on the amount of revenue that will be generated.

PPC Versus Display Advertising

Two of the most common forms of advertising are pay per click (PPC) and display advertising. Google AdSense follows the PPC model, in which advertisers pay a certain amount of money "per click" that the advertisement generates. So, a single campaign can reach 1,000 visitors (people who actually click on the advert) for a relatively small amount.

A proportion (usually small) of the cost per click (CPC) is returned to the Web-site owner as generated revenue. For each advert displayed, the expected click-through rate can be quite small.

Without a specific action, the site owner will not make any money at all. This model is, however, popular with advertisers, but less so with publishers of Web property that has a low CTR (click through rate).

On the other hand, display advertising works in the same way that traditional advertising does—the content provider is paid each time the advert is displayed, regardless of any ensuing action. This is also known as "banner advertising," although banners have become less popular over the years.

An alternative is to pay a set amount to the site owner for a certain length of exposure; this amounts to sponsorship of the game. The advertiser gets exposure for its brand, in return for which it pays the game creators for the prestige (or just the facility) of being associated with the game itself and having its advert displayed to the players.

Where to Allow Advertising

It is tempting to splatter a game with adverts. The risk, however, is that the value of each advert is diminished as it gets lost in amongst all the others. There are many ways that advertising can be incorporated into the overall game interface so that this does not happen. They all rest on one key point, however: They absolutely *must* be targeted toward gamers. If they are PPC adverts, this is doubly important, as no clicks means no income, and it takes an awful lot of online, registered, active, players to overcome poorly targeted PPC advert campaigns.

One model is borrowed from e-zine (electronic magazine) and e-mail list advertisers, where every now and again they slip in a *solo advert*. A solo advert is one that is sent to some, or all, of the list, with no other content whatsoever, and in addition to existing mailings that players receive. These e-mails can also be sponsored by allowing companies to advertise in the daily update or status e-mails. This is a useful technique, as it conforms more completely to recent legislation with regard to unsolicited commercial e-mail (SPAM). This use of solo adverts has to be very carefully deployed so as not to fall foul of Internet etiquette and legal restrictions.

Then, there is onsite advertising using banners. This is a form of display advertising that is similar to real-world billboard-style adverts. It is easy to implement, and works as well as the material that is provided by the advertiser. Gamers, however, might well be immune to banner advertising as they spend so much of their lives online.

Next, it is possible to provide advertising spots in top 10 lists and other non-game areas such as forums. These adverts can even be used to break up the content so that it reads rather like watching TV: Every now and again, there is an advert that must be tolerated in order to keep enjoying the show.

It is important to test and verify different locations for different kinds of adverts. This is important because display advertising yields a certain CPM (cost per thousand impressions) whereas PPC (pay per click) adverts only make money when someone clicks on them.

Thus, while the price that can be charged per click is higher than the price per impression, sometimes the CPC does not translate into money directly, as nobody clicks the advert. Here again, though, correct targeting will help, as the more relevant an advert is, the more likely the player is to notice and click, it.

Terms and Conditions

Designers must beware of trying to integrate advertising actions with the in-game currency or even the in-game mechanics themselves for advertising networks. These could well fall foul of the network's own rules on advertising.

For example, the terms and conditions often explicitly prohibit encouraging third parties to click on adverts or use automated systems to click on them. This usually extends to trying to offer players (viewers/visitors) some kind of reward for having clicked an advert.

Of course, if you (as the game's owner) also own the advert network, then this might not be an issue—but be sure to check with the advertisers first. The ramifications for getting it wrong aren't just that you won't be paid; your whole business model might well fall apart if you can no longer offer in-game incentives for real-world actions if that is the path that you have chosen.

Direct Sponsorship

Finally, we need to just mention a different form of advertising: direct sponsorship. This is different from adverts because it is equivalent to in-game branding. More importantly, it is the extension of a real-world brand into the game.

For example, it might be possible for a *Project Rockstar* game to integrate with record labels or real-world venues to lend their names to in-game equivalents. This produces a seamless integration between the advertising (sponsorship) message and the game's premise. And, as this example shows, it is often far easier to blend the sponsorship in with the gaming experience. Adverts will always be slightly obtrusive—even if we choose to ignore them—but a well-placed sponsorship message can even add flair to the polished end-game experience.

Even avatars can be sponsored—just like in the real word—provided that they require appropriate clothing, equipment, vehicles, etc. It is a complex engagement between the publisher (or game's creator) and the companies involved, so it is best handled by an agency specializing in in-game sponsorship and branding.

If it comes to it, it is probably a good idea to have all advertising and sponsorship deals processed by an agency that understands both advertising and gaming, as this leaves you, the game designer, with more time to actually create something that you are proud of and that advertisers actually *want* to be associated with.

COMMERCIALIZING A TURN-BY-TURN GAME

Turn-by-turn network games exist on several levels of complexity and time investment. *Project Rockstar* appeals to casual gamers but will eventually breed its own fanatics. The fictional turn-based space RPG described in this chapter, however. will probably attract more hard-core players because

- The rules are more complex
- The premise/environment is more difficult to appreciate
- It contains trading and combat—i.e., multiple skill sets

These three points are almost the diametric opposite of the *Project Rockstar* strong points—the rules are few and easy to grasp, it takes place in an environment that everyone can appreciate, and relies only on one set of life skills. This affects what I call the "pick up and play" factor.

Some games have a high pick-up-and-play factor, others a very low one. This does not necessarily affect their commercial success, just the audience at which they are aimed. Of course, the audience spread will indirectly affect some areas of the revenue-generation possibilities, and hence the commercial viability of a project.

A game with a very high pick-up-and-play factor and considerable audience reach, for example, can be easily commercialized through advertising and sponsorship. Like TV or radio, a large captive, targeted audience equates to advertising opportunities for which many organizations will pay reasonably highly. On the other hand, a game with a lower audience reach might have to rely on the audience providing the revenue through paid services. In addition, some of the avenues of revenue generation such as display advertising will be closed to the creators of such games, and they might only be able to use pay-per-click (PPC) models, which will usually generate less income.

One such category of games is the subject of the next chapter: real-time MMORPGs. Even *Second Life*, which ought to be one of the most accessible online games, has had to find revenue somewhere, and resorts to charging players. The reason—and this is speculation on my part—is that the complexity of the development effort, plus the day-to-day requirements, along with the huge audience reach, has meant that no amount of advertising or sponsorship can pay back the costs involved.

It's a salutary lesson: A Web-based game with modest requirements will be cheaper to put in place, generate more income, and have more potential revenue opportunities than a custom interface based full-scale MMORPG. But the latter games will still make money from a hard-core fan base.

As a side note, it is interesting that long-time indie stalwart Garage-Games has begun to marry the two together, offering real-time 3D gaming in browser-deployable environments. This kind of bridge between the two technologies may make some inroads into the issue of development cost versus income, and upset the aforementioned model somewhat.

It is also worth pointing out that Web-based turn-by-turn games (and also other kinds of turn-by-turn RPGs) lend themselves to being created and maintained without the help of a publisher. Since the goods are entirely virtual, have no physical distribution channels, and can be continually tweaked without recourse to rebuilding the package, the creation and financing model can almost completely ignore traditional publishing issues.

REFERENCES

The Infinite Game Universe: Mathematical Techniques, Guy W. Lecky-Thompson, Charles River Media, 2001.

Guinness World Records, 2008: Gamers Edition, Guinness World Records Limited (pub), 2008.

[BANKS01] "The Player of Games," Iain M. Banks, *Orbit*, 1991.

CREATING ARCADE AND MASSIVELY MULTI-PLAYER ONLINE GAMES (REAL-TIME)

In This Chapter

- Game Models Revisited
- Anatomy of a Game Model
- Revenue Models
- Merging Real-Time Gaming with the Internet
- References

To contrast with turn-by-turn games, this chapter looks at the issues behind creating online, real-time, massively multi-player games. Rather than rehashing the game-design arguments from the last chapter—many of the same principles apply—this chapter points out the differences, most of which stem from the following:

- **Client engineering.** Clients are generally custom-created due to the real-time nature of these games, which brings some additional burden for both the design and development.
- **Network inconsistencies.** These are hard, real-time systems; the Internet is not really geared up for that level of reliability.
- **Revenue model.** The additional burden of the client engineering and network inconsistencies means that the revenue must be mainly direct, coming from ongoing subscriptions.
- **Audience.** Given all of the above, the audience will likely be less casual, more discerning, and fickle—whilst also being very loyal, once won over.

Perhaps surprisingly, the server side does not change all that much. It's still a repository for all the in-game data, from player statistics and capabilities to the environment and all the artifacts contained within it. Most differences will be a reflection of the system's increased capacity requirements due to the real-time–update nature of the system. That means there is no such thing as a daily update; all updates have to take place in real time.

This facet of the client/server model naturally increases the complexity—and hence capacity—of the hardware systems. The result is that these games are more expensive to create, maintain, and run. Consequently, the price to the end-user will be higher. While turn-by-turn games can be free at the point of access, MMORPGs and online arcade games are rarely, if ever, afforded the same luxury.

This means that they have to be good. *Very* good.

GAME MODELS REVISITED

This section revisits the definitions of two kinds of online multi-player games:

- Massive multi-player online role playing games (MMORPGs)
- Arcade action games

Why? These games represent two extremes. The first, MMORPGs, represent an extreme in terms of the number (expected number, anyway) of clients that will be connected at once or exist in the database. That's the "massive" part—along with the size of the game environment, which has to be big to contain all the players. The second, arcade action games, represents an extreme in terms of the network speed and delivery of data. There might only be two players (or up to, say, four) at any one time, but they will be doing battle at a lightning-fast pace, thereby placing a great burden on the infrastructure in terms of expected response times.

MMORPGs

The general MMORPG environment inherits from the previous chapter, in that the same kinds of possibilities for customization exist. That said, there is one particular aspect of this genre that the turn-by-turn model does not share.

MMORPGs tend to be aimed more toward hard-core gamers than turn-by-turn games—although in-browser casual MMORPGs, which don't require the same investment in terms of time or money as the likes of *World of WarCraft* or *Everquest*, are on the way up. A few things make casual MMORPGs more accessible—simplified rules and less complex environments, for example—but essentially they are the same as their bigger siblings. MMORPGs in general are not turn based but are real time—meaning the environment has to be very reactive. This, in turn, means that the server can't be the only place that decisions are made because the Internet reaction time might not allow this. So, there will likely be a split between the functionality offered by the server and the client such that the client can maintain some of the game universe by itself, and therefore communicate to the game server in an appropriate fashion. Since this involves a special kind of game system, perhaps we should discuss that now.

The Game System Infrastructure

The game system will consist of:

- A fully functional client
- A server
- A database system

In terms of the investment required to create the game system, one thing is clear: It will be an expensive undertaking, whatever the client platform. The client must be capable of displaying complex graphics (and the developer has to decide between 2D and 3D renderings), contain enough AI to ensure that the game flows in the face of potentially uneven Internet connectivity, and communicate effectively with the player. The client itself could be anything from a Java-based in-browser client to a full game delivered as a shrink-wrapped product.

Meanwhile, the server must be able to maintain multiple connections at the same time whilst also ensuring that the players who occupy the same logical part of the game universe have priority communications *vis á vis* each other, as in the previous chapter. But now, rather than having a daily update cycle, the server needs to constantly update itself with respect to the evolving game. This is nothing new, but it does show that the complexity level has jumped somewhat from the turn-by-turn game dissected in the previous chapter.

The Playing Infrastructure

The playing infrastructure is very similar in many ways to the turn-based system you looked at in the last chapter. It is multi-player, but this time the interactions take place in real time rather than in a turn-by-turn fashion. Even real time–strategy games (RTS games) allow the session to evolve in real time. This also means that the player will be more or less constantly involved with the game during the session rather than it being a pick-up-and-play game, which can be put down as the player chooses.

Player Customization

Player customization is very important for MMORPGs, because the character (as in turn-based gaming), becomes the pivotal point. This could be as true for *Burnout*, a racing game in which cars can be customized, as it is for *Everquest*, *World of WarCraft*, and *Eve Online*.

It all comes down to a sense of ownership. This means that, as in the previous chapter, the individual characters should be completely customizable—not as a diversion for when the player has nothing else to do, but for recognition and in-game reasons. In addition, there should be a provision for the usual community functions, such as competitions, and a rendering of the in-game character as an avatar in ex-game areas.

Arcade Action Games

The arcade action gaming model is a little different. Here, the emphasis is on the client software, which has to stand up to the action role. That means it must adapt itself to the network flow, depending on how many players are connected at a given moment in time, whilst also providing an accessible interface for things like high scores. After all, these games are less about a progression and more about instant gratification and round-based combat.

The client, then, is highly unlikely to be anything but a real game developed for a specific platform. By "real game," I mean that it is not likely, for performance reasons, to be a through-the-browser experience.

Rather, it is more likely to be a piece of software that is designed to make the most of a specific platform, be that a console, handheld, or PC. The amount of data transferred via the network is likely to be reasonably light, which is just as well because the transfer rate is likely to be high.

For those reasons, the server will need to be fairly lightweight, offering only the barest of configurations for the sharing of connections. It might even be prudent to avoid putting any logic on the server at all, save for basic routing for the incoming data: a match-up service, essentially, for gamers.

The database does not need to be constantly updated; rather it is there to store the result of each bout. It will need to keep track of high scores, however, and be sophisticated enough that it cannot be cheated.

Anatomy of a Game Model

What the previous section has shown is that these game models have a very similar anatomy, sharing a lot of the same characteristics:

- High-speed reaction times (i.e., plenty of network traffic)
- Live database connectivity (i.e., a persistent gaming world)
- High-end assets (artwork and sound)

That means that unlike the turn-by-turn games you looked at in the previous chapter (with the exception of a real time–strategy game like *Civilization*), these games must be supported by custom client-side interfaces and will stretch the hardware to its limits. In this case, by "hardware," I mean the client (the player's interface on the game universe), server (where the player's moves are stored, relayed, checked, and verified), and network (the bit in the middle that facilitates the multi-player aspects of the game).

 It is important to note that you will have to substitute the standard game design stuff for yourself as it relates to the single-player environment. This includes, of course, everything that is related to the end-user experience, such as the control scheme. In addition, because this is a fundamentals book, it does not spend time discussing how the level design should be set out. You are likely already aware that there are different styles of multi-player games: capture the flag, cooperative combat, etc.

In addition, the maps that represent the levels must be defined with the multi-player environment in mind, where appropriate. That's because there are fewer constraints on what players will do in a given level when so many of them get together. Action games do not have this issue, as they tend to revolve around a constrained game environment (think of a fighting or driving game), but MMORPGs and FPSes have an additional dimension in that they are not constrained. That means the maps for such games have to stand the test of time, whilst also being as open as possible—and almost foolproof. In "Multiplayer Level Design In-Depth, Part 2: The Rules of Map Design" [GAMA01], Pascal Luban breaks this down into three *challenges*:

- **Durability.** The map must be able to withstand multiple challenges and game sessions, whether they be cooperative combat or *Capture the Flag* (CTF) based.
- **Accessibility.** Everything about the map should be pretty obvious; it's not a single-player map where you need to have hidden elements and traps or puzzles.
- **Entertainment.** It has to be fun, because if it isn't, nobody will want to play the game, let alone the map.

On top of this, other action strategy and MMORPGs have additional constraints—such as open game environments, quests, and so on—that require different map-making and level-design skills. Although these are outside scope of this book, I will touch upon them and the mechanics that must support them along the way.

Client Software Structures

Performance is an issue with this category of games in a way that it wasn't in the examples found in the last chapter. The gaming client is still a window on the game environment (which is stored on the server), but it reflects the changing state of that game environment, and everything in it, in real time.

 You might argue that a simple Telnet text-based RPG does exactly this, and that the number of players involved—and even the size of the game environment—qualify it as an MMORPG. That said, the text-based RPG is different in that it is text based, so the client requirements are that much less.

So gaming clients for real time action–based multi-player network games are custom created and must offer high performance. That means choices are usually limited to closed-binary or a Java-style play-in-the-browser solutions. This, in turn, leads to decisions such as whether to make the game available as a retail pack with some gaming hours included or a purely subscription-based model with a free download of the game client (*Eve Online* style). Games such as *Unreal Tournament* take the approach that the client and even some multi-player action is available for free, with the for-pay model adding to the single- and multi-player environments in a variety of ways.

There are, then, different kinds of clients:

- Single player at the core, with multi-player game modes
- Multi-player at the core, with no single-player game at all

The underlying question is, Where do you put the majority of the gaming logic? If you put it in the client, you risk being hacked (see Chapter 8, "Removing the Cheating Elements," and Chapter 9, "Testing Network Games"). On the other hand, if you put it on the server, you risk missing updates. And if you split the responsibilities between the client and the server, you risk getting out of sync.

To understand this, let us look at a client that takes all the decisions locally, a client that shares that responsibility with the server, and a client that does nothing. We'll assume that the game in question is similar to *Eve Online*, and a fighting game like *Street Fighter IV*.

The gaming client that makes decisions locally and relays the result to the server, and hence the rest of the clients, needs only to receive its view of the game environment. It will receive the commands relating to in-game entities from the other clients as the players make their moves. It will then calculate what happens next and relay the new statuses to the rest of the clients in the game.

In this model, it is imperative to put game logic in place to detect when one of the clients becomes hacked and prevent it from lying about the results of actions or the status of its own player in the game. This logic must go on the server. At this point, you may as well concede that the server should share responsibility for updates with the clients. In any case, it is the server that stores the persistent game state, so it might as well provide the logic to operate on that game state as well.

So, in this model, clients have the responsibility to display and calculate, but they relay that data to the server, which then checks and responds to all the clients with a central view of the game environment. In this way, it can detect and remove any cheating (we hope) and keep all the clients in sync.

The next step from this is a model in which the server handles everything and the clients just display the results. The issue with this approach is that, while it is secure, and while the client will be able to display much higher quality renderings of the game environment or be extremely lightweight (for Web use), it does require a very good network connection.

Clearly, deciding what kind of client to use is very important, and involves a trade-off of security against performance. Naturally, platform reach will come into play as well, in that if you want to reach as many potential players as possible, you need to create a client that covers that premise. On the other hand, many console gamers only play games on the console and not on their PC, so that has to be factored into the decision as well. The bit that doesn't really change in all this is the server.

PEER-TO-PEER GAMING

All of the above is based on the premise that the network model involves some form of client/server mechanism. It is feasible, however, to set up a peer-to-peer network to allow games to be pitted directly against each other. For one-on-one games this is simple enough, but for MMORPGs (for example) some kind of multicast will need to be set up. If this is the route you want to go, then security becomes paramount—and will probably preclude the platform being anything that is too open. For example, consoles would be okay, but a PC would be asking for trouble. In any case, it is more conventional, and somewhat easier, if communications take place via a central game server.

Building Server Solutions

The MMORPG server is built around the same basic premise as before: data storage and some game logic that helps to describe/manipulate the environment and the players within it. The difference is that the game environment, and the players and things in it, are all that much bigger—as is the game logic that describes the interactions expected within it. In contrast, the action server has one central focus: speed of reaction time. Although it will suffer from many of the same issues as the MMORPG server (i.e., there will be many games going on at the same time), its role is somewhat reduced to managing interactions and results rather than a game environment, per se.

One thing that the servers will need to be able to handle is multiple incoming connections—including supporting some way to make sure that they all receive the same attention. You'll look at ways of doing this in Chapter 10, "Network Programming Primer." The server is also responsible for security and cheat detection; these topics are covered in Chapter 8 and Chapter 9. It is important to remember, however, that the actual game logic and storage are only one small part of the responsibilities of the game server.

Designing for Multiple Servers

There are several kinds of multiple server environments, depending on the game and how the game environment and entire system is split up:

- **Server per service (split up game from support).** This approach is the norm for all game types, keeping the gaming servers separate from servers dealing with downloads, community issues, forums, and other kinds of off-game interaction. This might seem like overkill, but it is worth it in that it prevents something that happens on a non-game server from bringing the game server down. This sounds obvious, but like all obvious things, it can be overlooked.

- **Multiple game zones (big environment, many servers).** This approach is for those games where the actual environment is just too big for a single server to cope with (as in *Eve Online*). This could also be a split by number of clients, of course. Added to that, each zone might actually be a server cluster; a prime example of cases where there are just too many players for one server, as well as an environment that is too big for a single server zone.
- **Distributed gaming (different servers for different maps/ games).** This approach takes the view that specific servers will be set up to cover specific requirements, be that in the form of specific maps or game styles. So you might have a CTF server and a frag-fest server, where anything goes. This is just another way of splitting the workload—although it should also be noted that it is a good way to offer custom code bases, as well. That means two servers could run code with slightly different game rules, like the original *TinyMUD* customizations that led to MUCK, MUSH, MOO, and other derivatives.

How to break up the game environment and the players present in it is another one of those big questions in network multi-player game design whose answer differs depending on circumstances. Clearly, for example, LAN gaming doesn't suffer from the weight of this decision as much as, say, Internet gaming. For the latter, a lot rides on the complementary services—for example, the database.

The Role of Databases

A database is a heavy application in terms of memory and disk space as well as processing requirements. As such, while it is possible to run a database on the same platform as the server, often it will be on a different machine. The database also needs to be accessed by all players (albeit through the server platform); as such, it is often grouped logically with the server platform itself.

The database stores everything the game needs in order to function:

- Players' status, history, customization, and location
- Game environment
- NPCs
- In-game artifacts
- Ex-game artifacts (community, etc.)

As with servers, it is probably a good idea if the database is not part of the server infrastructure itself; in this way you can split tasks across databases. Of course, this split can be done in a variety of ways:

- **Split by function:** a database for the players, a database for the environment, etc.
- **Split by zone:** players copied from one zone to another

Any discussion of database design can wind up running in circles because there is no one answer to the question of how a database should be set up. One approach might be to put the players in one database and the game environment and their locations in another. Then, when a player moves from one location to another, all you need to do is a) change the player's location status in the PlayerDatabase, and b) display whatever the player might see, as taken from the LocationDatabase. On the other hand, you might choose to let the player move from one database to another, where the database contains the description of the players in a specific zone—and only those players—in conjunction with the game environment. This has a drawback, however, in that the player data must be copied from one database to another, which might be a time-consuming exercise. It does mean, though, that the load will be more evenly spread—which will make data access faster (you hope).

The discussion turns full circle when you consider the physical location and security of the database. Clearly, a distributed model is harder to keep in sync, but also potentially more robust than a model that sees all the data for one facet in a single place. The decision might be simpler for action games where locations just mean a place to stand and fight, but nonetheless, some of the same discussions will be had, especially when it comes to separating databases by function.

This follows much the same path as the discussions related to splitting the server park by function; you don't want a high-volume message board on the same database platform as the main game database, because it might well slow everything down. Where the main bottleneck is likely to be, however, is at the networking side.

End-to-End Networking Using IP

The protocol of choice for many games is TCP/IP—the same protocol used on the World Wide Web and the Internet as a whole. The reason for this is simple: reliability. That reliability comes at a cost, however: efficiency. In many ways, a more efficient way to use the network would be User Datagram Protocol (UDP); as its name suggests, it works by farming out much of the responsibility for the protocol's management to the user (or, more appropriately, the programmer).

This is the pivotal decision, addressed in Chapter 7 and Chapter 10: Do you go for the inefficient—but safe—TCP/IP approach, or do you go for UDP, which is faster but only because it ignores things like packet ordering and guarantees of delivery? Many network problems can be solved by selecting the right protocol for whatever task is expected of it.

For example, a good choice of protocol for a lossy application such as playing back low-quality video is UDP, which is a bad choice for anything that requires guaranteed delivery (unless the application is prepared to spend a lot of time checking that it has what it supposed to have).

 To make either of these protocols more efficient, yet another protocol can be used—this time at the IP level—known as multicast. Essentially, multicast means a single point sending data, simultaneously, to multiple recipients. It can help to make a networking protocol respond more quickly. That said, multicast lies in the realm of experimentation, having been tested in some very high-level military and virtual-reality applications, but not extensively in gaming.

As you shall see later in this book, there are three main problems linked with using networking in a real-time environment:

- **Latency.** Slow data rate
- **Jitter.** Unreliable data rate
- **Loss.** Unreliable delivery

I didn't mention these in the last chapter, because in that context they simply didn't matter. In this case, however, they suddenly matter very much, because we rely on them to convey the status of the game, and everything in it, in real time. In Chapter 7 and Chapter 10, you learn to implement solutions that tackle these issues head on. In the meantime, however, you need to understand in detail their effects on the game from a game design point of view rather than a purely mechanical one.

Problem #1: Network Latency

Network latency, easily defined as "lag," refers to a more or less constant delay on the delivery of data. This has a number of root causes, as you shall see later on. Latency is more common with TCP than with UDP, for the simple reason that TCP tries its best to deal with all the network issues at the source. UDP doesn't suffer from latency as much because it doesn't try as hard. If a packet is delayed, it tends to just forget about it, delivering it if and when it turns up. TCP, on the other hand, suspends processing until it gets a good packet stream or drops the connection entirely—in effect giving up.

The problem with latency is that it can make a game very slow. That sounds obvious, but it needs exploring a bit further. Latency exists on several levels, each contributing to the overall system latency:

- Network (of course)
- Control latency (the reaction time between the controls and the game)
- Client latency (the reaction time of the client PC/console/etc.)

- Internal server latency
- Database latency

Some of these—mainly network latency, control latency, and client latency—have a direct effect on the game as seen by the player. The effect of the network latency is compounded by internal server latency, which is in turn subject to database latency.

The solution to system latency is to make the network communication as efficient and consistent as possible so that it doesn't get flooded when the action increases in pace and complexity. The server latencies can also be attacked by judicious use of resources and good system and database design. Given the quantity of unknowns, however, all network connections will have a certain latency, caused in part by the fact that the Internet has no service quality commitment. In short, nobody guarantees that the Internet will "work," and there is very little measure of what's working and what isn't. The result is that, at times, the game will seem to be slow.

If you assume for a moment that all steps have been taken to reduce system latency, but that the Internet has a bad day, what is the net effect? Data will not be received in a timely fashion. That means the client will not be able to display the result of other clients' actions in a way that is conducive to the fast action of the game. Humans, luckily, are very adaptive, and studies ("The Effect of Latency and Network Limitations on MMORPGs" [NETGAMES01], for example) have shown that latency can be quite high (1250ms) before the game becomes unplayable. The reason for this is in the design of the game. If the game is still fluid at higher latencies, then players will slow themselves down to compensate. Even if the battle is taking much longer to play out, the players will not necessarily notice the full extent of the latency at work.

The secret, then, is to slow down the whole system to compensate. So in an action game, the fighting characters could feasibly be slowed to compensate for the lower data transfer rate; in essence, the pace of play can be artificially kept in sync with the data rate—as long as that data rate can be properly measured. By a similar token, the action in an MMORPG or RTS could be made to unfold in a similar fashion (remembering, of course, that the rate of play has to be set to the network transmission [latency] rate of the slowest client). Otherwise, some strange synchronization issues will occur—some of which are akin to cheating, as the local player might be able to move much more quickly than anyone else. This would mean that by the time the player's location data was sent in, he or she might have moved more than other players (something I call the "*Matrix* effect," after the movie).

One other thing to consider is that only clients in the same logical game space need to match their latencies. If client A cannot see or be affected by client Z, then client A has no need to match client Z's latencies until such a time as client Z moves within the sphere of influence governed by client A.

So this requires a more or less constant conversation between the server and clients in the same logical game space to allow the client software to match the latencies with the pace of play for that particular vector within the game environment. At the very least, constant latency enables you to create a workaround that renders the game playable—if a little slower.

Unfortunately, it is quite rare that latency is uniform on the Internet. Perhaps in LAN gaming, you can be fairly sure that it will be—after all, you control the network infrastructure. A more prevalent latency-related issue for online gaming is the so-called "jitter."

Problem #2: Network Jitter

Jitter is non-uniform latency. That is, it is latency that arrives in bursts. It is highly irritating to players, as it results in the game constantly trying to adjust for late and out-of-sequence data packets.

Causes of network jitter include

- Dropped packets, where packets arrive at buffers that are already full
- Delayed packets, where packets are re-routed onto routes that are slower
- Out-of-sequence packets, where packets in the same stream take different routes, which have different latencies

If the network protocol is UDP, then jitter is treated in a slightly different way than TCP; again, this is because the UDP protocol has absolutely no built-in defenses for packet control. As such, with UDP, there is less jitter, but the net result is that there are no guarantees for the correct delivery of data or streams in the right sequence. TCP, on the other hand, comes with jitter built in because it spends so much time trying to correct for the vagaries of Internet connectivity. If, suddenly, a part of the Internet goes down and packets are re-routed through two different routes, thereby arriving consistently out of sequence, then the TCP protocol will start to jitter as it rearranges the packets.

Let's assume you have taken the workaround option from the last section and made a game that dynamically alters its speed according to the prevalence of network latency detected across multiple clients all in the same logical game space. For one reason or another, let us assume, too, that the latency is variable—in other words, you are experiencing network jitter. This will result in the pace of the game also being variable. In turn, the player will be unable to adjust his or her own playing speed to match the latency because it is constantly fluctuating.

Somehow, this jitter needs to be smoothed so that players can (albeit unconsciously) continue to adjust their rate of play to match the system latency. Otherwise, they will be unable to settle into the game, as different characters will move at different speeds and the game environment will skip, lurch, and flicker its way to conclusion.

As with latency, however, there is no real solution to jitter. There are just things you can do to limit its effect on playability. The first is an extension of the solution outlined in the preceding section: to vary the latency in a way that gives the players time to adjust. Although this is a complex approach, if implemented correctly, it ought to give the game a chance to adapt properly. The second solution is to use dead reckoning and AI techniques to estimate the actual movements of players in the environment and then correct the estimations once the information is available. There are several kinds of dead reckoning; we deal, in Chapter 7, with two of them:

- Trajectory dead reckoning, in which equations are used to estimate movement of objects in the game
- Behavioral dead reckoning, in which historical observation is used to try to second-guess players in a very rudimentary fashion

An example of the first might be a bullet fired from a gun. Based on knowledge of the game environment and objects within it, you can deduce that a bullet fired from a gun will always travel in a straight line, and you can calculate the net effect without waiting for the clients to play out the sequence individually. This same trick can also be used with player-controlled vehicles and the like. If the vehicle is not traveling in a straight line, however, or comes to a point where it might have a choice as to whether it continues in a straight line, you need to swap to behavioral dead reckoning. For example, if the vehicle comes to a corner, you can roughly estimate that the player will try to cover the corner by slowing down, so clients (or the server) can calculate this and adjust its estimates to match reality as and when the data arrives. Sometimes, however, the data may not arrive—resulting in network loss.

Problem #3: Network Loss

Network loss can mean different things—loss of packets, loss of connectivity, and so on—but the net effect is the same: data that ought to have been there isn't. This manifests itself in the game in a variety of interesting ways, from stuttering movement to artifacts appearing and disappearing seemingly at random. At its worst, it can have an effect on the outcome of the game as players all try to do things at the same time, only to find that other players have moved the game on in a different direction.

Not only is this annoying, it can sometimes make it appear as if players are cheating. In fact, dropping data packets, as you will see in Chapter 8, is actually a rather good cheating tactic. The issue is separating natural loss of data from those trying to fool a dead-reckoned system by actively cheating.

One of the worst network loss problems is loss of the connection. This can happen at two levels: logical and physical. On the logical side, network connection loss is usually temporary. It happens when the network gives up for a time, usually due to a simple time-out. If the time-out persists, then the connection loss will become physical. In other words, the systems will become disconnected—rather than suspended—at the network level. Any of the resources assigned to the player on the server or clients will be returned to the controlling system, the player will no longer exist in a logical sense within the game environment, and his or her part is taken over by an AI controller.

We look at this in more detail later on, but again, there are no cures. There are only things you can do to make sure that when it happens, it doesn't affect the game too much. Clearly, in a two-player online action game, the game is over if the connection is lost—and can only barely continue if there is substantial data loss. In other games, such as MMORPGs and RTS games, players might even force a disconnect to save their position in the game (as a form of cheating) or they might need to be replaced by an automated player temporarily or permanently.

Dealing with data loss goes hand in hand with the various strategies that you looked at earlier for dealing with network latency and jitter. They are connected by the ways in which we choose to design solutions to the problems related to networking at large. These three problems are typical of all network games. As such, the bulk of the remainder of this book concentrates on ways to avoid these problems—or at least mitigate their effects.

REVENUE MODELS

This topic might be seen as a kind of footnote by some, but it is important to mention that the available revenue models are very similar to those explored in the last chapter—with one overriding exception: We have a direct method available through the client software, which we own and have developed.

That is, these games are usually

- A single-player version with multi-player add-on to justify the price
- A pure multi-player sold in a box
- A free client with a for-pay multi-player experience

That means most of the revenue will be generated through direct means, which, in turn, will help to fund the debt incurred by the development of the game. In essence, it is more like the regular game-development funding model that many mainstream development outfits will be familiar with.

The Direct Revenue Model

The direct revenue model is the easiest to leverage and appreciate—but a game with no pedigree will find it hard to get a foot in the door. This is because gamers already spend most of their available gaming time in their favorite MMORPG, and weaning them off it will be next to impossible.

In any case, the typical model used is based around sales of clients with hours of online multi-player time built in. These hours could be unlimited or they could come with a cap. In MMORPGs, it is usually likely that the hours are capped in some way, whereas for action games, there is not likely to be any cap with the retail package. In other words, for some genres of game, it is acceptable to expect players to pay for the online multi-player experience, whereas with others it is not. The latter usually follow some kind of subscription model for additional hours.

Using the subscription model to generate revenue is another way to leverage the multi-player environment. Here, it is typical (as with *Eve Online*) to distribute the client free of charge and then charge players for the possibility to play online with other players.

Expansion packs (the *World of WarCraft* model) represent another way in which players can be charged for buying what is essentially the same game, with some modifications and extensions, but nothing really ground-breaking. All they are designed to do is offset the cost of maintaining the game and make some profit.

Yet another way to directly generate money is via the in-game economy. Here, you charge players to buy credits that can be exchanged in-game for various things, be they items, playing hours, or virtual property.

One aside: It is possible to create a demo version of the game (single player) like the *Unreal Tournament* model and then get people used to the environment in the hopes that they will, eventually, actually give the developer money for it.

The Indirect Revenue Model

Less common with MMORPGs and action games is the indirect revenue model. The games discussed in the previous chapter relied on this model because they are delivered through a platform for which the developer could not charge. This was partly because the components used to build them were freely available, and partly because of the expectation of the gaming public that Web games are essentially free. You become less reliant on this model, however, in cases where the product, in a box, stands on its own and generates direct revenue.

Nonetheless, sponsorship is still a real option, especially for games based on some kind of intellectual property that has a real-world equivalent:

- Sports games
- Motor-racing games
- Music games

In addition, the advert revenue stream is available to games in this category, although not advertising schemes that require payment through a pay-per-click model. It is highly unlikely that a player will suspend his or her play session to click a banner while playing an MMORPG or action game. This may prove to be more lucrative via other parts of the game, however—i.e., related sites, community (forum, etc.) sites, and so on. That said, it should not be relied on; the best way to raise revenue will probably be through the direct method.

MERGING REAL-TIME GAMING WITH THE INTERNET

Real-time gaming and the Internet would appear, at first sight, to make very uneasy bedfellows. You might say that they, like water and electricity, are simply not designed to mix—and that when they do, chaos may ensue. There are, however, many tricks you can employ to deal with the worst excesses of the state of the underlying network, most coming from the programmer's own arsenal (covered in Chapters 7 through 10). Some will evolve naturally and some will need to be designed in, but all are made possible thanks to the increases in computing power that allow us to become ever more devious in our efforts both to create robust client/server game platforms and foil hackers and cheaters.

Most game engines, including, for example, the low-cost *Garage Games* engine (used in *Tribes 2*), come with networking support. This solution can then be built on, at a very low cost, to produce stunning gaming environments. It then becomes the task of the game designer to create a compelling gaming environment in which to play and innovative support for the in-game interactions. While arcade games like *Street Fighter IV* can get away with a less in-depth environment, MMORPGs like *Eve Online* need to offer more than just in-flight combat and must deliver over and above that simple core premise.

This extended attention brings money: direct revenue in the form of pay-to-play and indirect revenue in the form of trading in-game items and sponsorship and the inevitable books, guides, tactical manuals, and add-ons that provide the lifeblood of any network gaming enterprise: innovation and income. Without *both*, the game is in danger of perishing. In my opinion, any game creator who does not plan to mine every opportunity for both innovation and income generation is planning to fail in the long run. The strategy guides and offline concerns cannot be ignored; someone is going to profit from them, and it had better be the game's creators.

On the other hand, failure to recognize that these external critiques of the game will exist is to ignore a very constructive stream of criticism. With that criticism, expressed through the forums or in published guides, comes the understanding that the game can be improved upon. And improve you must to retain the interest of the paying gamer. After all, these are people who pay a premium and expect to get something more than just a single-player game against other people in return. Failure to deliver that experience will see the whole enterprise fall apart through debt. After all, it is unlikely that the game hardware will be pre-funded by the initial membership alone.

REFERENCES

[GAMA01] "Multiplayer Level Design In-Depth, Part 2: The Rules of Map Design." Pascal Luban, Game Design Studio, November 2006, http://www.gamasutra.com/features/20061108/luban_01.shtml

[NETGAMES01] "The Effect of Latency and Network Limitations on MMORPGs." Tobias Fritsch, Hartmut Ritter, Jochen Schiller, NetGames '05, Hawthorne, New York, USA, ACM 1-59593-157-0/05/0010

IMPROVING NETWORK COMMUNICATIONS

In This Chapter

- Network Communication Issues
- Solutions to Network Latency Problems
- The Principle of Minimum Data in Transit
- Data Loss and Dropped Connections
- References

The success of a network game often hinges on its ability to handle network communications. While strong network support and near-invisible connectivity will not necessarily boost the player's opinion of a game, bad networking will render the game less playable. And of course, the less playable a game is, the less it will be played—and subsequently, the smaller the market it will have.

Poor network communications stem from a number of causes, nearly all of them revolving around issues that are beyond the control of the developer: line speeds, underperforming network hardware, poor operating system support, and so on. Even so, there are many steps a developer can take to mitigate the worst effects.

Primarily, this chapter deals with the three core networking issues: loss, jitter, and latency, or lag. Innovative solutions are offered, including a discussion of ways to minimize the in-flight data, compress data being transmitted, and predict the state of the universe. All the techniques outlined here contribute in some way to the fluid playing of the game, as well as offering some level of protection against hacking and cheating.

 You'll learn more about protecting against hacking and cheating in Chapter 8, "Removing the Cheating Elements." This chapter is mainly concerned with helping improve the transit of data from A to B, possibly via C, in a way that is efficient, reliable, secure, and, above all, realistic given the tools at your disposal.

Besides the various problems that stem from unreliable data delivery, there are also issues relating to data that simply never arrives and connections that break completely. Solutions to these two conditions are also dealt with in this chapter—even if, at first glance, there seems to be very little that you can do about them.

A secondary goal of this chapter is to improve security with improvements in the networking layer. As you shall see, the two solutions are often intertwined, which goes some way to helping thwart the inevitable rise of cheating factions with a popular network game.

NETWORK COMMUNICATION ISSUES

Network communication issues affect different multi-player game models in different ways, depending on the technology and platform used to deploy the product. Clearly, the more networking (and more clients) there are, the more the various issues will affect the game. But there are also certain physical factors that affect the *performance* of the networking technology used.

From the most to least affected gaming models, the following is a short run-down of some of the common issues:

- **Internet multi-player games.** Internet multi-player games that are not Web based are clearly the most affected. In short, in this model, *everything* is out of the control of the developer. Developing for consoles will remove one of the unknowns (the platform), but all the networking unknowns will remain. These include the following:
  - Distance
  - Line speeds
  - Network hops
  - Reliability of lines
  - Internal networking issues
- **Private WAN multi-player.** The next most affected games are private WAN multi-player games. In this case, some of the communications will be out of the control of the developer. But this game type is also not generally used, as it is quite expensive to set up a gaming WAN just for one game—although part of the aforementioned Internet multi-player game model may be a private WAN, especially if there are communication conduits between servers. It is best not to separate the servers by the Internet if at all possible.
- **LAN multi-player.** One of the least affected categories is LAN multi-player games; these should run in a more-or-less predictable environment. Of course, there will be issues relating to networking support, but they will not usually be linked to the stability, reliability, or speed of the communication infrastructure. More likely, issues in this category will relate to the setup of the network as a whole.
- **Single-machine multi-player.** Of course, single-machine multi-player games are among the least affected. Although they might use some network game–style technologies (relating to the way in which the various players interact at the game level), these are outside the scope of this book.

In addition to these, network communication can have an effect on the following network game models:

- **Web-strategy games.** These games might be affected, but it is questionable whether this has a direct impact on playability. Web pages are inherently non-real time, and while it might be annoying for a site to be slow on occasion, slow performance is rarely a stopping point for the game. Of course, it will become an issue if the game is never available due to saturation—but this is more about scalability than it is about communications per se.
- **Play by e-mail.** By a similar token, play-by-e-mail games suffer almost zero effect from network-communications issues, even if the Internet goes down for a time.

Whatever else, the developer must remember one thing: Nobody controls the quality of service offered by the Internet, and there are no guarantees that it will actually be fit for use at any given time. So steps must be taken to make sure that, should the worst happen, the game will remain playable right up until the point that it is no longer possible to compensate for the underlying network service.

Lost data and erratic or uneven performance, as well as general network slowness must all be compensated for. This chapter now looks at the two principal culprits of network errors—loss and latency—before seeing how they are caused and how the effects can be mitigated.

Packet Loss

Data sent over a network is first broken into multiple packets, which vary in size depending on the protocol used and other key factors. These packets are then reassembled when they arrive at their destination, usually in the right order.

Sometimes, packet loss occurs—that is, a packet is lost during transit, presumably dropped somewhere along the line. In gaming terms, this could have a disastrous effect on the local game environment if the lost data is a piece of status data—although it may just manifest itself as slight jitter, which occurs as the environment adjusts to the missing data.

ON THE DISAPPEARANCE OF PACKETS

Packets can be lost to a variety of locations. Perhaps the most common is one that you will explore in this chapter as well as in Chapter 10, "Network Programming Primer": the dreaded buffer. A buffer is a place on a network in which packets are stored before they can be passed on to the next link in the chain. That could be a router, for example, operating at a slightly lower speed.

Suppose, for example, that as the buffer on a router is filling up, the ongoing connection stops—meaning the router has to find an alternative path for the packets. If it fails to do so, then when the buffer becomes full, those additional packets will simply be dropped.

Now, if the connection is a TCP/IP connection, the router will inform the sender that the packets must be resent. That's part of the protocol. With other protocols, however, such as UDP, this is not the case; the packets are simply lost, with very little information provided as to where they've gone, how many are missing, and what effect that has on the stream as a whole.

For now, let's assume that the loss occurs upon entry to or exit from routers or anywhere that the data has to transition from one interface to another via network hardware. In such cases, the loss is linked to the reaction time of the underlying hardware; if the hardware doesn't react quickly enough, the packet will be dropped. Regardless of the cause, packet loss is considered to be a reasonably critical event, as data will become corrupted or lost.

The TCP/IP protocol has built-in safeguards to combat data loss. Because it is a guaranteed delivery protocol, its underlying mechanisms try their best to obtain data intact, reassembling packets received in the correct order. When packets go missing, the protocol re-requests them, or else the connection fails in some way. This all happens before the data is delivered to the application and is transparent. Without the guaranteed delivery offered by TCP/IP, Web pages would not load reliably, and many applications simply would not work.

In contrast, UDP includes no such mechanism. Data is delivered to the application exactly as it is received, with no underlying safeguard against out-of-order or missing data packets—which, naturally, has some advantages and disadvantages. Advantages include ease of implementation and speed. The protocol is faster and, because it does not need to trap TCP/IP events such as lost and out-of-order packets, it can be easier to implement. The disadvantages, however, are that if there is any checking that needs to be done, it must be done by custom code. This will complicate the solution if guaranteed delivery is required, as will the relative paucity of flow-control information provided by UDP as compared with TCP.

As a game developer using UDP, you either live with the consequences (and revel in the advantages) of using UDP or build safeguards to protect against real data loss. These might include increasing the data-transmission rate to improve the game-environment sampling rate, incorporating prediction capabilities in the client and/or server, or just mimicking the TCP mechanisms to re-request missing data.

Different categories of data can also be dealt with in different ways. For example, a video stream using UDP can probably put up with lost data by degrading relatively gracefully (missing pixels, jittery display, etc.). But a pure digital stream, in which every piece of data is relevant (e.g., combat moves in a fighting game), cannot be handled in this way, meaning UDP would not be a good option. That's because with UDP, packet loss is *highly* likely to take place, whereas if the game uses TCP, then packet loss is likely *never* to take place. These inherent safeguards, however, slow the network—meaning you must make a decision as to whether you live with this or switch to UDP and handle things like flow control and guaranteed data delivery yourself.

This decision must factor in the importance of the data stream—which, in turn, depends largely on the kind of game you are creating.

Some games require guaranteed data delivery—especially RTSes and fight action games, where every piece of information counts. For such games, TCP provides a slower but more robust solution—but UDP can be used if the programmer is willing to take responsibility for ensuring the data flow. On the other hand, if the network portion of the game is just relaying a constant stream of frequently updated data (rather like a video of the unfolding events) without attaching importance to specific data exchanges, then UDP can be used to great effect because the flow control is less important. As long as out-of-sequence packets are dropped, the result will be solid enough to ignore the occasional dropped packet.

Network Latency

As mentioned, packet loss can result in latency—that is, a significant slow-down in network communications—as the network tries to adjust to the missing data. Repeated dropped packets will cause everything to slow down, as the underlying protocol re-requests missing packets. Other potential bottlenecks—which will be explored later on—include the following:

- Buffer overrun, causing lost packets
- Bottlenecks and hardware speed
- Distance and line speeds

In addition to slowing the network, latency can lead to synchronization issues between players' local views of the game environment and everything in it versus the server's view of the game environment. Indeed, different players may end up with different views—although this may not matter as long as the *outcome* of the game is not affected. In other words, as long as the players have a chance to catch up with each other, and the game plays out as normal, the fact that they take marginally different routes to the same conclusion doesn't matter. Web-based strategy games like *Project Rockstar*, for example, do not rely on fast network connections; if things are a little slow, there are no real consequences.

Sometimes, however, it *does* matter—most notably in online games that rely on speed and skill. For example, latency would be problematic in a first-person shooter (FPS) where a client reports that a bullet has not hit the player (because the player has moved), but everyone else sees that it has because their own view has not been updated with the new status information. (This example, courtesy of Jason Leigh [LEIGH01], is expanded a bit later in this chapter.) If nothing is done to address these types of issues, then playing becomes an awkward, frustrating, and unfulfilling experience.

Unfortunately, there is little you as a game designer can do to address latency, which is not a result of a design flaw in the game but rather is caused by the fragility of the delivery medium. It comes down to the manufacturer of the server, the owner of the Web-site hardware, and the Web-server software. You can, however, estimate the possible impact of latency on your game. To do so, you must first determine the game's bandwidth requirements, which you do by way of calculation and testing. One approach is to track the number of packets sent and received during test sessions in order to profile network usage. Profiling tools, such as those used for tracking the use of memory and other resources, will help in this respect.

Profiling tools are present in most modern integrated development environments (IDEs)—more specifically, as part of the debugging toolkit for most game-development platforms, both native and console. Failing that, the programmer will have to install profiling code himself or herself in the debug build, which will slow the build a little but also provide an accurate profile of the code as it is executed.

Beyond that, you can perform experiments to determine at what point raw network latency becomes an issue for players. This involves adding network inconsistencies to an otherwise perfect (or near perfect) connection, whilst the game is being played, with the goal to expose imperfections in the environment's ability to deal with such inconsistencies. So, while it is being played, you could introduce code in the network layer that drops packets, rearranges them, delays them, or introduces random amounts of jitter by combining all of the above. This will allow you to build up a profile of how the game reacts to network issues that relate to the gaming experience being delivered.

With this information in hand, you have two choices:

- Improve the robustness of the game so that should the latency spiral, the effect is less noticeable. This might include separating the data streams so that the important data is prioritized.

Some data is clearly more important than other data, and must be treated as such. For example, latency on status updates related to movement in a high-speed driving game (like Burnout Dominator*) will have more of an impact on the gaming experience than latency on status requests relating to the number of players in the system at a given moment in time.*

- Reduce latency in the system as a whole, as well as in the network component. This can only be done if the data transfer and networking have been adequately profiled beforehand.

As noted in the preceding bullet, you must consider general system latency as well as network latency. If the network layer produces a constant latency of 200ms but the database is not scaling properly, this might cause jitter (discussed momentarily). Also, if the database tends to freeze on certain operations, this will introduce additional latency.

For games operating in real time that use the Internet for networking, you will need to make some concessions locally to try to improve the communications and data transfer that you *can* control—because you *can't* control the Internet.

Latency is the principle cause of two irritating artifacts:

- Jitter
- Lag

Jitter

One of the most irritating manifestations of network latency is jitter, which occurs when latency is not constant, but fluctuating. In essence, jitter results from some—but not necessarily all—data being delayed. What's more, the length of time by which the data is delayed will usually vary, meaning it cannot be accurately predicted. Jitter can also stem from packet loss (e.g., video jitter in UDP), which creates holes in the incoming data screen. If this is vital data that has a direct consequence in the game, the result will be more than just an uneven experience. Moreover, the causes of jitter will negatively affect attempts at packet serialization, where packets are given serial numbers in an attempt to thwart hackers (see Chapter 8). This is compounded when packets arrive out of order or if the system throws them out because of the effects of jitter.

Some symptoms of jitter are evident on the players' side. For one, jitter prevents players from predicting movement accurately. If the movement data relating to other artifacts in the system is inconsistently delivered, the resulting movement will be similarly inconsistent. This will quite likely destroy an FPS, because players simply will not be able to exert the same amount of control over their in-game personae as before. Even if local movement is crisp and responsive, the game environment and other players' avatars will seem to move in an entirely unpredictable fashion.

All this is to say that jitter poses serious problems for high-speed precision skill games, such as driving-based games (*Burnout*) and one-on-one fighting games (*Street Fighter IV*). The fact that both of these games have central network gaming components implies that the issues relating to jitter are not insurmountable. Note, however, that network jitter has next to no discernable effect on the playability of Web strategy games. It *can* be mildly annoying, however, in text-based MUDs, in that screen updates sometimes fly off the visible area of the screen. On the whole, though, this is not a big issue.

Lag

Lag, a term that was coined in the 1990s to describe a general slowdown of the entire game environment, is a symptom of more or less constant (within a given time frame) latency. Because it is constant, it is less annoying for both programmers and players than jitter. It can also be predicted to a certain extent—or at least recognized by the game engine and corrected for.

Although it is less annoying and more predictable than jitter, lag can render a game unplayable if many different players have different levels of lag—meaning something must be done to mitigate it. This book looks at some ways to minimize the impact of lag issue in the upcoming section titled "Solutions to Network Latency Problems," but it is worth taking a moment here to explain the problem more fully.

What happens is this: The client on machine A updates in such a way that the player appears to be much farther away when his or her avatar starts moving as compared to the view of the same scene from the client on machine B. This is caused by the uneven reaction time. Luckily, in this simple case, the machines themselves can compensate quite easily through the clever use of status messages and minimization of data in transit, the aim of these measures being to enable fast updates when they're needed. There will, however, be a point at which the system breaks down—specifically, when the machines must adjust to the slowest speed of the system connected.

This issue is the subject of research studies [NETGAMES01], which attempt to gauge the effect on playability when clients update at different times due to lag caused by latency. One such study notes that the point at which a game such as *EverQuest2* becomes unplayable is when latency exists in excess of 1250ms. Up to this 1.25-second delay, however, there is quite a lot of room for machines to compensate locally for any network deficiencies. But of course, such maneuvering will involve a compromise between quality of experience versus security (see Chapter 8). That is, the more logic you put on the client side to enable it to make decisions on its own, the more scope there will be for foul play. For example, if a machine is tasked with relaying the result of any local decisions back to the server, the game is put at risk from the interception and subsequent alteration of status messages.

SOLUTIONS TO NETWORK LATENCY PROBLEMS

Key causes of general slowness include the usual issues: distance, hardware power, and wider Internet problems (software/hardware configuration, momentary DNS blips, and so on). In addition, dropped packets and other similar occurrences can also cause things to slow down somewhat.

Many of these issues are completely beyond the control of the game developer. Some might even be beyond the control of the service running the game (in the event that it is remotely hosted). Some, however, can be mitigated by running the game on your own hardware. Indeed, this is the solution of choice for most client/server games (like *Eve Online*, for example). But as you have seen, those games represent only a portion of the entire network-game genre.

What follows is a breakdown of the various steps developers can take to combat latency and jitter, and how doing so affects network game development. Some of the solutions are physical, while others are design based, but all center around the kind of network topography that the game uses to distribute its user base as well as to distribute the responsibility for updating the game environment and various clients.

Networking Topography

If you assume for a moment that a finite number of clients want to interconnect within a game environment that is part of a collective consciousness, then it is clear that this game environment can either be stored centrally (i.e., in a client/server network topography) or be distributed over the population (i.e., in a peer-to-peer network topography). Both approaches offer certain advantages and disadvantages with respect to latency and other issues, depending on the type of game you want to design and the type of data that needs to be transferred.

By choosing an appropriate network topography for your game, you can ensure that the system makes the best use of network resources. At the same time, you can make sure you get the right balance with respect to the system's ability to perform network-connectivity tasks and process data in the game environment.

TOPOGRAPHY DEFINED

Generally speaking, the topography of a network refers to the way in which the various pieces of the network are interconnected. In this discussion, however, there is the additional question of where the responsibilities for different networking operations lie, which must be included in the discussion of the topography. For example, you might decide to adopt a strict client/server model because the game environment is too complex to be distributed peer to peer and needs a big database. That would seem to indicate a topography that puts the server and database in the center of the resulting network. It is also likely, however, that the database needs to run on a separate shared machine, even when multiple servers are established to process the game environment with respect to the players. At this point, the topography will change to allow this. Furthermore, there may be some delegation of higher network functions to the client software (i.e., giving it limited but direct access to the database), thus changing the logical nature of the topography as well.

In a class (and associated text) entitled "Multiplayer Game Development," Jason Leigh identifies four kinds of multi-player video-game networking topographies (which he calls "connectivity models") [LEIGH01]. Paraphrasing his paper, these are as follows:

- **Shared centralized.** This topography is the basic Web-game or server-oriented action game topography. In this model, every client connects to one—and only one—central server, as in Figure 7.1. Here, the server maintains the game environment, acting as a hub to relay data between clients. The key limitation of this topography on real-time action games relates to the number of players a single server can support; any estimations in this area must be based on available processing power and how much processing is farmed out to client systems. The less work the server has to do, the more clients it can support at one time.

 Allowing clients to assume some of the processing tasks can help mitigate latency issues, but remember—the more the clients are permitted to do, the more scope there is for foul play (see Chapter 8).

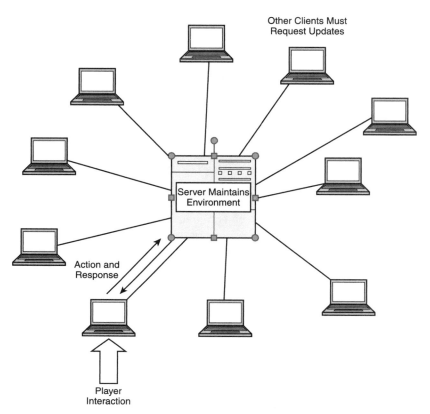

FIGURE 7.1 The shared centralized network topography.

- **Replicated homogeneous.** This model is the exact opposite of the shared centralized model; there is no central server in absolute control. That means every client is responsible for processing the game data according to the game rules. Clients then send updates to each other (i.e., a multicast solution). In this topography, each client must be connected either directly to all the other clients or via a central routing point, as in Figure 7.2. This approach can help reduce the role of the server to a simple routing hub or remove the central point altogether. Although such distributed processing has been used in the past for virtual-reality simulations, it is not widespread; that's because in this model, all the game logic typically has to be replicated across the participants. In other words, it is highly redundant. Although it is doubtful that a pure replicated homogeneous solution would work in network gaming, it is possible that some aspects of the approach could be used in network gaming to good effect.

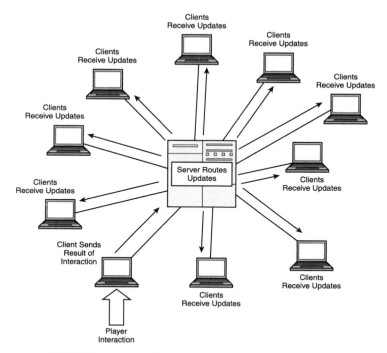

FIGURE 7.2 Replicated homogeneous network topography.

- **Shared distributed (peer-to-peer).** This model allows clients to connect to each other via some kind of central point, which also mediates. In comparison to the replicated homogeneous topography, the server in this topography has more of a role to play in making sure that the rules are respected. The topography is almost exactly the same as in Figure 7.2, except that the central point validates in addition to routing. The function of the central server is simply to keep on top of the game environment and maintain any persistent states. Local machines report the results of their own processing, and also include clever algorithms to present a smoother game experience to the player. This model will prove to be effective for some games, particularly where processing time is vital (i.e., most *Unreal Tournament*–type multi-player FPS games) and where a single-player version of the game already exists, because it ensures that the code base is accurately replicated across participants.
- **Shared distributed (client/server).** This is the topography of choice for most MMORPGs and large persistent-world games. It breaks up an enormous game environment into various server groupings, allowing clients to move between them and sharing the processing loads, making the topography scalable as well as robust.

Again, it is the same topography as the one shown Figure 7.2; only the responsibilities are a little different (and, of course, there are many instances of the client/server relationship). As in the shared distributed (peer-to-peer) model, there is ample scope for farming out local tasks. The key difference is that the game-environment processing is performed centrally; it is the game server that relays the results of actions to the clients. This topography provides for more central control, hence its use in MMORPG environments.

 As you probably noticed, the last two models above attempt to find a middle ground between the first two.

Most large-scale multi-player games are based around a cluster of interconnected servers in order to reduce internal system latency—the theory being that the less work a single server has to do, the more quickly it will be able to respond to the clients connected to it. A vast quantity of that work involves trying to receive data from and send data to clients—meaning that if you can reduce the number of clients, you also reduce the work. In other words, fewer clients over more machines means a more responsive playing experience.

Additional steps can be taken to further distribute processing—and, by extension, spread network traffic—with or without splitting the environment over multiple servers, depending on the amount of work each is supposed to do. For example, reducing the quantity of data (or the frequency of data exchange) will have a similar effect to reducing the number of clients on a server, thereby lessening the need to break up the environment into multiple zones. The problem remains, though, if one particular zone becomes overpopulated; in that case, you have no recourse if a strict zone-based server topography has been used. It would, at this point, be more logical to segment the population either geographically or by load sharing across two servers previously tasked to separate zones. Trying to do this dynamically probably won't work; moreover, an additional layer of network latency will creep in if the database becomes connected to two different servers at the same time. This database connection will usually take place over a (possibly inter-nal) network connection, thereby introducing another dependency on the weak link: the network layer.

Design-Based Workarounds

In addition to choosing the best topography to combat effects of network problems, you can also design in some solutions that address the twin issues of network latency and system latency. Given that system latency is a function of the network layer as well as the processing done outside of that bottleneck, you must design the whole system with this in mind. That said, it is the network connectivity that will likely cause most latency issues, as it is the slowest point as well as the least predictable.

This section deals principally with workarounds that are part of the design of the underlying game application software.

Poorly designed solutions waste time in various ways, all of which can increase system latency. Additionally, some of these ways are linked directly to network processing, and can exacerbate issues that emerge due to the natural latency of a network connection.

Many things can be done in the logic layer to make sure that overall system latency is kept to a minimum. In addition, you can make certain tweaks to mitigate the effect of intensive processing and network faults and thereby prevent jitter—although lag can rarely, if ever, be countered effectively. Examples include the following:

- Networking loops
- Bandwidth reduction and caching
- Sharing responsibility

Of course, almost everything you do in this arena is going to involve a balance of security versus networking versus available processing power—both on the side of the client and on the side of the server.

Networking Loops

Game designers and developers program in a loop fashion, with the following types:

- Input loops (from the physical world)
- Logic loops (processing the input with respect to the game environment)
- Rendering loops (the drawing and audio)

Each of these loops operates continuously. The input loop does so on an interrupt basis, waiting for feedback from the player via the man machine interface (MMI). The logic loop processes all the game logic, possibly on an interrupt basis, as well as performing a general monitoring function. The rendering loop ensures that those areas that need to be repainted are, and that the sound (spatial sound, background music, sound effects, etc.) is correctly overlaid with respect to the state of the immediate game environment. Normally, these three types of loops (although there may be more) are placed in separate threads, enabling the processor to try to farm out the processing in time slices in order to get everything done more efficiently and thereby improve the experience for the player.

Chapter 10 looks at network programming in more detail.

In addition to these, we must also create a network loop—both on the client and server sides—that operates on an interrupt basis for incoming connections and data, but on a regular basis for outgoing data. In addition, this loop is as important—if not more so—than regular player interaction, so this must be worked into the time-slicing algorithm that farms out work to the processor.

There are different algorithms for devoting time to various tasks based on their importance, available time slices, and other dynamic factors. All in all, the scheduling operates to make sure that everything gets done in such a way as to provide a consistent gaming experience.

The emphasis is slightly different for the client and server implementations (assuming that you are eschewing the capability to allow clients to contact each other directly). For the client, there is communication with only a single entity—the server—in the client/server topography being used. This enables you to incorporate into the network layer design a blocking socket call—which blocks until there is data to be read, and is ignored by the system until data is available—thereby releasing CPU cycles back to the system. (The alternative is to have the thread waste cycles in a busy-waiting loop, awaiting data. Even if the system operates on a time-slicing basis, it would still mean that for the whole time-slice, the network thread would effectively be doing nothing.)

In contrast, this would precipitate a disaster on the server side; the system cannot afford to block a socket when there might be data coming in from another socket. Because clients might be trying to send data to the server, it needs to have a thread that can poll multiple sockets but not block on any of them. This is the fundamental difference (with respect to network communications) between the client and the server.

This, then, is the first rule in improving network communications: Never waste time on a socket that has no incoming data—but do not use blocking sockets where multiple sockets are to be used.

This is also the case for replicated models, where each client has to multicast data to all other points in the game network. In such cases, each client is also a server, as it has to be in a position to both send data to multiple points and receive data from multiple points.

The interplay between the client input, network input and output, and game logic threads is the determining factor in overall system latency, manifested though the perceived reaction time of the game to the player's input, other players' actions, and the network component. Other game-development books cover these issues more completely; here, we are concerned only with the latter part—the network component. Experimentation and testing are the only ways that the developer can determine the best way to hook all the processing points together and facilitate communication between them at the game-code level.

Bandwidth Reduction and Caching

Improving network communications begins with choosing the best protocol—TCP or UDP—for the tasks that need to be carried out. As mentioned, different data-exchange requirements can take advantage of the different mechanisms used by TCP and UDP with respect to data delivery. That said, these protocols also share some key similarities—most notably the need to reduce bandwidth usage to the extent that it is possible. After all, both use the same underlying physical technology—a wire—to transfer data. And clearly, the less data you need to push around the network, the better.

Data comes in two flavors:

- That which is needed to run the game (communicate between entities)
- That which is needed to set up the game (level data and other re-sources).

One approach is to blend the use of UDP and TCP to make good use of available bandwidth—but care should be taken to ensure that the appropriate data is put in the appropriate protocol. On the one hand, vital data that would introduce latency into the system if it were lacking should be delivered via TCP, but the volume should be reduced. Data that is not so critical can be delivered via UDP—but if it has to be synchronized, then it is better to reduce the volume as much as possible in order to use less bandwidth and reduce processing overhead in correcting the transmission errors.

In addition to reducing bandwidth, it's a good idea to cache large data repositories such as level files and images. This is rather like a Web browser storing image files for later use; resources that are loaded frequently and do not change often are ideal targets for caching in networked video games. This can be done either as needed or at the start of the game session. In the first instance, the resources are delivered in-line via spare capacity in the data exchange so that they are available when needed. In the second, the user must actively download them (as was the mechanism used in *Unreal Tournament*) in order to have the correct shapes, sounds, level files, and graphics available at the start of the play session.

Sharing Responsibility

Another way to reduce bandwidth is to allow clients to take responsibility for some of the processing. In this way, they relay only the result of that processing, rather than every possible state change, back to the server.

Because state changes result from interactions between the player and the game—as well as other players and artifacts within the game environment—the processing of the game rules is outsourced to the collective clients. Earlier, this chapter covered an extreme example of this in its discussion of the distributed homogeneous topography. That model was deemed too high risk, but if each client is (separately) also calculating cause and effect, then the server could validate the decisions by comparison. This would be far quicker than calculating cause and effect itself, would reduce data transmission, and would offer a more robust solution with respect to possible cheating than the alternative.

One easy example is the aforementioned bullet fired within the game environment, provided by Jason Leigh [LEIGH01]. The message sent to update the clients simply relays the state change of the bullet. It is up to the clients to figure out for themselves who has been hit. In addition, they should play a role in computing how the bullet should fly and then relaying to everyone else the end effect—not the state changes, nor the position at a given time in their local rendering of the game environment, but the end result: hit or miss. In this way, we a) don't have to relay more data than is necessary, and b) don't have to wait for the data before showing the action to the player. This avoids the flooding of the network by state messages and also helps mitigate any natural latency or jitter in the system.

You should be aware, however, that this approach opens up possibilities for people to interfere with the game-client processing. For example, they might claim that the bullet hasn't hit anyone—when in fact it has—by intercepting the message and changing the status information. Feasibly, this could be achieved without other players being aware of it, as their system will simply render the data that has been provided to them. Until the bullet disappears in thin air, nobody will notice that there is something amiss.

All this is just another way of saying that as a game developer, you must find a balance between security and performance.

Minimizing Exposure to Latency

As you've learned, latency is roughly defined as a significant slowdown in network connections—but one that is more or less constant, meaning that unlike network issues like jitter, its effects can be predicted to some degree. Accounting for latency can sometimes simply mean anticipating certain things in the absence of real data.

TCP has higher natural latency than, for example, UDP. That's because TCP tries to validate the data stream. When a packet is dropped, TCP realizes this and tries to correct for it, waiting for the missing data to be relayed—which increases latency. One way to minimize latency, then, might be to use UDP. With this protocol, data simply disappears if a packet is dropped. Whether this is an appropriate solution, however, depends on the game type and the logic controlling the interactions in the game environment.

Using a game-environment update model that averages positions of in-game artifacts (avatars, NCPs, etc.) can both address packet loss in UDP (at least until a critical threshold is reached) and smooth out the effects of jitter in both TCP- and UDP-based networked games (again, up to a threshold of estimated positions). If this threshold is exceeded, a jarring effect could occur as the positions are re-established based on incoming data. Key to designing a solution that takes this into account is understanding how latency in the networking component of the system builds up in the first place.

Latency, Buffers, and Packet Loss

To understand how you can avoid latency, you need also to understand that network processing often employs buffers. A buffer is simply a place where data is stored before it is processed (either somewhere over the network or by the gaming client).

Systems generally have input buffers, where data is stored before processing, and output buffers, which need to be filled before the data is sent. The output buffer is also used to queue data in the event that the network beyond becomes saturated. In times of low traffic, the buffer can then be emptied, allowing the system to catch up.

Ideally, the interplay between these two buffers enables the system in the middle (be it a network or a processor) to be balanced such that it is always operating at maximum saturation when there is data to be processed. That means filling and emptying the buffers in an organized fashion, allowing just enough slack to be robust. (The slack is used to stock the buffer in the event the processor or network becomes saturated and has to take a brief time-out.) If an input buffer is not emptied quickly enough (i.e., the client is slow to process), then data will be lost. In essence, because the buffer is full, there is nowhere to put incoming packets, and as a result they will be dropped, causing data loss. If, on the other hand, the output transmission fails for some reason, preventing packets from being sent quickly enough (at the server), then the output buffers will also fill up. In this case, packets will be dropped unless you provide a solution for this on the server (see the section "Rate Adjustment Strategies" later in this chapter)—namely, backing up the system and making sure that no additional data is generated. This will potentially cause the gaming system to visibly pause—one of the worst effects of latency.

A network is also composed of various routers, firewalls, bridges, and so forth that deal with ongoing network transmission—commonly network transmission that you can't control. Worse still, you have no interfaces at your disposal that would allow you to adapt to the situation. Moreover, these devices also use buffers—and these buffers have the same limitations as described above. Packets are dropped because flow is interrupted by poor performance, either locally or remotely. Quite often, simply being in the middle of the flow is what causes packets to be dropped as buffers fill up.

This has a feedback effect in TCP networks because on the one hand, they try to retransmit to guarantee delivery, and on the other, devices using the TCP protocol will reduce transmission rates to try to reduce congestion. The net effect is that latency increases artificially—in addition to the natural network latency that exists. In contrast, in a situation involving high latency—with buffers filling up and packets dropping everywhere—UDP will not attempt to correct for it. It simply allows the data to drop into the ether, expecting the software application using the protocol to correct for missing data.

 In these cases, TCP is almost too smart; such occurrences of packet loss and latency can actually be a good argument for not using it as a network protocol. Indeed, most video-transmission packages use UDP and live with the data loss rather than use TCP and experience high levels of latency.

With large volumes of data, this might be a viable approach—as long as there is (as with some video transmissions) a high level of redundancy. If, however, there is a relatively low level of redundancy, and a high quantity of significant data, then this approach may not work.

Either way, a good solution is to control the rate of sending to try to minimize—or at least learn to live with—the effects of latency and packet loss on the network game infrastructure. This can be done at the client and on the server.

Rate-Adjustment Strategies

Rate adjustment simply involves changing the rate at which data is sent or received (or even requested). This can be a dynamic operation, with the rate being changed as the network components sense shifts in the state of their communications conduits, or it can be a set-and-forget option at the start of the transmission session. Clearly, the latter approach could lead to issues with latency and buffer overflow during the session, while dynamically changing the transfer rates can help to provide a more even experience.

Rate adjustment is common in many streaming applications; these enjoy the most benefits from rate adjustment because they tend to use the most bandwidth.

Rate adjustment occurs on two fronts:

- **The incoming packets for all clients.** The incoming packet stream must be dealt with in a timely fashion—that is to say, as quickly as possible. Otherwise, congestion will occur at the various endpoints, causing logical latency at the core game logic layer as it races to catch up. If, as the input stream backs up, the processor is tied up doing something else (i.e., in one of the other game loops), the processor will become flooded as soon as it turns to the packet stream to process the data. If this happens consistently, the system must consider requesting that the data-transfer rate be adjusted—either by slowing down the transfer or reducing the data in the stream. There is, of course, a balance here between the time taken to process incoming packets and the time needed to render the game environment. This is why, as noted previously, it is essential to position the network processing loop correctly in the system as a whole.

This is, naturally, more of a problem for action games than it is for turn-based games or strategy games. That said, these might also have streaming aspects that need to take account of the data rate.

- **The send rate across all clients.** On the server side, there exists the possibility that a sending rate that is good for one client is not good for the others. Being able to adjust the data rate on the server side to accommodate this is necessary when the clients must remain synchronized with each other (i.e., in an action or fighting game); otherwise, some clients will get ahead of others in a very visible way. After all, clients will naturally relay data as quickly as it is available to them, so the server must throttle the sending rate as it relays the packets. For a collection of clients in relative proximity in the game environment, the server must decide what the relay rate will be for each client, as only the server knows which clients are associated with in-game entities that are logically close to each other. The server then has to adjust the relay rate to match the slowest client so that all clients receive data at roughly the same rate. This data relay rate may be slower than the natural network latency; indeed, it's a kind of artificial latency that you can control and that is shared by all the clients.

The clients will also have to adjust to ensure that the game remains smooth even if the data rate is slower than they would expect. This aspect is part of the game design, and should not result in jitter.

Rate adjustment may also be necessary at the client side in cases where the server-side buffers are filling up too quickly. This can happen because the server has too much to do (too many clients) or because the onward transmission is much slower than the incoming rate of data reception. In such cases, communication between clients and server is vital to synchronize the data-exchange rate as well as to make sure that every client cuts its data-transfer rate as required. The result is a network-wide agreed (or negotiated) data-transfer rate that keeps all parties in sync without exposing the player to latency, lag, or jitter.

As a last resort, you can always send less data, less often. The result is not faster data transfer, as is the case with non–stream based data exchanges like status information, but actually transferring less data. While it means different things to different applications, this approach can lead to holes in the transmission. For example, in a streamed application, a lower data-transmission rate usually means a lower-quality result. This can mean something relatively benign, such as lower-quality sound or video, or something quite profound, such as jittery in-game movement. It really is a last resort, and is to be avoided as much as possible.

That said, because this approach is desirable due to its speed and efficiency, to improve on both, you could try to make sure that *each piece* of data to be transferred is smaller. One approach is to strip out all the extraneous data and make for a more efficient exchange of information—hopefully without any loss of quality or integrity. That's what the next section is all about.

THE PRINCIPLE OF MINIMUM DATA IN TRANSIT

This section discusses what I call the "Principle of Minimum Data in Transit," or how you can use network bandwidth more efficiently. It centers on ensuring that:

- You transfer only the data that you need to.
- The data is constructed in such a way as to convey maximum meaning.

The first point is easily made. If the game works on the principle of downloadable content with a purely distributed network game topography, then there will be very little reason to exchange data. Some, if not all, of the processing can be done on the client, thereby minimizing the data in flight—but also drastically increasing exposure to hacking.

This last is part of the problem with data in transit. It is not possible to talk about network efficiency without mentioning security and hacking. After all, in proprietary client-based games (refer to Chapter 1, "The Challenge of Game Networking," and Chapter 2, "Types of Network

Games"), the game's designer puts the entire game's content at the mercy of the end user. The whole framework is there—the game software; the resources that make up the graphics, sound files, and level files; the logic that controls it; and the engine that processes it. If the platform is a PC—or even a console with a hard drive—then the whole package is available to the end user. If he or she is even slightly devious, the end-user might just reverse-engineer the code to figure out how the game has been put together—including the exchange of data. From there, it is a short step to figuring out how to use it for his or her own advantage.

All of the following techniques require code on the client side to make them work. They are therefore vulnerable in some way to this kind of attack. The trick (as you shall see in Chapter 8) is to make it so hard to crack that hackers simply won't bother.

By a similar token, all of the following also apply in some small measure to games where the client is truly dumb—i.e., it displays only the result of passing requests to the server. Typically, dumb clients make no decisions for themselves. They merely query the server, without ever updating the game environment (see Chapter 8). You explored this approach in the first few chapters of the book—for example, while exploring text-based MUD games. Clearly, in this case, there's not a lot you can do to reduce the data being sent to the terminal.

On the other hand, data-reduction strategies can work for Web strategy games, even if the client is dumb. Theoretically, at least, these games should be less subject to hacking, as there is really nothing to gained by doing so; the game environment logic remains on the server. There might, however, be something to gain by automated playing—especially with online games in which spending hours performing fairly mundane tasks is rewarded—which can cause network congestion. That said, the kind of person who is going to go down that road will probably be a minority. The problem occurs when such people decide to propagate their creations, allowing others to take advantage of the loopholes they have discovered. Data reduction can help combat this in two ways:

- By rendering the data less immediately readable
- By mitigating the worst effects of network congestion, should the worst happen

Before you can address possible data bloat, however, you must know what the actual consumption is. That means some form of data measurement must be built into the development version of the game in order to estimate actual network usage. After you determine this, you can then concentrate efforts on the areas causing bottlenecks rather than trying to reduce all data to a bare minimum (whilst possibly sacrificing quality of streamed data and ease of development and maintenance in the process).

Basic Data Reduction

Of course, the first obvious data-reduction technique is to relay only the data that is absolutely necessary. This sounds obvious—but it is seductively easy to build game logic around the constant presence of data, which, in the network environment, might not be possible. Instead, game logic should be built around the *lack* of data—or at least the assumption that data will be delayed—rather than the necessity of having data every *x* cycles. This approach will reduce the refresh rate, which will help keep data in transit to a minimum—but it needs to be backed up by techniques to compensate for the "missing" data.

If you plan to use dead reckoning, you can dispense with many data-exchange cycles, intervening only when the player does something un-expected. Dead reckoning only works, however, in games where in-game artifacts have known trajectories that are not expected to deviate. For example, if a vehicle is traveling at a given velocity in a certain direction, you can more or less gauge where it will be a few update cycles from now. You don't really need to relay data that tells the clients that the vehicle is *still* following the same trajectory; instead, you can simply relay a status change message when that trajectory *does* change. In this way, you can dispense with a lot of intermediate data-refresh cycles. By a similar token, you need not send all the data pertaining to a client every time an update is processed. Rather, you only *need* to send data that has changed. This is related to the dead-reckoning example. (Note that for client-side updates, you also need some way for a client to request a refresh if something goes amiss.)

The data that does have to be sent should be combined in one set of data rather than sent in several spurts. This will put it all in one packet, rather than spreading it over several packets. It is worth stalling an update until a full packet can be sent—unless the data is time critical. Again, this is a design issue, not a development one. The decision must be made at the time of the game's design how the status data (for example) is to be organized:

- **One shot, all data.** In this case, each status update contains all the data—although it may overflow into additional packets unless care is taken to reduce the data that has to be conveyed (for example, by using special encoding rather than plain-text instructions).
- **Artifact-by-artifact updates.** This approach splits updates by in-game artifact role. Therefore, each entity in the game environment has its own update cycle. This can be detrimental to network performance, however, producing multiple data-transfer cycles, which can slow down processing and lead to synchronization problems.

- **Continuous stream.** This is the least efficient way to transfer data (in principle), but cannot be avoided for things like videos, which need to start playing before they can be downloaded in their entirety. This will involve the use of a buffer, as previously explained.

Which of these three possibilities (or something in between) you choose will depend on the game design and the number of individual in-game objects that the environment needs to support.

Although these three approaches have their differences, what is shared among them is that, as far as possible, only state data should be relayed, not individual interactions. This state data is either:

- A state change (from one state to another)
- A state value (score, resources, etc.)

The client should work out the effect of the interaction on the game state and relay that as a state or state change rather than the details of the interaction.

In cases where the topography is one in which all the logic is contained on the server, this approach may not be appropriate, as the clients will not process enough logic to be able to come to a conclusion. In such situations, it may not be possible to send absolute game environment state data—but it should still be possible to send state changes from the point of view of the client system. This will be the case for many games that are played in the browser, using AJAX technology to manipulate the client view and receive updates from the server.

The data should be encoded so as to be as small as possible (which also helps with obfuscation, as you will see in Chapter 8). That is, rather than transferring something readable, like the following:

```
money=100;stamina=10;energy=90
```

you should opt for a data-reduced version:

```
11 00 FF 20 10 FF 30 90
```

Not only is the second smaller, it is also easier to process on the client side—and difficult to glean meaning from it by casual means. It is, however, hard to debug, and relies on all members of the team having access to a suitable look-up chart. Generally speaking, the extra effort is worth it.

INTEREST MANAGEMENT

Interest management, a term used by Jouni Smed, Timo Kaukoranta, and Harri Hakonen in their paper "A Review on Networking and Multiplayer Computer Games" [TURK01], describes a methodology for reducing the amount of data transmitted between clients by sending only that data that is useful to each one. While interest management is relatively complex, and a detailed discussion of its mechanisms is outside the scope of this book, the basic premise is that each party isolates its area of interest (what Smed et al. call the "aura") within the confines of the game environment. If the server is in charge of distributing information, it can also issue updates that correspond to the intersection of these areas of interest. As the paper notes:

> "Thus, when two players' auras intersect, they can be aware of each others actions." [TURK01]

There are various complex and interesting ways to divide the game environment into regions, and which approach is taken will depend largely on the kind of game being implemented. But all the various ways of doing it rely on being able to relay and filter through a central point. It stands to reason that if the filtering were client based, it would be yet another loophole for cheating, as the client might filter out its own location data in an attempt to hide from other players and yet still be able to interact with them. Having a central dispatcher provides a cross check that should prevent this. The data transmission out toward the clients is then reduced to a minimum, as they will receive only updates that are of interest to them—that is, updates that are within their areas of interest.

If you've implemented each of these basic approaches to data reduction but are still experiencing data-transmission issues, then perhaps some more advanced techniques are required, such as compression.

Using Compression

All data-reduction techniques that require post processing of data that is received, such as compression, will increase processor load as the data is reconstituted. It is preferable if this can be avoided. That said, if you've exhausted the basic data-reduction options, then this can be a good option.

Compression is designed to replace expansive data with data that is encoded in such a way that the redundancies that most data contains are removed. For example, if you know that a rectangle is white and located at x,y on the screen, you do not need to send the location and color of every pixel in the square. Instead, you can just send the top-left corner, the width and height, the fact that it is a rectangle, and the color. This will take up much less space. And you can send the same amount of information to describe even the biggest square that the display can handle, making the compression scalable.

You'll note that there is a limit going the other way. If the square is smaller than, say, a few pixels in dimension, it is probably more efficient to just send the pixel information rather than the complex data structure that represents the square. Finding the balance between data reduction and the smallest units of non-compressible data is outside the scope of this book, but interesting food for thought nonetheless.

In addition to making data smaller, compression also ensures that casual observation will not yield any directly usable clues as to what the data packet might contain. Put another way, the benefits of using compression are twofold:

- **Efficiency.** Simply put, with compression, less data is transmitted. On the other hand, compression does result in a performance hit on the client *and* server as the compression/decompression algorithm is applied to the data to be transmitted. (Clearly, you must take care to ensure that any efforts you make to reduce data do not increase latency due to increased load on the processor. Only by measuring this will you be able to determine whether you are helping rather than hindering.)
- **Obscurity.** Obscuring the data ought to make it a little bit harder for hackers to figure out what the data contained in the packet is really for. As long as a relatively incoherent data representation is also employed (as discussed in the preceding section), the data should be relatively meaningless even if someone manages to decompress it.

You should be aware that hackers have access to the code that is doing the decompressing—especially in a distributed model—making reverse engineering a real possibility. The more paranoid you, as a developer, are about this, the better (up to a point).

Be aware that applying compression to multiple packets with UDP (for example) will yield some very odd results if data goes missing. The end result might even be that the data cannot be reconstituted, or that the effort required to patch the hole transcends any benefit from the data-reduction exercise. In this case, simple run-length encoding (RLE) might be a weak but efficient solution. It also might just be all that is necessary. Most compression algorithms work more effectively with sample data; if you restrict compression to small samples, RLE might offer the best compromise of efficiency over speed. Yet again, testing—or at least simulation—is going to be the key to ascertaining the best solution.

 Run-length encoding replaces multiple artifacts in the data stream with a number representing the number of occurrences of that artifact, thereby theoretically reducing the number of bytes it takes to represent a string of identical artifacts. An artifact can be a single character or a tuple.

COMPRESSION VERSUS ENCRYPTION

Not all encrypted data compresses easily (if at all). If encrypted data is designed to not be easily decompiled into logical units of repetition, it is, by design, not easily compressible. For example, with run length–encoded data, encryption removes patterns from the data in an attempt to obscure it—which renders most compression that uses repetition (including RLE) completely useless.

This kind of encryption is designed to make it difficult to derive content from form (representation, in this case) over time by sampling. That means hackers relying on a high incidence of pattern and observation of cause and effect will be thwarted by RLE and encryption alike.

Ciphers with a rotating or seeded key, however, can prove very useful. On the one hand, it is hard to glean meaning from data that is constantly changed based on a cipher system; on the other, the data itself is likely to be compressible because *some* patterns remain. The fact that the patterns are essentially meaningless—and any attempt to change them is likely to scramble the meaning so much that the built-in logic to process the data will flag them as corrupted—means that you have protected your data effectively. Of course, this only holds for as long as the cipher is not broken—which might make straight encryption a better option in many people's eyes. But for compressible encryption, a cipher has many useful properties.

Using Game Environment Prediction

One way to mitigate or smooth out effects of short periods of lag and especially of jitter—intermittent pauses in the game data stream caused by natural latency—is to use game environment prediction. This can be applied to three key areas to try to ensure that the effect of jitter is not felt by the player:

- **The player.** This approach involves trying to guess what the player will do next, and whether that varies substantially from what he or she is currently doing. It's a server-to-client technology, as the local client will know perfectly well what the player is currently doing. For this reason, player prediction is more about how you update remote clients (and the server) with respect to the way that the client is viewed in the game universe. You can afford to have the prediction lag behind slightly as long as it is not noticeable by the player at the remote client on the other side of the server. (After all, at some point, you will correct the prediction.)
- **Non-player in-game artifacts.** These are slightly easier to predict, as they typically follow in-game logic that has been fairly well tested. For example, a bullet, once fired, becomes such an artifact, and is unlikely to deviate from its initial path.
- **The game environment.** This is easy enough to predict, and would apply to things like planets in a space game or the track in a racing game. Much of the reaction of the game environment can be rendered locally; indeed, it barely ever needs to be relayed.

Prediction is particularly great for countering the network stutter that causes jitter, the theory being that updates are spaced with reference to actual events. If, for example, a car is moving in the game at a given velocity and direction, you don't need updates so regularly because you know where it is going; as such, the data sampling rate can be lower. This is fine as long as you don't mind a few differences between the clients' rendering of the gameplay.

But what happens if data is permanently lost? In that case, prediction becomes much more difficult—which is where AI could, in theory, take over. A word of warning, though: In this scenario, you are essentially substituting a real player with an AI equivalent. This has several ramifications, the first being that the player will be playing locally (or frozen out) whilst his or her alter ego, now controlled by the server or a remote client, continues to play on his or her behalf. If it fares poorly, then the player will be (rightly) irritated; if it fares better than the player would have, then the other players will be (also rightly) irritated. The use of AI prediction and player emulation comes into its own, however, when the player disconnects (permanently or temporarily)—something we will look at later in this chapter.

AI prediction is used in fast-paced fighting games such as *Street Fighter IV*, where small glitches in network connectivity cannot be tolerated. As long as the gaps are small enough, the system can emulate either player, realigning them once the data stream is re-established.

Fighting games in particular rely on a more or less constant stream of data updates. It's no good trying to post only when something happens;

things are happening all the time, and in discrete units. Sooner or later, an update will be missed, and it's up to the system to predict what happens next—and correct itself when it turns out to be wrong.

Prediction Correction

As useful as prediction is, it does pose certain problems, such as, What happens if the player does something unexpected? If, for example, the player is moving in a given direction but suddenly stops moving and starts hacking away with a sword at another in-game entity, you need to make sure that this new behavioral trajectory is correctly relayed.

There are two sides to this. One, the player has stopped moving. Two, the entity at which the player is hacking away probably also stopped moving. If the other system reacts too slowly, then the observed player may no longer be in the correct place at the correct time to effect the new actions.

So how does the system (as a whole) catch up with this sequence of events? Obviously, the first thing is to make sure that the game environment views never diverge too much from each other. That means reeling in the freedom that clients have to maintain their own world view a little bit. This, however, has serious implications with respect to security. For example, if you give too much decision-making power to distributed clients, that decision making might become susceptible to tampering.

For Web games, this not a problem, as no decisions are made in browser. Rather, all decisions are made on the server; the client simply renders them. So even if you need to smooth out the data flow in some way with local (JavaScript) logic to combat lag or jitter, you can't affect the outcome of the game. The same goes for other client/server games based on dumb clients (i.e., MUDs). That means the only thing you need to worry about here is reflex based. That is, there is the possibility that an automated player could be made to play faster than a human. (We'll deal with in Chapter 8.) If, however, a smart client is introduced, where some of the logic is implemented on the local system (for example, a shrink-wrapped MMORPG like *Everquest*), then you start to encounter serious problems. In resolving issues relating to jitter (and/or lag), you run the risk of introducing a security loophole that makes it possible for players to circumvent game rules.

The scenario runs something like this: In trying to ensure that jitter is almost undetectable by players, you let the gameplay out on several clients simultaneously. That means local clients take input from their human player and pass the status and consequences of that input back to the main server. (This was the approach taken in many multi-player strategy games, such as *Age of Empires*.) Any unexpected in-game moves can be priority-posted along with the consequences, and each copy of the game environment can be checkpointed using a variety of methods (explored in a moment) to make sure that they stay in sync. But what happens if a rogue player intervenes to relay false or augmented information to the main server? Examples might include a sword doing 10 times more damage than it ought to or a strategy game posting inflated resource figures after a certain period of time has elapsed. Once the inflated resources have been passed to the other game clients, the player will be able to do things that he or she ought not to be able to do—things that will allow him or her to overtake the other players in an unfair manner. This makes proper synchronization with respect to the server and other game clients an absolute necessity.

Synchronization

Synchronization involves checkpointing game-environment representations in order to keep all copies of the game environment in sync, even as updates based on decisions made in a distributed fashion are being posted. The checkpointing approach is designed simply to make sure that, at a discrete moment in time, all clients have the same snapshot of the game environment. This allows the clients to be sure that their predictions are true or at least that they can be corrected with real data so that they do not stray too far from reality.

Of course, one thing you need to be sure of is that no one has interfered with the data—which is very tricky. You can avoid packet insertion by following the guidelines in Chapter 8 in general. But what happens when you've just lost the plot and want to update?

Let's look at these in turn. Packet insertion occurs when a client has been modified—or augmented with additional software—to introduce data that should not be there. That data is then forwarded to all clients, thereby changing the way they perceive the game environment and the status of the sending client. Once replicated through the system, it becomes the "truth."

Checkpointing helps to stymie this cheat attempt. Its power is limited on its own, but when combined with other techniques on the server, all can help minimize the impact of packet insertion by offering a kind of centralized analysis of all client data and a decision as to who is correct (the majority carries the vote). That means if there is a client that has lost the plot and needs a quick refresh, rather than going to potentially corrupted clients, they now have the option of going to the server.

There's another reason for this too—especially for those who choose UDP for data transmission. Protocols like UDP have no mechanism for ordering data reception. That means each packet must be synchronized using a number that indicates the age of the packet so that older ones can be thrown away if they arrive out of sequence.

So, if you're trying to correct prediction on the fly, and the packets arrive in the wrong sequence, it will likely make a bad situation worse, unless these steps are taken to rearrange the data as it is received.

You should also implement synchronization detection by the server and other clients. This is as much to enable them to get back into sync as it is to make sure that the data stream still has integrity. It is the server that bears the ultimate responsibility, as it is the only entity that has overall control—not to mention the fact that it is the only part of the system that is more or less guaranteed not to have been tampered with.

Queuing Events

Queuing events—a technique frequently used by MMORPGs (such as *Everquest*)—can help solve a few issues relating to efficiency (and jitter), security, and prediction (although it is, of course, not appropriate for all kinds of games). The phrase "queuing events" doesn't mean holding up events before relaying them to the client, but rather refers to players being able to queue up events that take a certain length of time to play out. These events are queued on the server, probably one by one, and then passed, as a queue, to the client software. If you assume that the efficiency by which packets are to be transferred does not depend on their size, this approach makes sense, in that it sends as much data as possible at once. With respect to resolving issues relating to prediction, queuing events helps because the discrete wishes of the players can be relayed to the clients ahead of time—like a kind of action buffer that removes the necessity to try to keep up with fast-paced action. The result is that each client can play out the actions in its own time, as long as these buffers are kept fresh—and since they likely contain much less data than a complete environment update or sequence of discrete actions, this shouldn't be a problem.

This mechanism can be taken to another level by enabling the game system to also queue up events—as long as there is a way to take them out if the AI controlling the queuing changes its mind. This might even be used as a mechanism to return some of the logic processing to the server by allowing it some breathing space as the clients execute the queues of events attached to system-controlled in-game entities.

Of course, the client must make sure that the queue is invisible to the opposing player; otherwise, he or she might be able to cheat by knowing what is coming next. Also, if the data in the queue is delayed for any reason, the other clients will run into problems.

DATA LOSS AND DROPPED CONNECTIONS

So far, this chapter has dealt with cases in which data is delayed for some reason or the integrity of the data is threatened. In addition to these possible problems, there is the risk that data can go missing, or that the player's connection could be dropped.

Combating Data Loss

In the worst-case scenario—in which the data doesn't arrive at all, which sometimes happens when the UDP protocol is used—you have very little in the way of recourse to deal with this. Even so, you must try to combat data loss; otherwise, it may become impossible to play the game. First, however, you must have some way of knowing that data loss has occurred. Unless the underlying protocol reports a loss, it may not immediately be obvious.

Detecting Data Loss

With TCP/IP, if one packet is dropped, the whole connection tends to time-out—which is why, on occasion, a Web page will fail to load initially but, when refreshed, loads correctly. This same refresh mechanism can be used to re-establish connections and data streams in a networked video game using TCP/IP. In that case, however, the data will be lost forever because, unlike a Web page, the game environment is in a constant state of flux. UDP, on the other hand, is connectionless—in other words, each collection of packets is sent in isolation, and there is no need to even keep the connection alive between the sending of data. Furthermore, there is no guarantee for data delivery; therefore, the application itself is responsible for detecting dropped packets, which then become a fact of life.

Out-of-sequence packets are the first indicator of data loss. This is not to say that the packets arrive out of order (which, too, might also be an indication); it's more that there is a visible gap in the packets that arrive. This will be noted, however, only if the detection mechanism is built in to the network-processing logic of the game. Other indicators of data loss can be built into the protocol, such as detection of smaller-than-anticipated packets—for example, where the data header says that there should be 128 bytes, but only 64 are received.

Using some kind of serialization or numbering scheme to validate the stream of incoming data packets is a necessary precaution for UDP, but technically not required for TCP (at least as far as data reception is concerned). That said, serializing the packet streams for TCP is one way to make sure that the data stream maintains integrity, guaranteeing that the data is received as the sending client intended. By extension, you can therefore detect whether there is any data missing in the stream over and above any of the support for this that is built into the protocol. This is important because the client might send the data out in good faith, only for it to be tampered with by the network portion of the system (either inadvertently or maliciously). The underlying protocol might not be able to tell the difference, but the game should be able to detect this and take action.

Dealing with data loss goes hand in hand with detecting data injection, as the two are sides of the same coin. Data injection is at the core of many of the examples of cheating that you will read about in Chapter 8.

Dealing with Data Loss

If you think back to the example of the car traveling in a straight line, you'll remember that everything works right up until the player does something unexpected. This action (or the result of it) is first shown on their screen, after which it is supposed to be relayed to the server. If, for some reason, it is *not* relayed to the server, the result is that other players do not see the cause—just the effect. The data loss makes the *action* invisible, because the systems have synchronized to prevent the game-environment views from deviating from each other. The end result is that it just looks bad—in the worst case, as if the other player is cheating—which does not reflect well on the game.

Let's assume, for example, that the car is racing along, but takes a small diversion to pick up a power-up present on the road (like the power-ups in *Mario Cart* or *WipeOut*). From his own point of view, the local player jigs to one side and picks up the power-up. If this is not relayed to the server because of data loss, however, then a strange phenomenon will occur, the effect being that on the player's system, the object is no longer there, but for the other systems, it is. It is as if the player hasn't taken the object. This may result in one of the following (as viewed by remote player's systems):

- At some point in time, the object "disappears" with no explanation.
- Another player dives in to grab the object, resulting in two players having the same object.
- The server or other systems get confused.

Unfortunately, having chosen an update model that farms out the logic to the remote systems, the game designer can do nothing to prevent the object from disappearing or being duplicated. All he or she can do is make sure that the third outcome never happens, as it represents the worst-case scenario. Systems should never need to be reset because they are unable to sync themselves.

Of course, the worst hit will be action games. That's because in action games, maintaining the flow of action is usually crucial. This is also critical in strategy games that use data in the same way as an action game would.

In the most basic case, missing data can be treated as infinitely delayed data—that is, you can simply hope that the problem will resolve itself. This approach will work for non-action games—but at what point does the game decide that the data is really lost, and that the game has to take action? Some turn-based games, for example, use a counter to count down the rest of the players' moves based on the first to move (this is the *Civilization* approach). They also need an internal counter to make sure the connection is still alive, and that the connections can be polled to ensure that every client is still alive.

This polling approach helps in two ways: First, it helps prevent data loss. Second, it makes sure that the players are all still connected, even when they fall silent and no longer actively post actions. This might, at first glance, seem to violate the principles of keeping the data in transit as light as possible and avoiding noisy network communications layers. But it is actually vital in games where there may be substantial gaps in the natural communication between clients and the server. It is also vital for managing games that need to combat dropped connections.

Combating Dropped Connections

A dropped connection occurs when the network hardware or operating system encounters a glitch, either in the software (driver) or in the hardware. The connection becomes unusable in the short term, with the network layer possibly returning a "time out" error. The result is that the player will (temporarily, we hope) disappear from the game environment at the physical level (that is, the actual network infrastructure level). Of course, the player will still exist in the game environment—and you must decide what to do about that at the logical level.

There are some similarities between network jitter, data loss, and dropped connections, in that the server will not receive data required to update the game environment. Some of the symptoms are also very similar. The difference is that, if the server is correctly monitoring connections, it will know that the connection has been dropped—meaning that it can compensate more easily for the error than if it were just a question of some dropped data. Dropped data tends to be more silent than a dropped connection.

There are two kinds of dropped connections:

- Unintentional
- Intentional

While it may not be possible to tell difference between the two, they are very different phenomena.

Unintentional Dropped Connections

An unintentional dropped connection occurs when, through no fault of the user, the connection becomes temporarily unusable. Once a connection is lost—hopefully unintentionally—the server has several choices, depending on the authorization architecture. The general idea is to re-establish the connection as transparently as possible, depending on the level at which the connection was dropped.

Clearly, if a hardware failure that could lead to security issues caused the dropped connection, then re-establishing the connection is not going to be possible.

Some games store authorization data and can automatically re–log on the player. Indeed, the player might not even notice that the connection was dropped. This is probably the best form of auto-recovery after a dropped connection; the end result might appear similar to, for example, a jittery connection. (Note that this solution would usually be used with console games, but not for PC games, where the machine might be used by multiple people.)

If auto-recovery is not possible and the player needs to re–log on manually, then the server must remove the player from the game environment in a timely fashion. That's because there is no guarantee that the player will return right away (if at all); he or she might be faced with a long-term or permanent network-connection loss. This action will naturally have a profound effect on the game session in progress.

The following actions, which vary by game type, are likely to be the most appropriate from the point of view of the players:

- **Action games:** automatic re-logon preferred
- **Strategy games:** automatic/semi-manual re-logon
- **Web-based games, turn-by-turn games:** not critical

If the connection is lost but can be re-established, the game developer might indicate this in-game by briefly shimmering the graphical representation of the player to let other players know what has happened. This is purely an aesthetic nicety, but it does serve to inform players about the general network environment. Text-based MUD games from the early 1990s had a similar solution:

```
[character name] shimmers briefly as <he/she/it> reconnects.
```

In the game, of course, some form of prediction will be needed at the server or distributed client level. In principle, prediction should make sure that both the local player and the other, remote players notice as little deviation in the gameplay as possible. This is the same as the approach we took for data loss and jitter caused by irregular network latency. It is, in fact, more solid, because you know the reason for the lack of data—i.e., the connection has gone down—which means you can more accurately compensate for the problem.

In cases where the connection cannot be re-established, of course, the player's in-game representation must be replaced by an AI-controlled one (if the game requires that a certain number of players be present) or removed completely. The decision as to when to remove the player—and what to do with the in-game state—is left up to the game designer. At one extreme, the player can simply be returned to a known safe point in the system, and pick up from where he or she left off at some point in the future. At the other, the player loses everything that he or she had built up in the play session immediately prior to the connection failure.

Unintentional dropped connections should be dealt with sympathetically, without penalizing the player. Some players, however, might choose to manually disconnect—either physically or logically—in order to save their place in the game during an exchange that might lead to their in-game position being compromised. (We'll deal with this more concretely in Chapter 8.) That, as you probably know, requires a less sympathetic approach.

Intentional Dropped Connections

An intentional dropped connection occurs in its simplest form when the player unplugs the network cable to fake a network connection issue. This can be seen as akin to cheating, as you shall discover in the next chapter; in fact, it is hard to see it any other way.

The only reason that a player would disconnect his or her network cable would be to forcibly remove himself or herself from the game. It's not something that could happen by accident. Consequently, it ought to be possible to detect it at the physical and logical levels. On the physical side (assuming you categorize data synchronization as physical), you ought to be able to tell whether the client has disconnected manually by intervening at the operating system level (for example). If the connection is closed above the hardware level, you could reasonably infer that the disconnection was intentional and address the issue accordingly. (This relies, however, on that information being available to the server.)

If the cable was just pulled out, there would likely be no warning, so you can assume that it was either intentional or unintentional. You can then perform a few logic operations to try to ascertain the likelihood of the disconnection being intentional. These operations take place on the server, but could also infer the intervention of the client at the start of the next play session—kind of like a post-mortem of the connection failure. The server and client could then come to a decision together as to whether the connection was dropped intentionally.

A scoring system should be established to rapidly grade the disconnect in order to assess the chances of the disconnection being intentional. The aim is to use in-game and network-layer information to determine the likelihood of cheating. Although this is not a guaranteed method of weeding out those who seek to cheat by forcing their machine to disconnect from the server, it is as close as we are likely to come. (Scoring is covered in more detail in Chapter 8.)

This leads to the game developer's decision as to whether the player should be punished or whether to just let it go—that is, to live with the consequences of intentional disconnection, or try to continue playing using AI techniques so as not to disrupt the game from the point of view of the other players.

Most importantly, the trick is not to confuse the two—intentional and unintentional—forms of network disconnection, as this will alienate and confuse players.

REFERENCES

[NETGAMES01] "The Effect of Latency and Network Limitations on MMORPGs." Tobias Fritsch, Helmut Ritter, and Jochen Schiller of the Freie Universität Berlin, published as part of NetGames '05, Hawthorne, New York, USA, by ACM.

[LEIGH01] CS426 "Multiplayer Game Development." Jason Leigh, Electronic Visualization Lab, University of Illinois at Chicago, 2003–2007.

[TURKU01] "A Review on Networking and Multiplayer Computer Games." Jouni Smed, Timo Kukoranta, and Harri Hakonen, Turku Centre for Computer Science, TUCS Technical Report No. 454, April 2002, ISBN 952-12-0983-6.

REMOVING THE CHEATING ELEMENTS

In This Chapter

- What Is Cheating?
- What Are the Risks?
- What Are the Solutions?
- Hacks, Cracks, and Cheat Codes
- Communication Layer Cheats
- Logic Layer Solutions
- References

Lest you believe that you need not worry about cheating, you should perhaps think again. As PCs get more sophisticated, they can be used not only to play games, but also to cheat on them. Indeed, cheating can occur in as many ways as there are network games. It is the game designer's responsibility to make sure that the game cannot be cheated, and to police any infractions that do occur either manually or automatically. How seriously the designer takes this role will have an impact on the long-term popularity of the game.

While it would be impossible to cover them all, this chapter at least looks at why cheating occurs, what form it takes, and ways to combat it. Specifically, this chapter looks at two kinds of cheats:

- **Augmentation.** This involves helping the player to be better than (in some cases) humanly possible.
- **Logic-layer cheats.** These involve fooling the client and server into believing that the player is better than he or she is or that the game has progressed on the client side in a fashion not logically possible.

It also looks at key ways in which cheat detection can be implemented—not only to catch people using bots to play games in an automated fashion, but to catch other types of cheats as well, such as data insertion and other attempts to fool the server or other clients that the game is unfolding in a way that is both beneficial to a specific client and not an accurate reflection of reality. It then covers possible actions that can be taken against cheating within the game itself, with the worst offenders receiving a total ban and plenty of other sanctions in between.

 The kinds of cheats that are the most difficult to catch are ones who act within the rules of the game, including automated players. These are hard to detect and prevent, as they don't tend to draw attention to themselves.

Apart from this is the possibility that cheating elements can simply be factored out (ignored)—that is, either cheating doesn't happen in the first place or its effects are minimal. To achieve this, the problem must be approached on several levels:

- The network and the data that it carries
- The client, the decisions that it is allowed to make, and the data that it generates
- The server and how it processes the game environment

Before we get into that, however, we must first define what game designers perceive as cheating, and where the risks lie.

WHAT IS CHEATING?

Sometimes, a fine line exists between behavior that might be considered cheating and that which might just be considered competitive. Behavior that falls in this gray area might be ignored, as it doesn't detract immediately from everyone's enjoyment.

Despite the insistence of Greg Costikyan, in his 2000 article "The Future of Online Gaming" [COS01] that

> "An online game's success or failure is largely determined by how the players are treated. In other words, the customer experience—in this case the player experience—is the key driver of online success,"

many game designers, players, and those running the game turn a blind eye to a detrimental player experience caused by cheating as long as said cheating does not affect the bottom line. And that's at the root of the problem—or, as Matt Pritchard [GAMA01] puts it:

> "Cheating undermines success."

Pinpointing a single definition for cheating is a bit more difficult than you might think. Cheating takes many different forms, and its effects are felt in so many different ways, that it is hard to point to one single behavior as cheating personified. That said, a reasonable definition might be "a playing style that exploits the system to the personal benefit of the individual." The focus here is the fact that cheating should give the player an unfair advantage; otherwise, what would be the point? Another type of cheating might be behavior that is aimed at damaging the playing experience of the other players—but again, the player doing the cheating likely does so to gain an unfair competitive advantage (although in some cases, it might just be the thrill of disrupting others' gaming experience).

Then again, some things that you might think of as cheating may not be. For example, although the practice is usually frowned upon by game manufacturers—and may violate the terms of use—selling in-game currency, or entire accounts containing leveled-up characters, on the Internet is not considered to be cheating, as it does not detrimentally affect the game and those playing it. That's not to say that doing so is strictly on the up and up; after all, it enables people to artificially advance or benefit from additional weapons, removing the hard graft that comes with the natural progression of the player through the game's leveling system.

 Certain questions arise that transcend the issues surrounding cheating and automated playing, namely Is a player who spends time building up a character for the sole purpose of selling it on cheating? By same token, is the person who buys it also cheating? Either way, it is a waste of resources to try to deal with this kind of cheating when there are automated processes that can reduce overall cheating of the kind that is actually detrimental to the experience of all the players rather than just one or two.

There is a thin line between what might constitute cheating and what definitely is. It's hard to point to one particular thing and say that it is *always* cheating—except in cases where the natural capabilities of the player are enhanced or where the game is played outside its own rules.

Before you can look in any detail at the causes of, effects of, and ways to combat cheating, you must first consider where the risks lie. Clearly, single-player games are not at risk in the same way, because cheaters benefit only themselves by cheating—and if they want to do that, that is up to them. But where do the risks lie for multi-player network games?

WHAT ARE THE RISKS?

Different games have different risks associated with them. In other words, different games have different mechanisms by which it is possible to cheat—and in some cases, a game's implementation makes it more susceptible to cheating than others. For example, a game that uses text-based commands is at high risk for cheating of all kinds, the reason being that any game in which data that is transferred is encoded as pure text will be very easy to spoof. After all, in the case of a MUD with a Telnet-based front-end, for example, the server has no way of determining whether the client is a machine or a human. Furthermore, the plain-text nature of the commands means that the machine can very easily introduce them into the data stream. What's more, the cheater doesn't have to go to any lengths to try to figure out the game's command API, seeing as how it's the very same sequences of characters used to play the game. That is, there's no translation from keyboard to game, as there is in a sophisticated shooting game with a specialized client front-end.

By the way, speaking of sophisticated shooting games with specialized client front-ends: These are not safe, either. Indeed, client software games are very high risk, regardless of whether the client is a full game engine with a multi-player component or simply an advanced client front-end. The risk is high for one simple reason: The tools needed to construct elaborate hacks are placed right in the hands of the hackers. Hackers have access to the same tools as any other developer—plus some that regular developers might not even know about. They also have an in-depth knowledge of programming, machine code, and all the facets of engineering that go into building a game. That means if you don't take precautions, they can reverse-engineer the game and use the information that they glean from this process to cheat.

Genre-Specific Risks

As mentioned, MUDs with Telnet-based front-ends are quite vulnerable to cheating, as are client software games. These are not, however, the only genres that are at risk:

- Real-time action games are at risk from people using hardware or software to augment their own capabilities, which can happen at several levels and may not always be detectable. This might include anything from an auto-fire button on a joystick (is this *really* cheating? Some would say so...) on up to automated aiming and shooting software that bolts onto the client. These latter automated systems are universally agreed to be a serious threat, as are fully automated programs (bots or macros) that are capable of playing on their own.
- Strategy games are at risk from software cracks and message interception, the intent being to lie about the in-game status of the player. In this way, the player can artificially advance his or her position in the game. This usually occurs to the detriment of everyone else; after all, *their* clients are playing a straight game, so they cannot possibly enjoy the advantages that the cheater has, nor can they easily detect (unless the cheating is flagrant) that cheating has taken place.
- Games that reward repetitive in-game actions are at risk from people trying to use automated means to play more quickly, more frequently, or for longer than they are naturally able (or willing) to do. It is one thing for people to spend hours crafting a property in *Second Life* only to then sell it on eBay; it's quite another for someone to build an automated software package capable of looting and pillaging with the best of them for the sole purpose of racking up enough kills to build an account that can be sold to someone to go on a killing spree. That's just not playing a fair game.

Global Risks

In addition to these genre-based cheating strategies, there are also some more general cheating strategies that apply to games outside the strictly reflex-based action-game genre. The lack of twitch gaming does not preclude some advanced tactics for getting an illegitimate upper hand.

For example, games that rely on people being able to see what others are doing are at risk from cheaters taking another approach. Namely, they will wait until they see what everyone else has done before making their own move. That part is perfectly okay; it's kind of like a chess strategy. The "cheating" part involves using software to spoof the other clients (and the server) into thinking that the cheater has actually made his or her move *before* everyone else. Then, when the moves are evaluated, the cheater comes out on top—but not by chance.

As you saw in Chapter 7, "Improving Network Communications," in many action games, dead reckoning is used to estimate game moves—meaning that behind the scenes, moves do *happen at varying times. This places these games at risk in a similar manner as games that rely on people being able to see what others are doing.*

The other side to this coin is that games that rely on people *not* being able to see what others are doing are also at risk. Depending on the topography used to implement the gaming model, the client might need to have this "invisible" data in order to calculate the next iteration of the game environment. The risk is that people may try to intercept this data and use it to their own ends. Again, this type of unfair advantage—known as over-the-shoulder gaming—is usually detrimental to other people's gaming experiences.

In short, any multi-player network game that becomes more than a little bit popular is at risk from people trying to cheat. This only gets worse when the rewards for doing so are concrete rather than simply a question of personal pride—although personal pride and fame do incite people to cheat in equally large numbers for certain games. By opening up a game to many players (in an Internet environment, for example), hacks, cheats, exploits and so on are all going to surface at some point, because gamers tend to be an ingenious bunch of individuals. It's all you can do to stay ahead of them—or at least learn to patch quickly enough they cannot cause too much disruption.

Luckily, game designers have many solutions to consider, all designed to detect, prevent, or increase the difficulty of cheating. As you will see, that is the balance that needs to be struck: Do you solve the problem at the source, attacking the cheaters themselves, or make it hard to gain any benefits from cheating?

WHAT ARE THE SOLUTIONS?

The first part of any solution is to pinpoint possible loopholes in the design and fix them, thereby preventing cheating. To do this, some developers may want to turn to, well, a hacker or cheat. After all, these are the people who are most familiar with the weaknesses in games. Some will even do it for free, just *because*. Another way to prevent cheating is to police the game; in this way, you can at least reduce casual cheating to a minimum, because the vast majority of casual cheaters are scared of getting caught—not to mention having their account suspended. A third approach is to obscure data communications between the client and server; in this case, obfuscation capabilities are simply built into the game design, meaning that no further action on this point is needed once the game has been distributed.

This last bit is part prevention, part detection, as a robust system will be able to detect when obscured data has been tampered with and discard the data accordingly.

So prevention at the source is part of the equation—but so is detection in the game itself. For this reason, like so many of the network multi-player implementation strategies you have seen, detection capabilities—as well as prevention mechanisms—should become part of the design as well as part of the end implementation. Note, however, that although the detection mechanism should be *external* to the game to prevent reverse engineering, it should not simply be bolted on at the end. Detection should happen at the server, to the extent that it is possible. Smart clients may also be part of the solution—but unless great care is taken, they will be reverse engineered and subsequently cracked *if the game is popular enough*. The worst thing a developer can do is underestimate the popularity of his or her own game, and thereby under-invest in anti-cheating mechanisms.

Detection Approaches

There are several ways to detect whether cheating is taking place:

- Mechanical (i.e., network traffic)
- Behavioral (i.e., in-game behavior transcends what ought to be possible)
- Logical (i.e., errors are detected in data at the server side)

These three intervention points will crop up in one guise or another throughout the rest of this chapter; it ought to be possible to use any one of them as a basis for detecting cheating. To do so, however, you need to make an investment in time (i.e., implement human detection mechanisms), technology (i.e., implement automated mechanisms) or both (i.e., implement hybrid mechanisms). They all have their advantages and disadvantages.

Human Detection Approaches

Human cheating detection involves having certain players police the game from the inside. This requires that the person either play or watch for unusual patterns in the gameplay in order to spot cheats as they occur. The advantages of using human cheat detection is that doing so results in a relatively low rate false positives, coupled with the fact that when false positives—that is, when a player who has not been cheating is falsely accused of doing so—do occur, the subsequent experience is slightly less frustrating for the players involved. After all, a human can talk to the player and explain what the issue is, which will probably yield a better response than the player simply being banned by an auto-mated process. This makes the likelihood of retaining that player after a false positive much greater.

 You'll learn more about false positives in a moment.

Of course, the disadvantages include the fact that, as a detection ap-proach, human detection is highly expensive in terms of time. And time, after all, is money—human time much more so than computer time. There's also the possibility that a human will miss cheating behavior; in fact, it's almost guaranteed.

Automated Detection Approaches

Anything that a human can do in terms of detection, a computer can usually do faster, for longer, and more reliably. As long the areas of the game in which cheating might occur are correctly identified, you can cre-ate an algorithm to spot incidences of cheating in the system. The auto-mated system also has better access to the nuts and bolts of the game. The bits and bytes that make up the network interface, the various game val-ues, and even the timing of events are all better processed by a computer.

The advantages of using an automated system to detect cheating are various. For a start, no humans are required, which makes it cheaper. In addition, the chances of false negatives—that is, where a cheat is not identified, or is identified as a regular player—is as close to zero as the algorithm allows; in this regard, the machine will never make a mis-take. Cheaters *will* be caught.

 You'll learn more about false negatives in a moment.

Of course, the flip side of such an aggressive policy is that you may experience a higher rate of false positives. And since the system is auto-mated, this can be hard on players; it becomes difficult to explain why a player has been banned in the middle of a winning game if all they that player has to talk to on the other side is an automated system.

 Usually, the best detection mechanisms are those that detect automated playing (bots or macro scripts), but if the game is well designed, there's no reason that most cheaters cannot be caught 100% of the time.

Hybrid Approaches

Most developers tend to use a hybrid approach, which can work in one of two modes:

- **Discrete threshold.** This involves setting a low automated ratio of false positive/negative detection and dealing with those incidences of suspected cheating near the borders manually.
- **Layered referral.** This approach scores each incidence of suspected cheating according to criteria, with humans reviewing the whole lot before action is taken.

So you can automate processes to single out potential cheats, and then use police players to follow up if there is any doubt as to whether a single instance is really cheating or not. You can then set a threshold to separate cheats about which the system is 100-percent positive from borderline cases based on your ongoing experience with the game and its cheating elements. This also implies that the detection and reinforcement process is in continuous flux, always being adapted as the game is played.

Categories of Detection Mechanics

Several detection mechanics can be implemented, regardless of your detection approach:

- **Traffic analysis.** One of the easiest ways to detect mechanical cheats (such as bots) is traffic analysis. This involves examining traffic and trying to detect whether it has been tampered with. (The article "Identifying MMORPG Bots: A Traffic Analysis Approach," by Kuan-Ta Chen, Jih-Wei Jiang, Polly Huang, Hao-Hua Chu, Chin-Laung Lie, and Wen-Chin Chen [ACE01], describes this method in detail.) Tampering can take many forms, but the most telltale signs tend to be reaction time, packet sequencing, and alterations of in-flight data. This detection mechanism, which is a purely mechanical approach, is very effective—but only up to a point.
- **Behavior analysis.** This form of automated analysis is meant to detect cases in which the interface used by the player to connect to the server and other players—or to connect the player to his or her computer—has been altered to augment the player's capabilities. These alterations might include the implementation of aiming aids that, say, enable players to shoot out of their backs, or protective devices designed to ensure that the player is never hit—even in a hail of bullets. For this type of analysis to work, the automated system must have a very good idea of how a game ought to play out—making this approach more of a design-based solution (and one that will tend to be quite resource-intensive to carry out the processing required).

- **Status analysis.** Status analysis involves cross-checking the status of the player with his or her in-game actions in an attempt to see whether the client has been tampered with to improve the player's status (for example, giving the player more money than he or she should have in an RTS, or not diminishing the player's energy correctly in a real time–action game). Usually, the client system will have been tampered with in such a way that it incorrectly reports the state of the immediate game environment as well as the player's status.
- **Progression analysis.** This usually must be done by a human, with a flag raised by an automated process. It involves checking the progression of a player through a game over time as compared to the rest of the playing population. That is, if a particular player seems to be advancing more quickly than anyone else, he or she could be cheating. It should be noted, however, that this is typically a very subtle form of cheat, and will likely not be spotted. Besides, it doesn't disturb the game as a whole beyond an unnatural progression—unless it can be proven that the player is not human. In that case, a too-regular progression through the game would be a clue as to the humanity of the player in question.

All of the cheats detected by these mechanics can be prevented to a certain extent, either through the design of the game or the environment in which it is played.

Prevention Versus Detection

Being able to detect when cheating occurs is useless if you don't do anything about it. On the flip side, it is not enough to simply build in as many anti-cheating measures as possible but not invest in detection. It is simply not possible to create a game that both is cheat proof and maintains all the facets of the original design, balance, and technology that the developer envisioned. All this is to say that any measures you do implement with regard to detecting and preventing cheating will involve striking some sort of balance between the two.

On the subject of prevention, one possible approach is to make the rewards for cheating less attractive. This is difficult, however, because it usually means tampering with the very core of what makes the game fun to play. For example, anything that makes a game attractive in terms of achievement—i.e., the natural progression or advancement through the game—will become a target for cheating, as some people are naturally greedy.

Another approach to prevention is to take pains to make it as difficult as possible to actually cheat. This usually involves implementing mechanics at the design and implementation levels—which, inevitably, compromises the game's performance and/or flexibility in some way.

For example, you could move all the game logic to the server in order to ensure that the code needed to reverse-engineer the game would not be available to cheaters, but doing so would limit the sophistication of the game, as the complexity of the game environment would need to be reduced accordingly. In addition, the cost (in terms of the finished product) of doing so would weigh heavily against the benefit of having done it. Besides, cheaters could still carry out traffic analysis and would likely be able to decode for themselves how the game is put together.

If your game requires that at least some of the logic resides on the client (which is the case for most sophisticated FPS, action, and strategy games), you can at least make sure that reverse engineering doesn't yield any clues as to how the game rules are encoded. This logic should also be applied to network traffic—in other words, exchange as little detail as possible, and encode what you *do* exchange in a manner that hides its true nature. Similarly, you must take steps to protect the flow of data over the network, and generally pay attention to security measures. These might include additional layers of soft security, such as key phrases, passwords, and light encryption. Note, too, that detection can produce opportunities for prevention—typically changing the client or server software in such a way to prevent the type of cheating detected in the future.

Action Versus Inaction

Once cheating has been detected, the game must decide how to deal with the culprits. Should it be overlooked? Should action be taken to sanction the cheater? If action should be taken, what kind? In the worst-case scenario, the account is immediately disabled before being reviewed, leaving the onus on the player to try to get himself or herself reinstated. Clearly, you would have to be *very* confident in your ability to correctly identify cheaters to take this tack. Other possibilities include allowing for a human review and, if the reviewer concludes that cheating has indeed taken place, moving to disable the account.

Instances of cheating that are considered to be less egregious—such as intentionally disconnecting to avoid a fight—might be dealt with less severely than, say, players attempting to get a leg up on others by nefarious means during gameplay. Your response to the latter might, for example, be to permanently disable the player's account, while your response to the former may simply be to strip the player of goods, cash, or status within the game. Whatever route you choose, you must make sure that the sanction is effective.

An innovative solution might be to allow "cheat leagues," where cheaters can try to outdo each other. Provided players keep their cheating ways to those leagues, they might provide an outlet for some of these to let off steam. This, of course, will be predicated on the understanding that players will be permanently banned if they attempt to apply their cheating ways in the game proper.

The balance of action versus inaction is delicate. You don't want to punish so-called "rail-gun gods"—that is, players with a seemingly unnatural aim and trigger speed. But at the same time, you need to be sure that cheating is not taking place. Otherwise, you may well find that your game becomes a battle of the cheating elements, comprised only of a cheating community. This may lock you, the developer, into an endless cycle of discovering cheating loopholes, issuing patches, and just waiting for the cheaters to find their way around the newly installed anti-cheating code.

Added to this is the possibility of a misdiagnosis. These come in two forms:

- **False positives.** These are false accusations, wherein a stand-up player is identified as a cheat. False positives tend to increase in systems with very aggressive cheat-detection mechanisms, unless care is taken to establish the difference between a real positive and a false positive.
- **False negatives.** These occur when a cheat is not identified, or is wrongly identified as a stand-up player. False negatives are more prevalent in systems with less robust cheat-detection mechanisms.

Of these, false positives are particularly problematic. That is, being strict with real offenders is a good thing, but punishing an innocent party is damaging to the gaming population as a whole. But false negatives pose a problem, too, in that players who continue to cheat undetected can diminish the game experience for other players. Moreover, cheaters who are not caught burn system resources illegitimately, perhaps even causing service outages, server crashes, or other problems.

One way to reduce the number of false positives is to attack the problem of cheating by implementing preventive measures in the game's core to reduce cheating overall. This approach will hopefully involve less in the way of in-game responses—that is, cases where some kind of sanction is required—and, by extension, reduce the number of false positives (especially if an automated system is used to identify and punish cheats).

As such, any anti-cheating strategy should use testing to play with the ratio of false positives to false negatives until a balance is struck that is workable for both the developer and the player population. Specifically, the number of false positives should be kept as close to zero as possible.

(Anything above 5 percent would be considered the result of an aggressive algorithm [ACE01].)

The reason for this testing is simple: As the game becomes more popular, the cheating incidence will increase, probably beyond the capacity for the game to absorb it. In addition, the detection system must return high detection rates, with the emphasis this time on reducing the number of false negatives (i.e., cases where a player is assumed to be human when it is not). Here, anything above 95 percent is considered to be accurate [ACE01].

This implies that the game style of every single player is subject to analysis more or less constantly, with the burden of this processing placed on the server for security reasons. Clearly, an efficient detection system will be necessary to avoid slowing down the whole game.

HACKS, CRACKS, AND CHEAT CODES

In the pre-Internet days of gaming, "cheat code" referred to a small piece of code that could be introduced into the memory of a computer before a game was executed that would alter the game in some way. Cheat codes were shared on BBSes and in specialist magazines. Historically speaking, this practice is the forerunner of every hack and crack since, and has a special place in the development of games.

All games are susceptible to the introduction of cheat codes that will change the way that they operate, although the technology available to cheaters has increased exponentially since the first home-computer games (as opposed to console games) were popularized.

"Cracking" involves some kind of manipulation of a system (game or otherwise) to facilitate cheating. Crackers might crack their own client or crack the server. Either way, the implication is that some damage has been done to the system that renders it changed. "Hacking," on the other hand, generally involves opening up a system in some way in order to obtain information. Some hackers use their skills in the pursuit of something benign, such as trying to learn from a game's design. Others, however, share the information they obtain with crackers either for profit or in the spirit of cooperation—a kind of "honor amongst thieves" arrangement.

There are numerous online discussions relating to the difference between hacking and cracking. Here, we tend to distinguish them by whether the culprit simply obtains information or acts on that information.

Although a main focus for a developer is preventing hacks and cracks (as well as augmentation and the other mechanical cheats), you may also be faced with badly written (or at least incompletely tested) game software that yields holes that can be exploited by players. These are included in the category of "logic cheats"; these are usually easy to spot, as they tend to work against game rules.

How Hacks and Cracks Happen

Before any hacking or cracking can take place, the cheat needs an "in" to the game system itself; there are a number of such entry points in the system. "Locking" those entry points—protecting them from being used by hackers and crackers for ingress—is key to surviving in the network multi-player game business, especially in real time–strategy and action games, including MMORPGs. Fortunately, it is usually easy to identify and close most of these entry points—especially when players attempt to use them to do things that are outside the rules of the game. That means the detection of these holes post-development is also made easier (but should not be relied on, for reasons stated earlier—namely that it is possible to introduce data into the stream in a manner that does not rely on exploitation of these holes in the system).

If, however, a hacker or cracker does find an exploitable point of entry, your system becomes subject to the following:

- Reverse engineering
- Physical cheats
- Logical cheats
- Spoofing and spying

Reverse Engineering

Evaluating release code to try to determine the logic behind a game or where vital data is stored is known as "reverse engineering."

Presumably, you already understand the compile process:

Source Code → *Compile* → Object Code → *Assemble* → Machine Code

 For the sake of simplicity, this assumes that the link process can be expressed as "Assemble," which implies that the various resources, libraries, and other externally required pieces of the final system are rolled into the machine-code product.

Reverse engineering attempts to go backward in the chain. Although it is highly unlikely that the process will yield anything approaching the source code, many hackers understand the output of an optimized compiler better than the developers themselves. So even if they can't get back to the nicely formatted source code, they can at least scan the object code (having disassembled it with a disassembler) to find out how the game works, where the important data is stored, and other vital information.

There are any number of reasons why someone might attempt reverse engineering:

- To find the location of key data for the purpose of over-the-shoulder cheating (where the client stores values for the game environment outside the player's own sphere of influence). This can even migrate toward changing key values so that the progress of the player is adjusted according to the cheater's whim (the so-called authoritative client cheat category, discussed shortly). As long as the client software can be made to believe that the data values are legitimate, then the cheater's own world view will permeate through the game environment and become truth.
- To find loopholes in the game logic that can be exploited—for example, weaknesses in the underlying programming that might be used to win challenges. One such logical fault was found in a popular online game, where it became apparent that a player could teleport things into other players with disastrous results. (Of course, you're already aware that testing is a good way to trap these kinds of glitches.)
- To devise mathematical/logical solutions to puzzles revolving around how various things are calculated or the location of key objects in the game universe.
- To track back to network data that can then be modified in-flight in order to manipulate the natural progression of the game. If someone knows where key data is stored, he or she can find out how it is accessed and what it looks like just before or during transmission. (Note that in order to make the most of this approach, there must be something between the client and the server to process the in-flight data. The information on its own is not particularly useful.)

Of course, some reverse engineering is fairly benign. In many cases, people do it simply to try to get information that would help players be more successful. In the single-player world, this is reasonably common, as is trying to change values to help the local game. It is only when the information is subsequently applied to a network game with more at stake that it becomes an issue.

Physical Cheats

Physical cheats are usually facilitated by a machine that sits between the client and server, its sole purpose being to intercept packet streams at various levels and modify them depending on information derived from the in-game environment. Theoretically, this machine could be acting as a network relay proxy or even something between the man machine interface (MMI) and the game system. Any kind of mechanical auto-fire style button would fit into this category. Other tools include the following:

- More advanced systems of auto-play (as long as they are not solely software based).
- Automatic playing mechanisms that revolve around using screen sensing by peeking into video memory and testing values of pixels. That information can then be used to help the player control his or her gaming experience, augmenting his or her natural ability with logic.
- Advanced information packages that use the data exchanged between clients, and between the client and the server, to overlay information on the screen to which the player should not be privy. Even something as basic as a map overlay can mean the difference between success and failure in an online game.

 Most physical cheats apply only in cases where reflex time is paramount.

Many physical cheats can be detected using some of the techniques listed earlier. For example, you can measure behavioral reaction times to pinpoint cases where the reactions seem to happen too quickly after the event that caused them. If you use additional logic to determine the player's line of sight at the same time, you can use the reaction time and environmental data together to weed out cheats. Testing and balancing will then enable you to determine where the natural line can be drawn between expert players and automated assistance.

Logical Cheats

In addition to physical cheats, there are logical cheats, which can affect any game—not just those that rely on split-second reflexes. A logical cheat uses the game's design against itself, perhaps by directly intervening or maybe by finding a loophole in the game's design.

 No third-party programs need be running in order for the logical cheats to work— although some third-party software will be necessary (i.e., for writing to memory whilst the game is in session).

Games in which the client is assumed to be correct and informs the server of the progression of the game are particularly at risk, a key problem being the fact that the client doesn't know it's been hacked, and the server can't really tell because it does not have access to the data. In other words, although the data in the memory locations managed by the client is assumed to be correct, this data can in fact be modified by a hacker/cracker either to demote other players' positions or beef up the cheater's own. This is just one example of a logical cheat; you'll see many more later on, when we discuss kinds of cheating that have been seen in the wild.

Spoofing and Spying

In addition to the straight cheating techniques discussed previously, there are also some clever techniques that could be used to *help* a player—even if it might not be classified as cheating per se:

- **Spoofing.** Normally, spoofing refers to making the system believe that a player is someone else. Here, however, we use it to also cover instances when the client is making the system believe that there is a real person behind a virtual in-game one. This occurs when a pseudo player appears on a separate account, and is used purely to garner information, and to display that information for the real players's use. Examples of the information conveyed might be a detailed map with locations of other players or some AI used to predict events and the locations of other players. Because the pseudo player, which plays automatically, exists simply as an information-gathering entity, it doesn't matter if it is repeatedly killed and has to be reincarnated. It need only play at a level that makes it look human.
- **Spying.** This involves spying on data packets and using the information therein to track other players, even if they can't be seen in-game. This is a very stealthy approach that needs no actual in-game intervention by another tool. It's just watching, after all, and is nearly impossible to detect. For this to work, the spy's game client needs data from all the other clients in order to play out the game—which is also sometimes necessary due to jitter and other network issues. In other words, the very things you use to deal with the problems associated with network gaming, as discussed in Chapter 7, can be used against you.

Clearly, the only thing you can do to combat these stealthier types of cheating is protect your game—and hope that you do enough for *long enough* that it doesn't negatively affect the game. (By this I mean, of course, affect sales of the game or game subscriptions in a bad way.) Protecting the game can mean anything from obscuring data that is exchanged between clients to obfuscating the code base such that casual hackers cannot derive any information from it. Other protections are also possible, with the focus always being to ensure that it is as difficult as possible for hackers to do their damage.

Types of Cheats

In "How to Hurt the Hackers" [GAMA01], Matt Pritchard divides cheating into six categories:

- **Reflex augmentation.** This type of cheating occurs when the player augments his or her skills with a proxy or other third-party program. Auto-aiming, mapping, and other programs designed to give an unfair advantage fall into this classification.
- **Authoritative clients.** This is where client software relays false updates to the server and other clients, and is assumed to be *the* authority on that data. Because the game logic is considered sacred, the server and other clients have no reason to doubt it.
- **Information exposure.** This classification includes cases where the player can see—or has put himself or herself in a position to see—information that should remain hidden. All kinds of data is flying around the system, and it's your job to make sure that it cannot be used against the game.
- **Compromised servers.** In this classification are cases where the server has been hacked (either from within or without). This is quite severe and must be taken very seriously; it could very well happen if precautions are not taken to prevent it.
- **Bugs and design loopholes.** These are exploitable problems in the design or implementation of the game, either at the client side or on the server. Usually, these are uncovered by hacking or automated playing, but can be uncovered during testing in much the same way.
- **Environmental weaknesses.** In this classification are issues that become apparent only when the game is running, and may be detected only as a function of another facet of the network gaming paradigm—e.g., lag causing game-state suspension and queuing of multiple cancel requests for the same initial action in *Age of Empires* [GAMA01].

For the purposes of this discussion—and to look at possible solutions to the root causes of these problems (i.e., data communication and hacking code)—these categories can be further grouped to describe the cheating behavior:

- **Exploits.** Here, the code of the game is not changed, but players manage to gain an advantage using loopholes or other weaknesses.
- **Augmentation.** Here, the player or game is augmented by other software.

- **Cracking.** Here, the game code is compromised in order to obtain an advantage.

You can try to factor out cheating that you can prevent by paying attention to three key aspects of software creation:

- Rigorous testing
- Design
- Run-time detection

That is to say, anything that falls into the exploits category—bugs and design loopholes, environmental weaknesses, or perhaps information exposure—can potentially be dealt with by good testing practices. By a similar token, cheats arising from cracking—say, compromised servers and perhaps authoritative clients—need to be dealt with at the design level. Finally, cheats involving augmentation—i.e., authoritative clients or reflex augmentation—are countered using run-time detection (although there are things that should be done at the design level to prevent repeat occurrences). You may, in time, produce your own classification system, vital for tracking potential opportunities for cheating in the game that you are putting together.

I've introduced a paradigm that makes sense to me—that is, one that focuses on exploits, augmentation, and cracking—but that might seem to be too strict to apply to Pritchard's classifications. But the definitions are quite fluid, and will change from game to game, as will the roles of the various actors and facilitators in the system that make cheating possible.

 Some of Pritchard's classifications—information exposure, for example—describe facilitators to cheats more than active cheats in themselves. To deal with this, we might have created another classification that was more directly based on cause and effect. For example, suppose we tried to address a situation where the information exchange is too transparent, meaning players could use the information to create an authoritative client hack or for reflex augmentation. The resulting category might then encompass everything to do with data exchange, and solutions would need to be found for every possible cheat within that category.

Exploits

Exploits include bugs and design loopholes, where the code is examined to find ways in which the game logic can be fooled into allowing actions that are not normally possible. For example, someone might discover that it is possible to teleport into locations, including characters, and use that information to destroy in-game personae by, say, teleporting a bomb into them as opposed to it appearing next to them, which would give them the chance to run away. The bug in this case is treating players as locations (rooms) in their own right—handy for inventory management (you can put things "into" the player), but disastrous if those locations are known to other players.

The availability of a single-player version of an otherwise identical multi-player game will give players plenty of time to find out where these loopholes might be.

Related to bugs and design loopholes are environmental weaknesses, which rely on finding holes in the design of the game environment. For example, as noted in Pritchard's "How to Hurt the Hackers," there are cases in which players have been caught hovering between two server zones, knowing their enemies can't cross from one zone to the other (NPC controlled), and taking pot shots at them. Information exposure also falls into this category, as it involves the exploitation of a weak network transmission protocol or coding that has not been created to render data non-transparent.

The more you can do to mask data, the better, because a simple exploit can result in something more immediately damaging: augmentation of the player's natural abilities.

Augmentation

This category includes reflex augmentation, which is, as you will remember, a simple extension of the player's own natural ability. (Note that without information exposure, reflex augmentation would not be possible; in this way, these two classifications are intimately linked.) The category also includes authoritative clients, which augment the game data and forward it into the network as if it were the true status of the in-game entities. Of course, that data is changed in such a way that it masks the true state of the local player (usually) with respect to the game environment.

Cracking

Like the augmentation category, this category, too, includes authoritative clients, where the client is cracked such that it no longer follows strict game logic, instead generating results that are either possible but highly unlikely, or downright impossible. If there is no cross-reference to check whether the data is feasible, then the player might not really need to play at all, managing his fake game position with a cracked client. This is fairly unlikely, however—as is the possibility that there will be compromised servers (also in this category) on the game network. After all, one would hope, in modern systems, that security was sufficiently tight to prevent a direct hacking and cracking attack on the game servers.

That said, this does not preclude games' vulnerability to other forms of cracking, where the very fabric of the implementation is damaged through intentional misuse. For example, suppose some casual hacking of an online RPG game revealed to the hacker that all the descriptions are stored in a MySQL database with a PHP front-end. Given the well-known vulnerabilities in both SQL and PHP, a hacker might well introduce small scripts, which would be executed by the server and result in untold damage (the so-called SQL "injection" technique, for example). The bottom line is, once a hacker has exposed the relevant interfaces, he or she can use it to gain a competitive advantage in much the same way as any regular exploit or augmentation cheat.

Of course, all of these require a certain level of information exposure. Therefore, keeping data opaque is again proven to be paramount to maintaining an anti-cheat gaming service.

Bots and Automated Playing

An entirely separate category of cheating is described by the common term "bot." A bot, or script/macro, is an automated player that relies on scripted commands and a dose of AI and in-game knowledge to carry out tasks *as if it were a real player*. Players use bots—which might be, for example, a program that sends keystroke information to the game, thereby emulating the actions of a player—for many different reasons: some to gather information, others to build up accounts with large resources (which can then be sold to people who want to cheat by getting a head start in the game).

Some people wonder whether bots really matter, and where the dangers actually are. The way I see it, if a player can defraud the system by using a bot, then they do matter, and the dangers are clear. Besides, excessive automated playing can be a drain on system resources, especially since bots have one clear advantage over humans: They don't get tired.

*Dangers exist in many modern games (*Unreal Tournament *for example), where open scripting mechanisms are built in specifically to support bots, thereby revealing to bot creators how they might go about constructing their own to be used from a playing perspective rather than, as is common, an NPC perspective. In some games, the creation of these bots is encouraged—even necessary. But letting people build bots, and giving them information about how to do so, does rather open up the system to exploitation if not managed carefully.*

The only real way to deal with unwanted bots is to detect them—typically through network monitoring, with the "tells" being extended uptime, fast response times, repetitive actions, and the like, as well as through in-game logic—and shut them down. Prevention is not really feasible; after all, it is unlikely that you'll want to cripple the system by removing scripting entirely.

COMMUNICATION LAYER CHEATS

Any time a game sends data out over or receives data from the network, the game system as a whole (including all connected clients) is at risk. In fact, the communications layer is the most vulnerable, as it potentially exposes the most data to cheating by:

- Altering data in transit
- Adding data to the flow
- Changing the flow of data physically

The most danger is present when the data stream can be changed without requiring that the client software be changed, as this becomes impossible to detect.

Data-in-Transit Cheats

A data-in-transit cheat involves changing the data being sent by the client to the server (often by inserting rogue packets of data between legitimate packets to change their meaning) or examining incoming data. An auto-aim proxy, for example, makes use of both, examining incoming data and inserting packets to help the player hold his or her aim on an opponent. Specifically, the proxy software might use the incoming data to determine the location of the nearest opponent and then check the direction in which the player is firing. Based on this, the proxy will then insert packets before the fire command to focus the weapon such that it is aiming at the chosen target (here, the nearest opponent). When the other clients process the incoming data, they perform the aiming adjustment and shoot, reporting that the target has been hit. (This is unless, of course, some kind of spoofing is in place, by which it is reported by the targeted player's client that the player, in fact, moved just before the shot was fired, thereby avoiding it completely. The game then becomes a battle between the efficiency of two proxy gaming clients.)

In addition to handling data-in-transit cheats occurring on the communication layer, you must also address those data-in-transit cheats involving the authentication layer. These include more traditional hacking and account-hijacking cheats—which, while irritating from those concerned, are outside the scope of this book as they deal more with security than competitive advantage.

Lookahead and Update Dropping

"Lookahead" is roughly defined as the ability of a player to see events that seem to happen in the future from the point of view of the client, or a player's ability to project his or her own moves into the future *as if* the player had the ability to see other players' moves before they are made. This can be achieved in different ways:

- By waiting until all moves have been made before making one's own move, pretending to be on a very slow connection (i.e., no response packets). This approach might make use of a technique known as update dropping, in which a proxy system drops data as if it were a slow or unreliable interface.
- By changing ongoing data to reflect an earlier posting time.

 Naturally, both lookahead and update dropping require an intimate knowledge of how data exchange occurs on the network.

These work because of a system for managing updates known as "dead reckoning." As you learned in Chapter 7, dead reckoning is a way to project the known movement data into the future in order to combat the effects of jitter and latency on the network. The trouble with dead reckoning is that, with every time-step that passes without a checkpoint of the data (i.e., without real data coming in), reality and perception potentially diverge. It is only when the packets finally arrive that the local copy of the game knows what the "real" reality is. In the absence of that data, the game plays out using its best guess of the state of the game environment.

Obviously, at some point, the dead reckoning will be so hopelessly out of date that the system will have to take drastic action. This could involve one or a combination of the following:

- Disconnect the player
- Continue playing as a local NPC bot
- Continue playing as a server-based NPC bot

The most common way to use lookahead to cheat is to spoof the client's latency to fool a dead-reckoning system by time-stamping its own moves in the past. In this way, the cheating system can wait until it sees the honest players moves before making a move of its own—whilst appearing to have made the move earlier. The other players might not even notice that this has taken place; it will probably just seem as if they are playing against a particularly gifted (almost clairvoyant) player.

A similar cheat is to exploit a system that waits for a number of packets to be dropped before classifying a client as disconnected. In these cases, the cheater need only forcefully drop his or her packets—which are usually required to inform the other clients and the server that the player is still connected—until such a time as he or she has seen all the other moves, and then send out his or her own update. In doing so, the player simulates a connection experiencing severe jitter/latency, tricking the system into believing that it is simply taking a long time to receive, process, and respond to update packets.

Intentional Disconnections

The final type of communication-layer cheat is one that I alluded to in Chapter 7: Intentional disconnection. There are two sides to dealing with this type of cheat:

- **Determining whether the disconnection was intentional.** The disconnection should be scored according to the likelihood of it being intentional, what the player has to lose by not disconnecting, and prevailing network conditions. Complicating things is the fact that declining network conditions may have contributed to the predicament of the player—meaning that the player either felt that he or she *had* to disconnect, or that he or she was eventually disconnected by the client because network conditions had deteriorated to a certain degree. But if network conditions are otherwise stable, and if the player would stand to avoid in-game penalties by disconnecting, then you can probably say that the disconnection was intentional.
- **Making the punishment fit the crime.** You should take action that reflects what the player has gained by intentionally disconnecting during an in-game exchange. What you want to avoid is a case where a player disconnects in the middle of a battle and is returned to his or her last "safe" point, with his or her in-game properties restored. Otherwise, you remove the risk associated with intentional disconnections, thereby rendering the game much less enjoyable for everyone concerned.

Note that the issues surrounding intentional disconnections really only apply to action games. With strategy and other game types, such a quick fix wouldn't help—for example, in Civilization, *where the game has to play out from start to end, there not being any real persistent link between game sessions.*

Solutions to Communication Layer Cheats

In order to prevent cheating that involves taking advantage of the data-exchange model or the actual data exchanged between the clients and the server, you should attempt to put in place some mechanisms for discarding data that you judge to have been tampered with. At the same time, you can prevent the cheating from taking place at all by making sure that a casual hacker cannot extract meaning from the exchanges in the first place. At the core of the solution, however, is ensuring that the data stream remains unaffected.

Packet Serialization

You first encountered the idea of packet serialization—where, typically, packets are numbered and sent in sequential order—in Chapter 7 as a way to prevent data loss. Because many communications layer cheats involve tampering with data that is reminiscent of real data loss (refer to the lookahead cheats outlined previously), packet serialization can be a good way to combat them.

The key here is being able to detect whether data is missing or has been inserted. Packet serialization enables the server to do just that. It also helps to identify out-of-sequence packets, especially if a suitable input and output buffering system is used (Chapter 7 explains buffers more fully). That said, it's relatively easy for someone to figure out which serial numbers factor into a series of packets—meaning a cheater can fiddle with the values whenever he or she wants to insert or remove a packet.

This assumes, however, that the packets are numbered sequentially. That is, you might combat this by assigning a pseudo-random number to each packet, derived from an algorithm generated using the contents of the packet (timestamp, data, etc.) as well as its place in a queue of packets. Alternatively, you might serialize bursts of packets, with one packet containing a header, one containing a trailer, and a hash calculated across all packet identifiers—thereby building a value that can be quickly validated without needing to examine each identifier in turn. In this way, disturbances of the stream can be detected by the server or client. This will, however, require that the pipeline be at least wide enough to consume all the packets in a burst, which can introduce jitter, which must then be combated using dead reckoning (again, seen in Chapter 7).

The Lockstep Protocol

The paper "Cheat-Proofing Dead Reckoned Multiplayer Games" [EECSD01] isolates several strategies to combat cheating in dead-reckoning systems—including one called the "lockstep protocol." Although this protocol is quite involved—and the actual implementation of it falls beyond the scope of this book—its usefulness as an anti-cheating mechanism requires that the theory behind it be detailed here.

In the basic lockstep protocol, at a given cue—usually when all packets have been received—client systems will evaluate the state of the game environment as one. In this way, problems of dead reckoning are immediately solved, because every player must wait until moves from all other players arrive before the next frame can be calculated [EECSD01]. The problem with this approach is that the game runs at the speed of the slowest link—and if latency is a factor, this could be quite slow indeed (as you saw in Chapter 7).

You can, however, use these synchronization delays to your advantage by employing something called the "pipelined lockstep protocol," which enables the system to send out frames before the frames from other players are received. Frames sent will contain only the data pertaining to the client doing the sending, and will represent the player's commitment to a move—hopefully in absence of knowledge of the other moves—at just the right time so as to smooth over network latency.

The drawback to this approach is that it does not protect against late-commit cheats, as clients can wait until all the other players' moves have been received before committing to their own move. The so-called adaptive pipeline (AP) protocol, however, combats this by adjusting the lockstepping to match the frame rate so that it is close to the natural frame rate. In other words, AP tries to combat late-commit cheats by establishing a frame rate that seems reasonable and assuming that anything outside of that is an attempt to defraud the system. (This does mean, however, that you must use traffic analysis to spot occurrences of cheating, as it is still a possible—although very difficult and unreliable—way to do so.)

Another interesting solution is the sliding pipeline (SP) protocol, which adjusts the so-called pipeline depth to reflect the prevailing network conditions. The distinction between the SP and AP protocols is that in the SP protocol, there is a buffer that holds moves while the pipeline size is adjusted.

Using one or a combination of these protocols, you can minimize cheats that rely on exploiting the dead-reckoning algorithms used to combat network problems. In order to combat other cheating mechanisms involving the actual data transferred, however, you would also want to secure the data—discussed next.

Data-Level Solutions

First and foremost, you must provide a solution to prevent authoritative client cheating—specifically, by making sure that data cannot be tampered with once the client has sent it out. Simple hashing and subsequent encryption of the hash value can prevent this, as long as the keys are hard to determine. In this way, you can also reduce the impact of encryption by passing over a hash value only once rather encrypting/decrypting the whole packet.

Of course, this doesn't prevent someone from looking at the values, using them to determine what is going on in the game environment, and subsequently cheat. To address this, you can also present data in a variable way. For example, you can constantly change the layout, the data names, or even the meaning of the data in a randomly variable way. Something as simple as adding a pseudo-random offset value to all positional data can go a long way toward foiling many cheats.

Logic Layer Solutions

You can do a lot at the logic layer to make sure that cheating is made more difficult, as well as allow for detection. These solutions, however, must be designed in rather than added as an afterthought. Many of these solutions also apply to other kinds of games. For example, non-networked games could use logic-layer solutions to try to detect when a player has introduced a cheating mechanism.

These techniques also help to prevent other kinds of cheats, such as mechanical cheats—for example, keyboard trapping and auto target selection. These cheats are different from those that are introduced in the logic layer itself (i.e., cheats that involve changing the client or the client data), but they can be combated by the logic layer.

These cheats require a combination of game-universe knowledge and interaction. If you can remove one side of the equation—the game-universe knowledge—you can tackle the problem head-on. To that end, rather than allowing game-universe information, such as the positions of enemies, fly around in the communication layer, thereby making things easy for hackers and cheaters, it is better to transmit status information balanced against some kind of checkpointing to avoid ad-hoc detection. The checkpointing needs to be robust enough to be able to track status data with respect to the entire game environment, including the logic layer. Additionally, as pointed out in the Gamasutra article "How to Hurt the Hackers" [GAMA01], you must also use AI to try to spot cheating when it takes place. In other words, if you assume that the logic layer will be compromised, there should be some kind of cross check to make sure that you detect this as soon as is possible.

As noted in Chapter 7, part of the problem is that local clients make decisions to account for jitter and lag. These decisions aren't just at the level of dead reckoning, but are also actual in-game decisions that relate to the processing of game universe data (i.e., authoritative client cheats, where the client is assumed to be correct even when the logic layer is compromised). The logic layer is all-important in these cases. To prevent the client (or the server) from being hacked in such a way as to give an individual a competitive advantage (i.e., cheat), you must make sure that the code and data provided cannot be easily used to reverse engineer the game. Perhaps the best way to do so is to use code obfuscation to combat information exposure.

Code Obfuscation in the Logic Layer

Because information exposure is at the root of many hacks, bots, and other cheats, it is an important part of the anti-cheating equation. As mentioned earlier in this chapter, the purpose of hacking is to reveal places in memory (during run-time), places on the disk (level files), or even places on the network that are used to store information vital to the running of the game session. If that data is easy to decipher, it will be easy to crack and spoof.

One way to prevent this is through the use of code obfuscation—that is, taking things with logical, easy-to-remember (and identify) names, and making them much more difficult to remember and identify.

There are many ways in which code can be intentionally obfuscated:

- Using illogical, impossible-to-identify names
- Dynamically changing names and/or locations
- A combination of these

Employing any of these techniques ought to make it more difficult for a hacker to find the data—meaning the hacker will not be able to give it to a cracker or use it to alter the natural path of the game to his or her own advantage (or at least everyone else's disadvantage).

Before you continue, it bears mentioning that there are inherent downsides to using code obfuscation in these ways. First, the result is very hard to debug; it is difficult to trace back the meaning from the code, even for the developer. Second, the resulting code will likely be slower to execute (especially using dynamically changing names or locations for data), as the machine has to spend time managing the process. Finally, even if all these forms of obfuscation are applied, the code is—in addition to being prone to error—not completely secure. There is always a lynch pin that holds it together; once found, that pin can be used to pull it apart. Testing for that point can be time consuming; the developer must be sure that it won't be more trouble than it's worth, even before starting out. The purpose of this discussion is to help you make that judgment call.

Static Code Obfuscation

The first technique is to change type and variable names statically—in other words, to make them less readable by assigning unique, but possibly random, names or by following a scheme that seems to have no underlying meaning.

So, for example, a very readable set of location data might be specified as follows:

```
struct PLAYER_LOCATION {
  int x_position, y_position, z_position;
};
// declarations
PLAYER_LOCATION * oPlayerLocationTable; // player one is at [0]
// example function calls
void AllocatePlayerLocationTable ( PLAYER_LOCATION oLocTab ) {
// code to do allocation
}
PLAYER_LOCATION * GetPlayerLocation ( int nPlayerID,
PLAYER_LOCATION * oLocTab ) {
// return the player location of nPlayerID
}
// etc.
```

From this, it would be very easy to find out, once compiled, where the player table is located in memory. Since the code contains a symbol table, a hacker would be able to trace backward from the variable name, data type, and even the function names that are tasked to do the work.

So a basic, first-level obfuscation might take this code and, using an automated tracking and allocation solution (discussed momentarily), allocate names that are less readily identified with specific parts of the game. This can be done at the source-code level or using an external tool that obfuscates names at the linking cycle. The end result might look like the following:

```
struct AAA-001 {
  int AAA-002, AAA-003, AAA-004;
};
// declarations
AAA-001 * AAA-005; // player one is at [0]
// example function calls
void AAA-006 ( AAA-001 AAA-007 ) {
// code to do allocation
}
```

```
AAA-001 * AAA-008 ( int AAA-009, AAA-001 * AAA-007 ) {
// return the player location of nPlayerID
}
// etc.
```

The lookup table that gave rise to the preceding would then look as follows:

```
PLAYER_LOCATION                          AAA-001
x_position                               AAA-002
y_position                               AAA-003
z_position                               AAA-004
oPlayerLocationTable                     AAA-005
AllocatePlayerLocationTable              AAA-006
oLocTab                                  AAA-007
GetPlayerLocation                        AAA-008
nPlayerID                                AAA-009
```

There is, however, a downside to this technique: It yields really unreadable code. Not to mention, when debugging, it becomes hard to trace back from the disassembled code to the source. You could try to get around this by only obfuscating at the end—but what happens if, for some reason, the act of obfuscation itself introduces errors? The answer to that question is twofold. One, it becomes very hard to distinguish between errors due to obfuscation and errors in the underlying code. Two, it requires double the amount of testing at the end of a development schedule that is likely behind anyway. The result might just be that it is dropped at the first sign of difficulty because, after all, the rest of the game works.

In addition, a hacker simply needs to observe the byte levels of data to begin spotting patterns that will yield its use. So no matter how good the obfuscation is, if a hacker has access to this level of detail, a dynamic solution is needed.

Dynamic Code Obfuscation

You can obfuscate data at the logic layer before it is passed to the network communications layer to make sure that the data is not easily deciphered. To do so, you can use a dynamic scheme for changing the names and offsets of data. Hence, a variable name and value that might normally be represented as

```
player_x:100
```

can be obfuscated through the addition of a simple random offset. To avoid patterns creeping in (i.e., repetition of _ and : characters), that offset must also be dynamic with reference to the position of the character in the packet of data as a whole. In this way, you can create a stream of seemingly meaningless data for very little processing overhead. And provided that you are using a scheme, you can always get back to the original (using a code-wheel approach, for example),

 A typical networked first person shooter usually sends and receives thousands of bytes per second. Subsequently, we cannot spend too much time with encryption, so obfuscation provides a very easy solution.

This same kind of obfuscation can also be done with level files, which would technically make it harder for hacking to take place locally. Whether this would be worth the effort, however, depends entirely on the kind of game being developed. Games that are predominately about teamwork within a relatively simple level file would not benefit overly from obfuscation. In contrast, games built around the level file in such a way that the level file itself is an important part of the challenge (traps, puzzles, etc.) are clearly going to benefit more from adequately obfuscated level files.

Dynamic obfuscation of code and data location is also a possibility. This includes moving data (and even code) around in memory, thereby making it difficult for a hacker to track. Even if a hacker were to try to fiddle with the data, he or she might well be fiddling with data that is either no longer there or now another part of the system entirely. Disadvantages to using this approach include a possible performance hit from the constant reallocation of memory blocks, and the possibility of introducing loopholes in the allocation process that could be exploited by cheats.

At design and development time, the source code should be readable (respecting software engineering practices), which makes it more easily maintainable. So for source code, you might have a preference to compile-time (i.e., at the time that the code is created for the game) or run-time obfuscation (i.e., whilst the game is running). In the latter case, the variable names and values (and possibly function names) are changed according to a scheme that has been designed into the software.

Possible Pitfalls

Naturally, there are things that can go wrong. For example, it is no good having a sophisticated run-time obfuscation strategy if the code doing the obfuscation is not, itself, obfuscated. In addition, there are the aforementioned dangers of the obfuscation causing run-time errors. In the final analysis, the game developer will likely have to attack this problem with a two prong solution—run-time and compile-time and/or design-time—if obfuscation is actually required. For any games where the central server is the authority, of course, none of these approaches are needed. Even a game such as that, however, is not immune to attacks from bots.

Identifying Bots

Bots are discussed here as a logic-layer cheat—although they actually occur somewhere between the communication layer and logic layer, as does the detection of bots. For this reason, the solution must look at both the behavior and the network components involved.

The main issue is, as noted in "Identifying MMORPG Bots: A Traffic Analysis Approach" [ACE01]:

> "Identifying whether or not a character is controlled by a bot is difficult, since a bot-controlled character *obeys the game rules completely*."

 It is worth noting that "Identifying MMORPG Bots: A Traffic Analysis Approach" [ACE01] was one of the first (if not the first) papers to address bot detection using traffic analysis. This came at a time (2006) when the standard practice was to dialog with the bots as a way to determine whether they were human. Clearly a more effective and efficient approach was needed.

Solutions to these kinds of cheats are expressed in "Identifying MMORPG Bots: A Traffic Analysis Approach" [ACE01] and involve measuring various traffic metrics because certain key indicators in the traffic profile usually point to an automated system. The idea is to try to build a profile of normal traffic and to compare it with the actual traffic in the hopes that an automated system will be caught out. Luckily, bots have some key identifying characteristics:

- Reaction time
- Unfailing memory
- Inability to dialog

 Without the possibility of comparison, one can only use generalizations—which might increase the number of false positives (or false negatives) in the detection algorithm.

First, you must make sure you can collect traces (i.e., reports of network activity, each line relating to a unit of data transfer) so that analysis can be done during the testing/development process. That way, you can get a handle on what regular play, tested play, and test cycles using your own bots look like—which makes detection in the end product much more reliable and easy to implement.

One of the key measurements, as identified in "Identifying MMORPG Bots: A Traffic Analysis Approach" [ACE01], is release timing, or how long it takes to issue the next command following the last command. The theory, borne out by analysis, is that because human players use a mouse or keyboard, their reaction times vary as the action increases. In contrast, bots use a decision loop and periodic timers—meaning that when you look at their response times coupled with data-packet arrivals, it is much more regular. On top of that, it scales, so increases in activity don't change the response times—or, if they do, it's because the bot recognizes that it has to reply more quickly to be ready for the next cycle.

For the purposes of discovering whether a bot is playing, the actual measurements of interest are as follows:

- **Prompt response.** The time elapsed between when the packet leaves the server and the response arrives at the server is unfeasibly brief.
- **Regularity in response times.** Response times are too regular to be human;
- **Traffic burstiness.** The amount of traffic in a given time span should be smoother than when compared with a player because the algorithms are artificial.

In addition, "Identifying MMORPG Bots: A Traffic Analysis Approach" [ACE01] noted that human players automatically adapt to network problems that change the pace of the game. That is, as latency begins to creep in, human players will naturally generate in-game actions in response to things that are happening at a gentler pace. A bot, on the other hand (unless very cleverly written) remains crisply responsive—in this case totally unnecessarily, as the latency means that there is no need for the bot to be ready immediately for the next cycle.

Actually identifying a bot involves performing a variety of tests to determine whether the observed peaks and troughs in the various timing graphs are significantly different from what might be considered to be the norm. Most of these tests require statistical analysis of observed behavior to ascertain the chances that a specific traffic profile can be identified as a bot (or, conversely, as definitely *not* a bot). The tests are ongoing, and the traffic profiles have to be dynamic so that the weight of experience can be brought to bear on the analysis. When the system can do that, it ought to be able to detect with a great deal of accuracy the presence of bots in the game network.

References

[COS01] "The Future of Online Gaming." Greg Costikyan, 2000 (http://www.costik.com/ogrfinal.zip).

[GAMA01] "How to Hurt the Hackers: The Scoop on Internet Cheating and How You Can Combat It." Matt Pritchard, Gamasutra, July 24, 2000 (http://www.gamasutra.com/features/20000724/pritchard_01.htm).

[EECSD01] "Cheat-Proofing Dead Reckoned Multiplayer Games." Eric Cronin, Burton Filstrup, and Sugih Jamin, Electrical Engineering and Computer Science Department, University of Michigan (http://warriors.eecs. umich. edu/games/papers/adcog03-cheat.pdf).

[ACE01] "Identifying MMORPG Bots: A Traffic Analysis Approach." Kuan-Ta Chen, Jih-Wei Jiang, Polly Huang, Hao-Hua Chu, Chin-Laung Lei and Wen-Chin Chen, ACE 06 June 14–16 2006, Hollywood, California, USA.

TESTING NETWORK GAMES

In This Chapter

- Principles of Testing
- Testing the Network Layer
- Testing the Logic Layer
- Re-Using Prediction Code in Testing
- An Overview of Testing Options

Thisis chapter is about testing games that have a network component—
a task that is not as easy as it might at first seem. Take a minute now
to think back over everything that we covered in Chapter 5, "Creating
Turn-By-Turn Network Games," Chapter 6, "Creating Arcade and Massively
Multi-Player Online Games (Real-Time)," Chapter 7, "Improving Network
Communications," and Chapter 8, "Removing the Cheating Elements."
Now realize that we have to test every aspect of that—not just the game, but
the mechanisms that we have put in place for:

- Communication
- Multi-player systems
- Cheating/hacking avoidance
- Improving network performance
- Persistent world data storage
- Etc.

This makes testing one of the most important parts of the development paradigm. Part of the reason for this is that a game is one of the
most unpredictable computing systems one can design. Added to this, a
multi-player game is a strongly emergent system in which it is very hard
to tell what kinds of internal states the combination of diverse players
and complex rules/systems will create. The interplay of all the variables
make it very hard to be sure that everything is working as intended under
normal circumstances, and adding a network *and* a multi-player component only compounds this.

Not only do we have to test the game, but also all the supporting systems that make sure that the game delivers in the multi-player networked
environment where not every player has the same skill level or is honest.

This chapter is broken down into several areas:

- **Principles.** This outlines the basic principles of the testing process,
  and how to track and measure it.
- **Network testing.** This encompasses various considerations for the
  different kinds of network-game models (including Web games), at
  the network layer.
- **Logic testing.** This ensures that the code that drives the game is
  tested beyond the usual test cycles required for single-player games.
- **Code re-use in testing.** This novel approach to testing isolates code
  from the system (game) under test and associates it with data that
  can drive automated test processes.

It is also important to know what needs to be tested explicitly with
scenarios designed by humans, and know what is tested implicitly
when those scenarios are executed by play testing. Added to this, it is
worthwhile to break down the scenarios into those that must be tested
by a human play tester as opposed to those that can be tested in an automated fashion.

There is a balance to be struck between the cost of employing people to test and developing the technology to test in an automated fashion. In the latter case, the game developer is reduced to desk-checking the results, which is far cheaper than employing human play testers. However the testing is to be performed, we must always strive to cover as much of the game as possible, knowing that 100% coverage is often an unrealistic dream.

This is a book on the fundamentals of development, and one chapter on testing will not replace the kind of experience and skill that comes from actually *doing* it. That said, this chapter will teach you how to approach the subject and what questions to ask when preparing a network-game development project.

PRINCIPLES OF TESTING

One bane of network programmers' lives is testing. It is difficult to test non-networked single-player games, but when the basis for the game is that geographically diverse players must interact in a virtual environment, it becomes much harder to ensure that the game has been adequately tested.

There are three aspects that need to be given attention:

- **Process:** the various stages and milestones of the testing process
- **Components:** what is going to be tested
- **Types of testing:** how each component is going to be tested, taking account of the process

Once these three points are addressed, you can move on to more specific testing theory and practice, but first we need to be clear on exactly what we mean by the word "testing."

The Testing Process

Broadly speaking, from a real-time software perspective, we can often break down the whole testing paradigm into two principles:

- **Testing for correctness.** This tests to see if the right software has been implemented correctly—i.e., there are no programming errors in the logic. Testing the correctness of the software essentially ensures that the game logic has been correctly implemented on a case-by-case basis. For example, if the game logic dictates that when a player enters a room, the light goes on, and when the player leaves, the light goes out, this can be tested for correctness. If, when the player enters the room, the light fails to go on, then the software has not been correctly implemented. And if when the player leaves, the light stays on, by a similar token, the software has not been correctly implemented.

- **Testing for robustness.** This tests to see if the software will stand up to a barrage of unexpected data and/or logic flows. A robust software application will continue to be correct, even when unexpected data or logic flows might confuse it. For example, if a second player comes into the room and then leaves, and the light turns off, then you could say that this is a case of incorrect implementation because the first player would be left in the dark. But if the players do something unexpected, like try to shoot the light bulb, then the software has to be robust enough to recognize that the light will go out permanently.

This is where it gets more complex for video games, and even more so for networked video games. In any real-time system, there will be issues relating to the response time and ways to make sure that the system responds within a time span that does not cause behavioral issues that have a detrimental effect on the entirety.

However, when a network is involved, lower response times can often be attributed to substandard network programming or unfavorable network conditions. Therefore, it can be hard to figure out what the cause of an issue might actually be—the system, an individual component, or the network in general.

The trick is to make sure that the correctness and robustness principles are both observed, even when simulating network issues, and therefore factoring them out of the equation early on.

Earlier, we noted that programming network games was a case of not bolting it on to an existing (tested) game. This opens up another set of problems: If there is no single-player game, then there is nothing we can test for integral robustness and performance before adding network functionality. So, we might seem to have shot ourselves in the foot by tackling the development process in such a way.

Nonetheless, there are plenty of techniques that can be used to reduce the impact whilst keeping high span of test cases. Some of these involve a little extra work, such as simulating parts of the system that are not available or that we want to react in a predictable manner. (As an aside, when we use the term "predictable," we do not necessarily mean "correct." Predictable behavior that would be unexpected or erroneous in normal playing circumstances is a valid form of test data that is required to ensure that the correctness and robustness of the system is adequately exercised.)

Testing in video games is a whole other possible book, and can involve any, or all of, the following:

- Play testing
- Simulated play testing
- AI-versus-AI testing
- Test-data replay

No doubt each development team will have its own way of doing things, but these four have been selected because they have special significance/application in network-game testing. The reason for this is because they allow wide coverage for low investment—if the game has been developed correctly.

One prerequisite for the above is that we can hook into the game code in such a way as to be able to measure (or *profile*) the performance of each component. In addition, we should be able to inject data into the various interface streams—the interfaces in this case being that which exists between the player and the front-end (otherwise known as the "man machine interface," or MMI), between the client and the server (should this exist), and the between the sever and its component parts. This last will include things like the database, which should be based on third-party components and therefore tested for behavior, at which point it is the data model and any database-side scripting (such as SQL-stored procedures) that are being tested rather than the underlying database system itself.

The first of the above list, play testing, is easy enough to appreciate. The player sits in front of the game (with a real server or simulated behavioral model behind the front-end) and plays through various scenarios. Afterward, the player reports his or her findings. This might seem easy enough, but it is very expensive in terms of people power. If you were to test an entire game from first principles to final shipping copy with 100% coverage, it would likely be prohibitively expensive—hence the need to know how to achieve maximum coverage with a minimum of test cases.

Of course, the next item in the list—simulated play testing—helps to an extent, but it can be tricky to know how far to exercise the system. In other words, a dumb client can be built that will try to achieve 100% coverage, but we don't really know whether the system has been adequately tested for *all combinations* of behavior. This is where in-game AI-versus-AI testing and test-data replay come in. In the former, we allow the AI of a system to play the game, based on mapping input stimuli to responses in the game. In doing so, we assume that the in-game drama that unfolds over several runs allows us to fully exercise the system. This can be helped along by adding some randomness to the finite state machines (FSMs) that govern the versus AI's behavior.

Now, we won't know if we have done this without some kind of empirical measurement, and test-data replay is supposed to help. The principle is that test-data replay takes a set of known test data representing situations in the playing environment that fall into one of three categories of probability of occurrence:

- **Can:** the usual rule-abiding flow of play
- **Cannot:** things that are against the game rules, or could be spoofed by a hacker
- **Should not:** things that are unlikely, but could happen

The first two are obvious enough, but the last grouping includes things like players intentionally running into walls or trying to go through a window rather than a door.

We then replay this test data through a simulated entity (with or without AI) and see how the system responds. This is great for multi-player networked games as we can have several sets of test data and replay the game over and over whilst changing (tweaking) other aspects of the system.

As long as we can measure the results, it makes testing more efficient and effective. There are even possibilities, in a multi-player environment, to play several sets of test data and simulated entities against (or alongside) each other, thereby exercising even more of the system. (Clearly some of this code, and even the data-replay models, are going to be re-useable in the game proper if correctly programmed, but we deal with code re-use in the last section of this chapter.)

Taking into account this suggested methodology, the basic testing process then becomes:

1. Develop the test approach—play testing, simulated play testing, AI-versus-AI testing, or test-data replay.
2. Develop the test data based on in-game actions/stimuli.
3. Apply the test data to the game environment (test).
4. Refine the test data based on results.
5. Refine the game based on results.
6. Change as little as possible/practical and run again.

There are a few things from this process that get lost in most game-testing processes. For example, the test analysts have to take the time to refine the test data in an intelligent fashion, and the developers have to be careful to change as little as possible before running the tests again.

There is a temptation to throw everything but the kitchen sink into the test data during the so-called refinements, and programmers might spot things that they believe need changing (often calling for "improvements") that have nothing to do with the last test run, but that nonetheless have an effect on future test runs. It is easy to get stuck in a loop whereby the test data and code changes are constantly cancelling each other out. But the feedback process is very important, as testing should be a process of continuous refinement—of both the test data and approach as well as the system under test.

On the other hand, nothing beats a devious human when it comes to stretching a system, and there is no substitute for real play testing. These play testers will still need an approach, complete with scripts to follow (the parallel to test data in automated testing), as well as a period of refinement. Again, this refinement should cover what they're supposed to do and how the system is supposed to react.

So, what are we testing? There are several key components that should be tested in this manner, and we shall look at each in turn.

Components

Briefly, the following are the main components in the system that need to be tested:

- **Network:** the connection/data transfer code
- **Interaction:** what many people would classify as the game proper
- **Middleware:** anything that connects the underlying system (hardware or software) with the custom code that makes up the game
- **Database:** the back end that stores all the player data

Different game models may have other components, such as specific hardware controllers (think of steering wheels or *Guitar Hero–/Rock Band*–style peripherals) that need to be tested as well, but this list ought to be fairly standard across all game types.

Network

Obviously, in a book about network-game development, much of the emphasis is on the communication between systems. The network component includes the communication, encoding/encrypting, and session-management aspects of the system. Each must be tested for data throughput, correctness, and simulated network problems and recovery. The reason we do this is to make sure that any mechanisms we have put in place to counteract the problems isolated in Chapter 7 are working correctly.

These include the correction of the following:

- Latency, lag and jitter
- Data corruption
- Out-of-order reception
- Etc.

In addition, the game logic must be tested in cases where we fail to correctly address any of these issues in the network layer to see at what point (if any) the behavior becomes corrupted by the inability of the network layer to cope. Only then can we decide if the system is correctly implemented. Simulating network errors will likely be a large part of this component, and there are third-party tools that exist to synthesize network problems.

Interaction

Principally, this component involves testing the MMI. Luckily, it can be tested using people or automated scripted testing tools. There are two sides to the MMI: the actual reaction of the interface to the player and the communication of the player's intent to the core system.

It is also important that the network indicators and network-level interaction be tested to make sure that even if there are underlying network problems, the experience degrades as gracefully as possible. Part of this should be dealt with in tandem with the network component.

Looking at these aspects may lead to some redesign, redevelopment, and subsequent retesting of the interface and/or underlying network-communications architecture to make sure that, as far as possible, the interaction is not damaged by issues out of the player's control.

Middleware

This includes anything (up to and including off-the-shelf components) that facilitates the relationship between the interface and the game environment. The interaction with the middleware must be tested, as well as the way it performs given the information that it is provided with as part of its integration with the game.

Testing is important because the middleware is often the link between two solutions. For example, cell-phone middleware exists to make porting of games from a non–cell phone platform easier. Therefore, it provides facilities that might not exist in the standard development environment. As such, it has to be properly tested.

The temptation is to assume that some functionality will have already been tested. This is most frequently the case if off-the-shelf components have been used (i.e., forum software, CMS, network-layer tools, etc.). However, it would be unwise to assume that any testing that has been conducted was either complete or correct.

Of course, if the middleware is present in a non-critical part of the system, then the emphasis on testing it can be reduced in favor of spending more time testing those aspects that provide core functionality within the gaming system.

Database

The database is usually where the whole game environment is stored. As such, it becomes one of the most important components in the system. In addition, it is also usually on the critical path, as it needs to be in place before most of the game-environment persistence testing can be performed.

As mentioned, it is vital to test the stored procedures created to help manage the back-office systems. These are like little programs running on the database server that execute tasks better done on the database rather than in memory used for the game proper.

In addition, the various interfaces into the database environment must be checked for correctness (ability to process data) and robustness (in case they receive bogus requests). This last could relate to hackers, rogue software, or just bad client-side programming leading to unexpected behavior.

The database middleware ought to have been tested already. That said, the behavior, capacity, and robustness of the database itself has to be tested in this component. One particularly important aspect of these tests is the stress test, and it is one that can be hard to address. To help in this, stress testing the database can draw from many of the previous techniques, especially in creating sets of randomly populated test data that can be applied en masse to the database to see how it reacts.

Testing Harness

Finally, all of the above must make use of one or more testing harnesses. A test harness is usually a piece of software that makes use of the functions under test, usually in isolation of the larger system. However, several parts of the system can be grouped and tested using a test harness to manipulate them. Other uses for the test harness are to subject the system to simulated behavior and measure responses. This is a key use for the test harness in network game testing, where testing must be extensive to allow for the added complexity of multiple simultaneous users—and a test harness is often the only way to achieve this. These are designed to manage the parts of the system not under test. One guiding principle is that the testing harness not add substantial load to the system. Otherwise, the results can be skewed, particularly in capacity and stress tests.

There are two ways to look at this: as a performance-analysis safety net or as an unfortunate side effect of placing additional load on the system. Whichever camp you fall into, one thing is clear: Any effect that the test harness has needs to be measured and taken into account in the final analysis.

All of the aforementioned components will require some kind of test harness, so it is not something that can be ignored. The fastest-performing test harness may also turn out to be a harness that simply replays test data sets as it does not have to think. Of course, this comes with an additional set of issues: Dumb test harnesses may not be much use in certain circumstances.

On the other hand, AI-based test harnesses may turn out to be potential bottlenecks. This will undoubtedly be the case if many are asked to run on the same system. Again, it is important that any conclusions drawn from results based on load, stress, or testing under conditions of duress are taken with the knowledge that there may have been other influences at work.

An example of the extrapolation that is required is to take a system designed to offer a gaming environment for 1,000-plus players. There is no way that the test team can hope to simulate the attachment of

1,000-plus clients to the system using 1,000 PCs, so there might be one or two PCs (or at most five to 10) tasked with running up to 100 clients each. One thing we can say for sure is that this is highly unlikely to result in the accurate testing of the client interface, because part of any problems might be due to the fact that we are asking so much of each individual PC. In addition, the game server is unlikely to be stressed by 10 PCs running 100 clients each; their combined performance will be well below any stress thresholds in the system. Again, their reaction times will be very slow due to the fact that they are running so many processes.

Of course, this is unrealistic, and we all know that the only way to test the server for capacity is to load up several machines with low-impact test harnesses and let them generate work for the server. Nonetheless, it is this kind of thinking that needs to go into the careful construction of the test cases.

An important consideration is the type of tests that must be conducted at each stage of the development and testing process.

Types of Testing

There are two main types of traditional test methodologies:

- White-box testing
- Black-box testing

We will look at each in turn in a generalized fashion. (Note that the definitions, while standardized in general test theory, have been bent a little to fit into the network game–development paradigm being presented in this book.)

The first type of testing, white-box testing, is totally transparent with respect to the system under test. We can see what each component is supposed to be doing, and what data it processes during the design of the test cases. The game programmer's knowledge is used to make sure that all aspects of (and logic paths through) the system are covered.

The drawback is that if any aspect of the system changes, then the test cases will need to change too, because they are intimately related to the actual data and logic that is inherent in the game. So, white-box testing is really only appropriate at the unit-testing level, before the game is put together for the first time with all the components in place.

Black-box testing, on the other hand, derives test cases from the external behavior of the system. As such, it will usually not be able to trap all the control paths, and the test cases are constructed without knowledge of the internal construction of the system. In game terms, this means that the test cases are prepared from the perspective of the interface (be it the MMI or a logical interface). This might include automated testing using third-party software to take the place of the player, play testing with a human, or substituting parts of the system with dumb test harnesses.

The important point is that the tester should not use any knowledge of the internal structure of the system to perform the tests. The reason for this might not be obvious at first, but relates to the possibility that the tester will unconsciously create a test set that avoids possible problem areas given his or her specialized knowledge.

Strategy

Before starting the testing, it is important to have a high-level strategy that will uncover problems as early in the development process as possible. The following is a best-case strategy, but it will often transpire that not all the various bases can be covered due to budgetary constraints. It is important to understand at what levels which kinds of testing are important, and where testing activities can be trimmed down if required by the realities of the business cycle.

Development Testing

This is white-box testing, hopefully done at the component level so that each one is completely tested before they are combined together as part of the integration phase. Reality dictates that this will rarely be the case, and units may well move into integration before they have been completely tested.

Each tester should know what the behavior of each component will be given a set of inputs, and these inputs should feed forward into future test iterations. This means that it should be possible to trigger certain responses based on inputs to the system on a repeatable basis.

Automated testing is the only way that enough coverage will be achieved that the testers can be confident that each component has been adequately tested. Since white-box test methodologies are being used, it ought to be possible to create test harnesses and replay test data sets that provide nearly 100% test coverage.

There is a drawback: The test harnesses themselves must, of course, be tested. Because of this potential problem area, it is advised to keep the test harnesses as simple as possible, with as little standalone and as much re-used logic as possible. In essence, the more re-use of existing solutions can take place, the less chance there is that the test harness itself will be at fault rather than the system under test.

Alpha Testing

This stage in the test strategy occurs when the first build is ready to go, and should apply to the complete system or at least a completely interactive system. In other words, all the components should be in place in a broad sense, but they may not have the detail that they will later on. For example, there might be wireframes rather than textured objects, or levels might not be as large as they are intended to be in the final game. Nonetheless, all the logic of the game must be in place, as it is at this point that we will also get a first look at the playability of the game and a chance to correct the balance.

Automated testing should play a large part here. It is made possible by the fact that the system can still be tweaked relatively easily without a big impact on the time scale. Removing and adjusting components is still feasible; making changes in the underlying game design, less so.

Beta Testing

This is the first time that the complete system is tested in a black-box style, and probably the first time that a human gets to play the game properly. Of course, different components may find themselves in beta testing at different times. So, the first play through of the client interface may well take place with a simulated server side presented as a set of test-data replayed through a test harness, or as a simple, rule-based, reactive system, designed more to demonstrate the game than to challenge the player.

Again, the play testing probably needs to be mixed in with automated testing, possibly even in the same sessions. This allows one play tester to play in the same system as several simulated players, which helps to make better use of the available person power than having them all play together for extended periods of time.

You must remember that there is a need, at this point, to have strict reporting criteria and key goals. If the play tester is experienced, there may be a temptation to give vague instructions along the lines of "Play the game and see how you get on." If this is the case, however, then the play tester will likely miss some aspects of the game that ought to be tested more fully at this stage. They will still add some unpredictability to the game, though—if not quite as much as in the public beta stage.

Public Beta Testing

This part of the overall strategy is where the general public is permitted to play the game for the first time. It can be a spooky moment for the development team as they wait to see what the playing public makes of the interface, game balance, difficulty levels, accessibility, and so on.

It is also a very labor-intensive phase, as the testers need to be monitored along with the game itself. This makes it an expensive part of the process, and not one that should be extended or repeated unnecessarily.

At this stage, anything beyond minor upgrades will be prohibitively expensive to repair and will more likely result in reducing the available features rather than trying to fix something that could have an impact elsewhere in the game.

It may well also be the first time that the production game servers are exposed to networks other than the private LAN used by the development team. As such, all manner of things can go wrong, and experience has shown that a phased approach is best. After all, if time is taken before the play testers are put into place to bring the system up and check that everything works as far as possible without them, their time will be far more efficiently used when the testing of the game proper begins.

TESTING THE NETWORK LAYER

The network layer includes everything up to and including the client-side networking, but does not include testing the back end or logic. What it *does* include are the bits and bytes that facilitate the transfer of data from one point to the other, as well as the guarantee that the data arrives correctly, in time, and tamper free.

The idea of testing is to get a handle on what the network capability is, but not to see what kind of capacity the whole system has. There is a necessity to check how stable the network-processing layer is and how it can, if need be, be improved—but not with respect to the rest of the system. This is because it is likely that things like the database are scalable—i.e., if you add more hardware, they get faster—and also because they are generally shared resources. So, it is of little interest, when testing the network layer, to have to take account of other potential bottlenecks.

What we do want to know, however, is what kind of load our networking layer will handle. The only way to do this is to try to break it—both at the physical level, with overwhelming traffic frequency, and at the logical level, with corrupted, hacked, delayed, and otherwise tampered-with data.

Simulating Network Issues

Again, there is the need to check for robustness and performance. The system has to be able to cope with both high volumes of traffic (performance) as well as situations in which that traffic is somehow corrupt (robustness). Part of the robustness testing is also to see what happens when the performance threshold is exceeded.

This section deals exclusively with robustness and performance as it relates to the actual transfer of data. To satisfy both these criteria, we also need to make sure that *both* the network layer *and* game logic can deal with the following:

- **Latency:** not getting the data on time once
- **Jitter:** unreliable delays between data bursts
- **Lag:** continued temporal difference between request and response or broadcasts

These can all be simulated using tools that introduce (simulate) network-connectivity issues between one of more systems. These tools typically exist in either hardware or software, or as a system that sits on the network between the client and the server.

Latency Simulation

This is at the base of all network issues, and is a vital part of robustness testing as well as in testing the correctness of any software solution to issues surrounding uneven network communication.

In some cases, this can be simulated as part of the game framework. For example, Microsoft's XNA Game Studio includes a latency and data-loss simulator as standard to help developers test networked games. These are typically used to simulate issues from the *client* side (i.e., as a bolt-on to the client software), but the server side cannot be ignored. To this end, it is worth understanding how latency can be introduced in a test harness. In fact, it is not a complex matter, and simply requires introducing debug code in the network handling layer. This code must be compiled to allow the following

- Delaying packets
- Dropping packets

In addition, it should allow for some basic statistics to be recorded, which will allow for post-mortem examination of the debug code. These should include the following

- Data throughput rates
- Packet loss as a percentage of traffic

In addition, the latency simulator must be capable of being tweaked to allow the following:

- Changing data order
- Variable delays
- Variable packet-drop rates

The key is to make it lightweight (so as not to adversely affect processing) and to place it between the actual interface to the network and the game code itself. An alternative would be to place a piece of hardware that mimics a router but allows the user to introduce the effects noted above on individual connections.

The latency simulator is at the base of the network error–simulation package. From it, many other situations can be simulated, including jitter and lag.

Jitter Simulation

Jitter is sophisticated latency caused by random dropped or delayed packets that results in the data being delivered in an inconsistent fashion. In essence, it can be simulated by changing the rate of data delivery in such a way that the latency varies over time, across a normal distribution curve, in a random fashion.

This last is important, as it requires that the jitter simulation be able to pick a data packet (or data group) at random and subject it to a random amount of latency such that only a small percentage is affected. The data that is affected should be affected in such a way that is unpredictable and where the extent varies.

The effect can be bolstered by randomly changing the order of packets and intermittently dropping packets. Note that these last two are discrete events, whereas the latency part of the jitter simulation is scalar: It has an extent, rather than just a decision as to whether to change the data.

An extended period of jitter eventually becomes lag.

Lag Simulation

This is a simpler form of latency, where the latency simulator is set to delay (drop or swap) packets for an extended period at a constant rate. This is very useful for testing logical workarounds in the code to deal with extended periods of data latency, which are the main cause of the lag effect.

The Network Testing Process

Naturally, introducing such a device will also have an effect on the database-side, and possibly server-side, as well as client-side performance. In other words, network issues can affect the LAN as well as the WAN connections, and it is vital not to ignore the possibility of local problems that will affect the system as a whole.

The key to the testing process is the ability to introduce these facets into the system and then see how it reacts. This should be done in both in an automated way as well as with real humans on the client side. Automation enables us to test a large number of occurrences, whilst the human testing enables us to get an idea of how it feels to play the game when the errors are introduced.

Therefore, we need way to measure the effects on the client interface and the end user (player), as well as the end effects on the system.

This will require quantitative analysis as well as qualitative analysis of the results, with statistics being measured in game by the test harness, as well as question-and-answer sessions yielding information from the players themselves.

Once we have performed the analyses, we can draw conclusions as to the appropriateness of the network programming and logic behind the network handling. Explicitly, we will know if the safeguards that have been written into the system to handle network errors are sufficient.

There several things we can do to simulate network errors:

- Drop packets (especially if using UDP)
- Corrupt packet data
- Delay packets
- Change order of packets
- Etc.

Each of these aspects will attempt to test the network and game logic in a different way, and improvements to the network handling in the game are likely to be made as a result. Because of this refinement process, it is important not to throw too much at the system at once; otherwise, it might become difficult to trace back the origins of a specific handling defect.

On the other hand, if the game is using layers of network protocols for communication, then it can become very important to quickly perform as many corrupted-data and data-delay tests as possible. For example, if UDP is being used, with logic implemented to help counteract the issues that can arise when a non–stream oriented protocol is used, then this has to be tested first.

If the game uses TCP/IP, which is stream oriented and has the benefit of almost guaranteed delivery, then the testing irregularities that are introduced will be different. The logic used to handle the packet synchronization, for example, may be vastly different, and reliant on the inherent stream-handling capabilities of the protocol.

Despite the special nature of the test equipment, testing the network layer in this way follows the same principles as laid out in the beginning of the chapter, so all the same processes and testing types are equally applicable.

Apart from introducing errors and behavioral artifacts into the stream, it is also important to spend time making sure that the network is resilient to high loads.

Load Testing

Load Testing the network layer (and system behind it) requires the following:

- We can throw a lot of data across the network (be it LAN or WAN).
- We can treat that data.
- We can get a response that tells us it was processed.

This means that we need to be able to make some important measurements:

- Requests made (per timeframe)
- Requests treated (per timeframe)
- Response time (per request/response)

While carrying out this testing, there should be limited game functionality behind the network components. In other words, only that game logic required to process the request should be present—i.e., no database connectivity code, and stubs for everything else that uses a server-side shared resource that might be external to the system under test.

The reason for this is simple: We need to be able to measure the network performance in isolation so that when we measure the system's performance as a whole, as part of determining the scalability, we want to be able to factor out things over which we have less control. The network interface tends to be such a thing.

The test team needs to measure and track everything in a spreadsheet. This is useful for creating predictions as to the point at which the network component will fail in the absence of enough test hardware to force the issue. In addition, you must remember also that any encryption and compression needs to be taken into consideration at the server side, as it will affect performance. The client side will be less critical if a strict client/server relationship exists, with all communication passing through the server.

This emphasis will change, however, if the server re-routes data to clients without processing, or where each client may receive direct messages (i.e., for in-game communication between players). In these cases, although rare, it will be necessary to also test the client software under similar conditions and gauge the network performance for them in tandem. The added complication is that a client may need to prioritize server communication over *personal* communication if and when the network becomes saturated.

We start, however, with the assumption that traffic is almost entirely one way.

One Way–Load Testing

Depending on the gaming model being used, it is possible that the vast majority of traffic in the network game will be one way:

- Server → clients
- Clients → server
- Client → client (rare)

Generally speaking, the relationship will be either one to many or many to one, as shown in Figure 9.1.

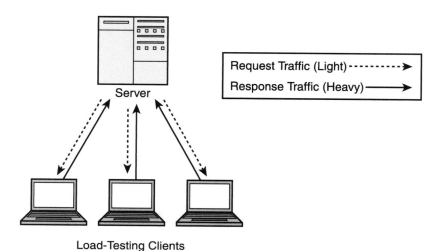

Load-Testing Clients

FIGURE 9.1 Load testing with predominantly request traffic.

From the point of view of the server in Figure 9.1, it has a one-to-many relationship with the clients. Conversely, there are many clients, all communicating with a single server.

Pushing data from the server to the clients can be simulated by simply not putting any "real" systems on the other side. If there is no response to be created (or if there is just a token one), then this can be handled by a single machine pretending to be multiple clients. This can be a simple harness with no logic behind it beyond what is necessary to make sure that the data arrives and can be processed. The idea is to do as much work as possible and make sure that the network can keep up with the data at the physical, logical, and interface levels.

This harness can double as a system for capturing the data, measuring response times, and analyzing network behavior. Of course, the more complex it becomes and the more overhead it requires, then the more distorted the results will become and the fewer clients can be simulated.

This testing model can also be used for e-mail updates in turn-by-turn games, for example; here, it doesn't matter if there is no reply, and we need to test the volume of e-mails that can be reliably sent within a given timeframe.

Load testing the other way round (from client to server) presents more of a problem. Even if an extremely light-weight, trimmed-down client is used, a single machine is less likely to be able to put enough stress on the server. Hence, multiple machines, or a spare server, will be needed to perform the testing correctly.

It is important to put pressure on the network layer, but also to remain realistic. If the game is quite niche (i.e., a specialist game with a low expected following), it is unlikely that it will get 1,000,000 subscribers in a short term. Given this, it is useless to use that as a target figure. Maybe a couple of thousand simulated simultaneous connections, of even a few hundred, will be enough.

Client-to-client testing follows similar rules, but each machine will be required to simultaneously emulate multiple clients. This means that the testing overhead will be even greater, especially since more logic will be needed to effectively simulate the dialog between the two machines.

It is up to the test team to find a balance that is realistic and yet provides test coverage that makes it worthwhile to carry out the tests in the first place.

Duplex-Load Testing

Duplex-load testing involves traffic in both directions, at the same time. We assume that this goes beyond the simple request/response dialog where the flux of data is predominately in one direction—from client to server, or server to client. Figure 9.2 shows the bi-directional nature of the traffic.

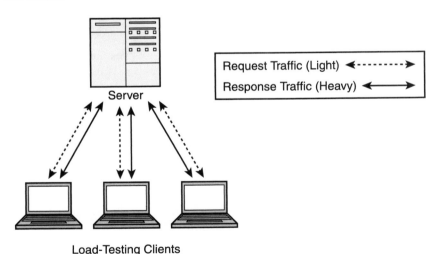

FIGURE 9.2 Load testing with full duplex loads.

Most of the games in the action genre will fall into the network model shown in Figure 9.2. It is especially important for games where the client needs to send data *to* the server whilst it is also expecting to receive updates and other data *from* the server. This goes beyond a simple request/response architecture.

Again, the rendering of the results of the dialog between the two parties is not tested as part of the network load testing. However, there are two points to make. The first is that the data used for testing should not be too artificial, and the data should be processed and a meaningful update posted. It might be randomly generated, but it should follow the profile of data that might occur in the game. Second, it is important to make sure that the client can keep up with the server and vice versa, so any overhead has to be more or less equivalent on both platforms. You should bear in mind that, after all, we are only trying to establish that the network layer is robust enough to process under heavy loads.

This is less important for other gaming models (where a little lag is not an issue) but critical for action games. Consequently, the network, even more than before, is only half of the story; attention must also be paid to the performance of the logic layer, discussed in section "Testing the Logic Layer."

Sustained-Load Testing

The previous sections have assumed that we will be testing peak load. We must also be sure, however, that the network layer is robust under sustained load as well. Note that the volumes of data will likely be lower than during peak-load testing due to the impracticality of being able to generate enough data and the lower likelihood of a sustained load in the production system.

We can tentatively define "sustained load" as a given number of network events (transactions) at a reasonable load (say 60% of total capacity) for an extended period of time (on the order of half to a full day). This is designed to simulate unusually high traffic during a specific in-game campaign, concerted player movement, special event, or just vacation/weekend processing.

The end goal is to ensure that if every anticipated user was active at the same time, the system would be able to cope. The data profile in this case is likely to be a spike (peak-load test) followed by abnormally high activity, but spread in a more typical way, over time (sustained-load testing).

Again, perhaps this is slightly more relevant for action games and games, where the conversation between the client and server is duplex in nature, than in other game forms. However, even a Web game can suffer the ignominy of a false restart when everyone tries to log back in at once after an outage, so this testing is valid for any online game.

This type of testing is especially important for subscription-based services, because there is a relationship between the hardware available and the income generated by players. The cost of increased hardware requirements brought about by an increase in subscribers (users, players) will be offset by the additional income.

If we can't measure the existing capacity, then we cannot estimate the new requirements based on additional players, and therefore have no way of knowing whether the system is cost scalable. By "cost scalable," we mean that the cost of supporting new players has to be balanced out by their subscription payment. That is, obtaining the first new users must not tip the capacity such that extra hardware, which has not been budgeted for, is required. Only after there are sufficient additional users to pay for new hardware can that hardware be implemented.

If the budget assumed that the existing hardware will support 1,000 users (sustained-load test), and the cost of maintaining that has been spread over 1,000 subscriptions, then the 1,001st player to come online will increase the hardware cost disproportionately. In other words, that player's subscription payment will not balance out the cost of supporting him or her—especially if a duplicate system has to be put in place.

Therefore, anticipating how much extra capacity can be gained, whether it will be enough, and how much it will cost compared to the subscription fee should all figure into the measurements being taken during the sustained-load testing.

If the variables are correctly taken into account, a system should be budgeted for whereby the capacity of the server is *overcompensated* by the income that it generates. Then, when the tipping point occurs and new hardware must be acquired, at least it is already partially paid for. (Of course, at this point, the logic behind the synchronization of the two systems has to be revisited, and a whole new set of testing problems present themselves as the game environment becomes spread over multiple machines.)

For Web games, however, this cost might not be relevant or useful to estimate, since the cost base is usually much lower than for a dedicated gaming server. In essence, Web games can be implemented more cheaply because they do not place high loads on the server, especially if they are turn based with daily activity limits. Incidentally, it might seem as if this only applies to Internet games, but the same exercise should also be done for LAN games, as it will be important to know how much hardware must be taken to the next LAN party.

Peak-Traffic Testing

The peak-traffic tests stress the system to a given point, simulating the simultaneous actions of a collection of players. This could also be called a "bulk sign on," as experienced by *Eve Online*, which holds the record for the number of simultaneously connected players. During the *Futuris Powerplay* gaming show held in Brussels, Belgium, one of the *Eve Online* servers seemed to fall over, and the team on the desk held its collective breath as we witnessed the re-logging-in of thousands of players. Testing for this kind of event is vital to maintain the image of the game. (*Eve Online* managed to cope with the sudden influx of players re-connecting, and, indeed, the only reason that anyone knew there had been such an event was by the fact that the players went offline and then came back.)

After such an event, the system is usually given time to recover—either naturally or by enforcing play limits—as the system caches are emptied and the databases re-aligned. While peak activity takes place, there are likely to be some tasks that are suspended until time can be found to service them, and it is important that they are not put of indefinitely.

Peak-traffic testing should also test these safety systems. Likewise, for systems that cache requests and process them internally at a different rate than that at which the requests arrive, peak-traffic testing will be important.

Depending on social and geographic trends in the target audience, there will likely be different usage peaks during the playing day. This will mean that there will be occasions where there are many players online at once and the system has to be robust enough to cope—or fail gracefully if a certain threshold is reached.

Client-Side Considerations

We have looked mainly at emulating multiple clients with a single machine, but for WAN gaming, it is also important to look at some other situations. For example, players might be connecting over thousands of kilometers of fiber-optic cable, or dialing in using a plain old telephone line.

Getting geographically diverse clients might be an issue, and the cost of doing so has to be weighed against the expected performance bottleneck that it creates. It is likely that the bottleneck is elsewhere than at the network level, given the performance of networks today. If, however, the server is located in a place that is not well connected to the Internet, then this may well be a problem—especially if the majority of the expected clients are located in places that have ultra-fast network connections.

In addition, many of the same tests have to be conducted with diverse client systems such as hand-held or cell-phone devices, which cannot be easily simulated. The question here is, How can we be sure that the clients can cope with the data being thrown at them? The answer, of course, is that we cannot—unless we test. So, load, sustained, and peak testing will also apply to clients in these circumstances, and it all goes hand in hand with making sure that the logic layer, as well as the network layer, is up to the job.

TESTING THE LOGIC LAYER

Having tested the network layer and everything that manages the transfer of data in safety and with a modicum of guaranteed delivery, we must now turn our attention to testing the logic that is behind the game itself. This follows the usual testing practices for single-player, non-networked games, and these aspects are covered in more detail in other books on the subject of game development.

There are, however, a few things that are worth mentioning in the context of network games. First, we shall assume that the logic layer in this case comprises:

- The front end (Web browser, plug-in, proprietary front end, etc.)
- The game server middleware logic (everything that is not network related)
- The back-end database
- Supporting third-party components

It is important to note that this list leaves out the network communication, compression, security, and encryption layers. We will only mention those aspects where they touch the above components—for example:

- In scope: peak login requests, player logs in, session tested against database, session updated in database, password decoded and verified, etc.
- Out of scope: peak network requests for static encrypted data

An obvious part of being able to test this is being able to simulate player interaction with the game environment.

Simulating Player Interaction

Player interaction can happen at several levels within the game, from the front-end to the logical interaction of the players' in-game representations with each other and the game system. This section looks at the interaction with the game environment, not necessarily via the front-end interface. Actual testing of this component is covered later in this chapter, in the section "Testing the Client Software."

Given that the network layer has already been tested and the capacity of the network is known, this aspect can be left out. This, in turn, means that multiple clients on the local system can be simulated over a much faster, higher-capacity network connection. This is very important because we want to get as much testing of the logic done in as short a time, and in as automated a way, as possible so as to reduce the cost of testing and make the whole process more efficient.

To make sure that we are exercising the logic in a way that touches as much of the game design as possible, scenarios have to be created that consist of sequences of actions:

- Valid action chains
- Non-valid action chains
- Mixed action chains

These should feel vaguely familiar, as they are very similar to the approach we used in testing the network layer. Here, again, the system is therefore being tested for things like

- **Robustness.** It doesn't fall down when multiple bad requests are made.
- **Scalability.** It can process multiple good requests in sequence.
- **Interoperability.** It correctly detects close-proximity player actions.

The last point is primarily important for massively multi-player games (action or turn based) where the action sequences can change based on other actions taken by players in close proximity to each other. This does not mean close *physical* proximity, but *logical* proximity within the game space. If you are finding this hard to grasp, then try to imagine two players approaching each other in game space, and the list of actions that could be carried out. If one of the players chooses to talk rather than fight, the context-sensitive logic has to be able to deal with the fact that there are two possible action sequences that can be offered and that they are not mutually exclusive. In other words, just because one player chooses not to fight doesn't preclude the other from taking a more violent stance.

The first item, robustness, means creating situations that are unexpected. Clearly, only the game designer can decide what those might be, and the best way to actually do it is to generate huge amounts of test data and throw it at the system (see the section "Re-Using Prediction Code in Testing" later in this chapter). Robustness testing is, of course, important for any game, but it is essential in testing network (and particularly online) games, which are much more unpredictable. As we have pointed out in the course of the book, multi-player games are by their very nature strongly emergent systems; as such, only extensive testing will ensure that they are working correctly at every level.

Scalability simply means trying to make sure that the system can cope at various levels. This should not be confused with the playability of a game designed for thousands of users that only gets tens and is hence rendered unplayable. That is a design problem, and as such is important, but not part of this book, which is about turning a design into reality. Scalability in this case simply means making sure that the in-game logic can handle various levels of player interaction.

A final point worth making: What happens when there is a usage mismatch and the network can't cope with the peak processing, or vice versa? This aspect also needs to be tested. By stripping out the network layer when testing the logic part, we can be sure that the logic layer is at least as capable as the network layer. This ought to suffice.

Bearing the above in mind, you ought to be able to devise some devious plans for testing the logic. However, we cannot neglect two important stress-testing parts: the middleware and the database, which we shall look at now.

Stress-Testing the Middleware

It is important to make sure the server can keep up with the expected number of clients—a task that is largely dealt with at the network layer in the network tests. This is only the front-end bottleneck, however, as there is also bound to be a lot of facilitating software, which I choose to place under the general umbrella term "middleware."

Thus, the middleware, in this case, includes the operating system as well as any file-sharing mechanisms, backup software, and other programming items that support the game whilst not actually being a part of it, per se. Naturally this also includes third-party components and in-line tools. An example of a third-party component might be a graphics-rendering subsystem (either online or off—i.e., Torque), and in-line tools might refer to data-generation systems that create bits of the game environment procedurally as the players explore new areas.

These all have to be subjected to stress testing, even if you believe that they have been tested adequately for the services they bring. One of the key advantages of using middleware is that it speeds the development process, and a big part of this is being able to rely on the fact that the components are tested. That said, you never know to what level they perform until you try—hence the necessity to stress test them at every level. The same goes for subsystems, such as databases.

Stress-Testing the Database

As with other third-party components, it is important to check that the database can keep up with the rest of the system. If caching has been implemented (where updates are posted during quieter times), then this also needs to be exercised to check that it is working correctly *and* that in-between caching the system still operates as expected.

Again, like network testing, stress testing can be thought of in terms of sustained traffic and peak traffic. This enables us to check that the database is durable, scalable, and robust:

- Error conditions (peak/sustained)
- Number of objects (players, system artifacts, player generated and system generated)
- Reaction time (i.e., does it slow down as more data is added?)

The same kinds of questions need to be asked about the scalability and organization of the data-storage component as of the server layer as a whole. This is especially true in terms of pricing the system. In other words, we need to know how much it would cost to add another user, another 100 users, or another 1,000. Stress testing lets us know at what point the database will begin to fail to support the operations that we throw at it.

At some point, we have to make the decision to split the game environment over several databases. Besides the logical separation, and the change in game logic that supports this, we also need to know who will bear the additional cost. Stress-testing the database, as before with the network layer, lets us find the cost of this tipping point—but it does take rather a lot of data, using white-box testing, to get accurate results.

Database Test Automation

Lots of database testing can be automated, both by throwing data at it through a proprietary front-end as raw database access statements or through automated manipulation of the client system. The first approach is faster and easier to deploy; the second is a step closer to reality. Different stress-testing tasks will require different levels of automation. Clearly, it is useless to spend time on unrealistic test cases, so a balance must be found.

The data itself need not always be meaningful, except in the context of the game environment, design of the database, and possible values of the various data types. As long as the database scheme is adhered to, the data can be generated more or less at random.

For example, in test terms:

```
Guy W. Lecky-Thompson        is just as valid as
Eud m. Nohbd=hgcwuyei        or even
Abc D. Efghi-Jklmnops        but not
123 4. 56789-01234567        (interpretation = numerical)
```

Some of the test data will also need to contain specific items designed to break the schema, and this falls into the general white-box testing of the system as a whole. Again, it is useful to have a concept of valid, invalid, and unlikely (borderline) test cases to draw from, designed by those involved in creating the database infrastructure.

Part of the logic and stress testing is to check how the logic layer responds to database errors. There are many ways in which errors at the database level can be dealt with—from simply reporting the error and standing down the system to gracefully recovering and trying not to affect the flow of the game at all. Different systems and different designs will have different solutions, but it remains important to check that, even if the most benign solution (system halt) has been chosen, the required operations take place if errors are encountered. Again, this requires a high level of test data.

Vast amounts of test data can, and therefore will, need to be generated. This technique is especially useful when testing non-interactive, multiplayer network games, as we shall now examine.

Testing Non-Interactive Games

One might think it would be easier to get non-interactive network games right, but this is not necessarily the case. Part of the problem is that they tend to take longer to play out, and therefore it takes time to achieve the same level of coverage. This means they can be expensive to test manually, so the emphasis ought to be on automated testing (see the last section of this chapter, "Prediction Is AI in Practice"). This reduces the need to involve humans to play the game at the regular speed, which is not usually cost effective. So, testing non-interactive games requires some ingenuity to make sure that they are correctly exercised.

In addition, with Web games in particular, there is an additional aspect to test—the presentation layer. This is something that the game developer only has limited control over since different browsers may render the results differently.

Web Games

There are a number of techniques that must be used to test the Web interface of a game, and we have to attack the problem at several levels:

- **Visual keys:** i.e., reading data returned by the system
- **Interaction with the simulated user:** i.e., clicks and key presses

In order to link the simulated user actions to the result, it is necessary to scrape the HTML that is returned for information (status), and then interact using something like AutoHotKey (AHK) or WinRunner (or other Mercury tools) to simulate mouse and keyboard action.

To help the scraping process, it is sometimes a good idea to put comments in the generated HTML, using the following syntax:

```
<!-- comments -->
```

Advanced interaction can be done via JavaScript (pseudo AJAX), again through AHK, or by direct manipulation of the browser through an externally scripted interface. This interface must be capable of sending key presses to the main window to emulate the user behavior.

This key-press approach is easier than trying to manipulate the mouse unless it is known exactly where each of the elements will appear on the screen, because different browsers may well put them in different places. Where the only interface is mouse based, without keyboard handling at all, a human has to be used to check the interface across different platforms. However, since all browsers respond to the Tab key for moving between fields/links/controls, and the space bar for activation (as well as the Backspace key for navigation), it can save time to take this approach for game logic testing.

A simple example is in testing a sign-up form. If we assume that there are two fields—player name and e-mail address, both mandatory—we can test various data-entry possibilities and scrape the results page to check whether the constraints have been correctly applied. Again, we can use generated data for this to expand the test data set beyond what would be feasible if real people were expected to sit in front of the machine and type.

The mechanics include sending Tab-key-presses followed by normal key presses, and making sure that the form is submitted. An alternative is to retrieve the document object model (DOM) using JavaScript and XML, and set the fields explicitly.

The final step is to trigger the form submission This is marginally more complex, but also linked explicitly to Web gaming using clients that support JavaScript and an HTML, XML, or XHTML front end.

Part of the testing solution will also need to measure the critical performance indicators. However, it is unlikely that you will be able to test for a large quantity of simultaneous clients unless a large number of machines is available; that will likely have to be left for the public beta.

On the other hand, multiple, faster-than-human requests can be made using the browser over a local network (the end product will likely be delivered over a WAN/the Internet) by using the above mechanisms. This enables us to measure

- Server reaction time
- Client rendering time
- Mean time to failure

From the above, we can estimate the capacity as well as whether the game logic works at all. A similar approach can be taken for e-mail games, where the data transfer is purely on the basis of an exchange of plain-text e-mails; obviously, here we can simulate many, many clients on a single PC platform.

E-mail (and Text Message) Games

One of the great aspects of play-by-e-mail games is that they allow the ultimate flexibility in terms of platform. In fact, any platform with e-mail can play. But the drawback is that there is the widest scope for misinterpretation or erroneous submissions. This means that the server has to be robust enough to accept everything from valid requests to spam without falling over. Ideally, everything in between should be be tested, just to make sure that the parsing logic is robust enough to deal with variable levels of player competence in presenting their action requests. Cell-phone text-message games have an advantage in that there is less possibility to spam the server with erroneous requests.

It is easy to test the logic locally, too, by supplying text files that can be parsed by the server and the relevant changes effected on the back end. This enables the developer to create vast sets of test data and measure the responses of the game server.

At the same time, because of the batch nature of the game, performance is also less of an issue—after all, for a daily-update game (likely to be the most frequent of update cycles), the server has several hours to perform various tasks. Each of these has to be tested, and will include the following:

- Processing incoming e-mail
- Deciding the consequences of players' actions
- Generating the new game environment
- Forwarding status e-mails to players

It is the last three items in this list that are likely to be the most time consuming and error prone, provided that a pre-processing software solution is used to remove any e-mails that are clearly garbage from the queue.

To avoid denial of service (DOS) attacks, the mechanism that separates the three categories of e-mail must also be extensively tested. These categories are as follows:

- Valid requests: actionable
- Possibly valid requests: return to sender
- Junk (a.k.a spam): drop

This last is vital—you don't want to spend time processing spam. Again, you should see echoes of the test data sets from previous sections—valid, invalid, borderline—which point to the correct strategy and processes to use.

One point to note is that the possibly valid requests should be rejected in real time to allow the player a chance to resubmit. Each player might also be required to send in several e-mails to secure his or her move (action) quota, depending on the game model implemented. This approach is midway between online and offline gaming.

Online/Offline Games

One genre of multi-player network games provides a real headache for testing: what I call "online/offline games." These include games like *Perplex City*, for example, where there is a very tangible link between the real and virtual worlds. It becomes impossible, at this point, to test every aspect, because it is an extremely complex gaming model to apply.

These games also unfold at a leisurely pace such that it is unlikely that an error at a given time will substantially affect the outcome of the game. The game can even be in a state of perpetual development as the end goal is reached, as long as the whole thing is planned correctly from the outset—including provision testing.

The thing with test data is that each piece would just be one isolated incident in a socially advanced game model. Thus, the notion of test data changes slightly. The socially advanced aspect is important. More than other kinds of games, the model benefits from a slow unfolding of events. Each piece of interaction between players (at all levels in the real and virtual world) helps to spread the clues. These clues are destined to eventually provide the solution to the game, as well as opportunities for espionage, false leads, and other devious "trust nobody," conspiracy-style gameplays by the system and players alike. (As noted in Chapter 8, this is not classified as cheating unless the game's creators have taken explicit steps to prevent/punish such behavior.)

Testing such a complex interplay of various beings in the virtual and real worlds is, sadly, impossible in quantitative terms. In qualitative terms, however, we can plan for various test cases that comprise detailed "what-if" scenarios. But this approach is naturally more about blue-sky thinking and discussion than it is about empirical results. Nonetheless, all the stress, load, and interface testing still holds. After all, the game might become very popular, and the players still need a way to communicate, be it through online forums, live Web chat, or a virtual world such as Google's *Lively* or *Second Life*.

Testing the Client Software

In a nutshell, we test the client to make sure that it can cope with the demands placed on it. If the network game under development is based on a single-player action game, then it will, of course, have been tested as part of the normal development cycle.

In addition, multi-platform online games that use the Web browser to access the system will have different capabilities than those used in development. These cases need to be tested as well.

We shall make a distinction between testing a Web-browser (virtual) interface and a client package that is completely under the control of the software developer. The latter has the advantage that it should, from a software point of view, be completely understood, making white-box testing that much easier.

Proprietary–Client Software Testing

The proprietary client is the piece of software that is used to interact with the game environment. In a sense, it is the portal through which the game environment can be manipulated by the player, and the tool that the player uses to interact with other entities in that game environment.

The capability of the client software has to be tested on several levels:

* As a gaming interface
* As a conduit for player actions
* As a relay for the state of the game environment

This last item includes other players. It is important that the client software is capable of reacting to changes very quickly. In reality, it must react at least as quickly as human players can perceive that those changes will have an effect on their progress through the game and/or their immediate situation.

Clearly this means that the test harness must be the ultimate player, able to respond quickly and evaluate the situation almost immediately. All the other principles of performance and measuring that performance also apply, which places additional burdens on the developer of the test harness to make a robust test platform. In addition, testing across multiple platforms might be important to maximize reach. Of course, if it is a single-platform release, this will be less important.

Web-Usability Testing

Despite fact that HTML, XHTML, XML, CSS, and JavaScript (the most likely development languages for Web games) are all well-documented standards, different platforms do react slightly differently.

There are many browsers, and some of these are platform dependent:

* Windows: IE, Firefox (Opera)
* Mac: Safari
* Mobile: Opera
* Linux: Firefox, Opera
* Etc.

Often, the best solution is to pick something that is closed binary platform independent like Macromedia Flash, or up-and-coming cross-platform solutions like Adobe AIR, Yahoo! Widgets, or Opera plug-ins.

With the exception of the last, these have the advantage of being non-browser dependent, and of rendering results in a similar way across all supported platforms.

In addition, there are the various open standards like the Facebook API, which allow games to be deployed under slightly more interoperable standards. These are linked, of course, to the platform (Facebook, MySpace, etc.).

All target platforms need to be tested using the same scenario and the same set of supposed player actions, and must be verified by a human. It is currently very difficult to test Web interfaces of this nature automatically. This makes the testing process very resource intensive—more so, in fact, than with a proprietary software application that accesses the system via the network component, where the actual code can be linked into and vast data sets used to test the system. The final outcome is that Web-usability testing often has to be performed by a human, and that makes it expensive.

RE-USING PREDICTION CODE IN TESTING

There are many things that we can do to help produce a good test platform, but all of them rely on some measure of programming. Code re-use at the testing level—i.e., taking code that has been tested in unit testing and redeploying it for use in alpha and beta testing—is not a new idea. It is, however, one that is not always appreciated, and so it is worth taking a few moments to outline how code that is used for prediction in a game can be turned around and used to test the logic of the game.

When the network game is created, in order to help mitigate some of the effects of network disconnection and/or slowdown, it is possible to use local processing power to try to predict what will happen in various situations. Games such as *Street Fighter IV* use this technique to level the playing field between players of differing network experience.

For example, a player positioned at a certain place in the 3D space that represents the physical (virtual) game environment might have limited movement options. It ought to be possible to predict, given the player's position and trajectory, where he or she will be in the next time slice—provided the player does nothing to change it.

Lots of things cannot be predicted, but enough *can* that we can make up for network stutter and provide a smooth experience. The reliability of inter-network connections (between networks that make up the Internet, for example) does not allow us to be sure that packets of data will always arrive in a timely—or even regular—fashion. This means that, depending on the choices made regarding the sampling frequency for the data to be relayed (by the client, usually), there may be a gap that needs to be filled in by the AI until such a time as the next bit of information is relayed. Prediction helps us to fill that gap.

Prediction Is AI in Practice

Any game with non-player characters (NPCs) has to have AI in it to manage them. This AI code can be re-used in the testing process, which means that we are redeploying some (tested) core game code for higher-level testing functions. The game is, in a way, playing against itself. In-game entities that are not controlled by the players will, after all, need to react, but also preempt, based on what the player is likely to do next. They are, in a sense, also players.

The only advance knowledge that is required is that of the system and the capability to synthesize behavior that is known to exercise that system. This is an abstraction that can be coupled with the AI that makes up the prediction/reaction of the system. The result ought to be a robust test bed that can be used to exercise a large proportion of the system. The temptation might be to also test the initial AI in this way, but clearly that approach will work only if we also admit that the AI will be in a state of flux as we uncover issues with its behavioral modeling. This also makes the testing process that much more complex and should be avoided.

The exact proportion of automated testing against human testing is linked to the stage at which we are doing the testing. The aim is to present a mechanism by which we can approach the testing at various stages in the most cost-efficient manner. For example, early-stage testing should be automated, as we expect more basic errors (and more total errors) to be present in early development of the game.

What is important is to concentrate on testing at the anticipated level of player involvement. This measurement of involvement is what sets network-game testing apart from other testing projects. Potentially, there are more players, more systems, and more situations in which the system can be placed. Therefore, we need more data and more active entities to be able to test the system fully than in a single-player non-networked game. This is why we look to a combination of AI, simulation, and data-set generation to provide extensive test coverage at a lower cost point than we might otherwise anticipate.

Alpha Testing

In an ideal world, alpha testing occurs when the previously tested modules of the game are brought together for the first time and the emergence takes hold. It might also be the first time that some of the unit-tested modules are brought together.

At this stage, we might anticipate that the players will not be able to fully explore the game system. This might be because not everything is fully functional or because of constraints brought about by the game being variously halted during testing activities, by system errors, or by other issues identified by the testing process itself.

So, we might be able to establish limits such as the following mix:

10% player
90% simulated

This means that we anticipate that 90% of the system should be tested in an automated fashion—in other words, by applying test data to in-game entities controlled by the test system at high speed. It should, logically, catch most of the more basic errors that could be present in the system. Only 10% of the time spent testing will be done by real players, who should explore the higher-level functions of the game system under test. This 10% should begin only after the system is 90% stable following the automated testing.

Beta Testing

The beta phase may well introduce the game to external players (i.e., a public beta) for the first time. It is also likely the first time that a more or less complete gaming environment is deployed for testing. Due to this, the game environment as a whole should therefore be populated in the following fashion:

20%–30% player
70%–80% simulated

This implies that the game environment, as it is being played, consists of a number of simulated players playing either with or against the human players, and the aim is to completely exercise the gaming mechanisms.

Whereas before we broke the testing process down into two separate processes, player and simulated, in the beta phase, because all the basic errors should have been removed by unit and alpha testing, we are now suggesting that the actual in-game AI entities play side by side with real players.

Whether or not the game developer chooses to actually imbue the virtual players with any kind of AI beyond being able to just play the game, one thing must be certain: that the testing is appropriately exercising the logic of the system such that every possible avenue of play is explored.

AN OVERVIEW OF TESTING OPTIONS

The topics we have covered relate to all aspects of testing—from the client to the server. If the advice here is followed, it should yield a stable, robust, yet high-performance gaming platform.

The cost of the testing process should be realistic if the code that is deployed has been fully tested and if appropriate bits have been re-used to reduce the chance of untested code making its way into the chain. For example, testing Web games can often be reduced to automated interface clicking and validation of interface artifacts. In this way, the game can be very rapidly tested, and the rough edges smoothed over before human play testing begins. If a human has to play test a Web game from first principles, it is often a very tiresome and frustrating process—much more so than for testing other platforms—because of the nature of the Web interface.

Client/server action games have a slightly different spin: the interface software (the game proper) has to be tested apart from the server-side software. However, here we have the advantage that the client side can be simulated, even before it is ready, by software that essentially becomes the test platform. We stated that the network component should not feel as if it has been bolted on as an afterthought. In the testing paradigm that we describe here, the old argument that the client side has to be ready before testing can begin becomes obsolete. We do not even foresee the possibility of a single-player game that might need to be complete before testing can begin, so that would make that particular argument redundant. The game has to be tested as it is being developed, and developed starting with the logic and network component, with the visible part of the game tested last.

All the disadvantages that this might appear to represent—specifically in terms of the lack of visible progress as the server side is developed without the client side—are outweighed by the amount of re-use for testing and development of code.

In essence, the server side is tested in isolation, while the client side is tested against an abstraction of the server that uses the same test code as the simulated client that was used to test the server. This circular testing methodology helps to make sure that everything is tested to the same standard, using *the same scenarios*, but reversed.

A MUD-style, turn-by-turn game lies somewhere in between a Web game and an action game. Communication jitter and lag are often more important and less able to be glossed over than in an action game. Every word counts, and so the emphasis has to be on testing the weak link in the chain: the network layer. We can afford to do this level of network testing and streamlining in a turn-by-turn game because the remainder of the system is, by comparison, less complex than other kinds of networked multi-player games.

Testing can, in general, be handled by throwing technology or people at it. Both come with costs, however. The pertinent question becomes: Does the cost of the technology (probably created by people) compare favorably to both the results achieved by that investment and the equivalent cost of doing it manually? Clearly, re-use at the testing, automation, and even coding levels will increase the likelihood of being able to say that the automated testing has achieved a higher efficiency and therefore lower total cost than using armies of play testers.

Developers and testers understand this, but designers need to be aware that the system they want must be able to be tested in an efficient manner. The risk, if testing is not designed in, is that there will not be enough resources left for testing, and an unfinished product will be shipped and almost immediately patched.

Automated test technology ought also to be reusable across projects if it is to satisfy the above criteria. Although it is also likely that testers could be re-used on future projects, it is often less of a concrete investment—not to mention the tax benefits of being able to write off the cost of actually *creating* something as opposed to just hiring people on a short-term basis.

So, testing is not just about letting a few college students play games for hours on end. It's part of the design, part development, and part business strategy that powers any game, and is even more important in networked multi-player games than in almost any other kind of computer software system.

10

NETWORK PROGRAMMING PRIMER

In This Chapter

M uch of this chapter is really only applicable to online real-time network games, which need to communicate using a local area network (LAN) or wide area network (WAN) connection. Some parts deal with logic that is equally applicable to other gaming models, and these are noted where appropriate.

Other types of game—for example, Web games played through the browser and so on—don't directly manipulate the network interface, and therefore do not necessarily require an understanding of the details of network programming in order to make them work.

However, it is essential that we follow up the theories and abstract implementation details with some concrete discussion of the building blocks of network programming. These fundamental topics include the following:

- Sockets and socket programming
- Polling and other techniques for multi-player processing
- Client/server game programming
- Open source code libraries

The aim of the chapter is to ensure that, having designed and developed a well-behaved network game, the underlying networking can be implemented using off-the-shelf code to speed development, whilst keeping the principles of stability and security that such projects require. It is, however, merely a discussion of the fundamentals. There are details and implementation tricks that network game programmers will learn over time. Nonetheless, what is presented here should allow you to hit the ground running.

An Introduction to Socket Programming

A "socket" is a programming construct that allows the software application (in this case, a game) to talk to other instances of software applications over a network connection. It hides the actual implementation of the bits and bytes communicating with hardware behind a logical abstraction.

Each piece of network hardware (wireless, wired, Bluetooth, Wi-Fi, etc.) has its own particular foibles. These are encoded in the driver, thereby abstracting the problem away from the programmer—that is, the programmer only needs to know what he or she wants to implement, and leave the actual hardware control to the driver. What we are left with is a clear interface, common across most (if not all) code libraries, that allows us to implement networking easily and fairly portably.

Sockets are associated with ports as a way to identify them in the system. While it is perfectly possible to open a socket that is not linked to a specific port, it is often a great help if the port is used as a way to separate communication streams. It is one possible way of identifying multiple connections. As we shall discover, however, there are many other ways of implementing multiple network connections from the point of view of the server. And that is the crux of network gaming: It is multi-player, which implies multiple network connections.

Before we go on, it is worth pointing out that the networking bottle-neck is more likely to be the processor than allocating sockets and ports. By the time you run out of ports, the chances are that the machine is approaching saturation.

Types of Sockets

There are two principle types of sockets:

- Stream sockets (sometimes referred to as SOCK_STREAM)
- Datagram sockets (sometimes referred to as SOCK_DGRAM)

A "stream socket" is oriented around a permanent connection, and is part of the TCP protocol. This connection may bounce up and down, causing jitter, but every packet sent ought to be received in the correct order by the client system. This statement glosses over some of the more technical aspects of how this is achieved, but as far as the network library is concerned, it is more or less true. This doesn't mean that you can dispense with logic to detect out-of-sequence packets, but in principle, they should not be prevalent in the system.

A "datagram socket," on the other hand, is one that operates on the principle of "open, send, close." In other words, it is not permanently connected to the remote system, and as such offers no guarantee of flow control or deliverability whatsoever. In practice, this means that if you want to build a game over UDP/IP, you need to add a layer that makes sure that the packets arrive as intended. This includes checking that they are in the right order, because the only guarantee in the UDP protocol is that if the data arrives, it will be error-free.

The networking protocols that we look at here are TCP/IP and UDP/IP. The "IP" stands for Internet protocol, and deals with routing issues, which are not covered in any detail here. They mainly concern themselves with how the data gets from A to B. We are more concerned with the data itself.

Many streaming data services, including multi-player video games, use UDP. These implementations have a layer that deals with the vagaries of the UDP protocol. UDP can be very useful simply *because* no connection is needed, rather than despite it. Due to this, we care much less about things like dropped packets and jitter because UDP is part of the equation. In many ways, UDP makes the whole networking paradigm easier to implement, as long as we accept that there will be some natural wastage in the information exchange.

This means that we have to explicitly compensate for the following:

- Lost packets
- Delayed packets
- Out-of-sequence packets
- Dropped connections

As long as we can compensate for this inherent lack of a permanent connection (by only exchanging data in very small, isolated chunks for example) then UDP is a great protocol. However, if we have to exchange larger, more frequent chunks of data, then the TCP protocol offers much better intrinsic flow control.

Naturally, TCP does have some overhead, which might make it less attractive, but this overhead is there to make sure that the data arrives correctly. This is vital for things like Web pages and MUDs, where any loss of information means that the page or displayed data is corrupted.

For a game like *Quake*, however, it can be relatively unimportant that there is the occasional bit of lag, network latency, or dropped packet causing jitter because it can be compensated for. Academic studies (for example, "The Effect of Latency and Network Limitations on MMORPGs" by Tobias Fritsch, Hartmut Ritter, and Jochen Schiller [FRI01] show that players are very resilient (and tolerant) toward these kinds of issues, as long as the outcome of the game is not unduly affected.

In short, as jitter and latency increase, the game flows less and less well—but players are willing to put up with an enormous number of problems before they abandon the game completely. It's nice to know, but not something we should build into our network handling; we must always strive for the best communication possible.

In addition to the two protocol types, there are also two ways in which we can use sockets:

- Blocking sockets
- Non-blocking sockets

We deal with these in detail later on; for now, we should just mention that blocking sockets are the usual default. The problem is that lots of functions used in socket programming run the risk of blocking the sockets.

The worst-case scenario is that a program can find itself in a busy waiting loop, blocking the socket even when there is nothing to do, as control will not be returned to the program until data arrives to be processed. One way of avoiding this is by using non-blocking sockets. Non-blocking sockets are simply not allowed to block. Each call to the socket will return regardless of the presence of data. This has its own problems, however, as polling for data in this way eats up CPU time. We look at some ways to make the polling process slightly more efficient later on in the chapter.

There is, however another option, called "multiplexing." Multiplexing means that you need only to *monitor* a set of sockets, and then send or receive over the ones that actually have data. This removes the risk of causing a block on one of the sockets, and removes the need for using CPU-intensive non-blocking sockets.

Multiplexing is necessary for server applications or smart clients having more than one socket connection. For example, any system that is communicating with multiple remote hosts will benefit from multiplexing, but it is less necessary for clients that are running one connection, as they can use non-blocking sockets.

The point is this: The game should never, as a client or a server, get stuck in a loop waiting for data, because if it does so, there is a risk that *nothing else* in the game will be able to run. No more screen updates, database accesses, or serving other clients. Blocking is bad and has to be avoided at all costs.

Protocol Layers

The socket is at the sharp end of the network programming paradigm. It is the point of communication with the outside world. However, the data itself has to be correctly presented to the interface for the network communication to work.

For each protocol that is used (TCP, UDP, IP, etc.), the data needs to be correctly encapsulated. This essentially means that the data is put into an envelope, with the envelope itself containing information that is pertinent to the network protocol but not necessarily to the game. For example, the envelope might have instructions as to what to do with the data, usually contained in some kind of header, when it is picked apart by the recipient. This might include specific encoding, encryption, or in-game identification data. The outermost layers (envelopes) contain address information so that the transport layer knows what to do with the packet of data. This is depicted in Figure 10.1, which shows layers of data encapsulation.

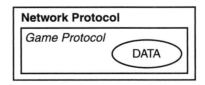

FIGURE 10.1 Packet headers and layers.

Figure 10.1 is a very simplified representation of the layers that are involved in network communication. There can be more or fewer layers, some added by the protocol (networking) library, and some that are proprietary to the game itself.

At the heart is the payload data, which is then usually encapsulated in a layer that is part of the game logic. This inner envelope may or may not be present, depending on the complexity of the error checking and security that is deployed. Then the resulting data is treated as payload and encapsulated in a layer that is used by the network to deliver the data to the end point. To understand this separation more fully, we can look at the OSI Layered Network Model in gaming terms:

Application	Data delivered to the game
Presentation	How the data is represented for transport
Session	How the communication between systems is managed
Transport	How end-to-end communication is managed (TCP versus UDP)
Network	Addressing and routing (IP)
Data Link	Physical addressing between network (MAC) and system
Physical	Mechanical transmission of data

In this book, we deal with issues at several levels of this list, but not the physical, data link, or network layers. These are transparent to the network game developer. We are more interested by the logical representation of the data. The implementation of the transport and session layers are also usually transparent but included in the networking code supplied by the API developer. For PCs, the network is handled by the operating system, with drivers supplied by the network equipment manufacturer. The code-level interface to the hardware is standardized. For other platforms, the development kit supplied by the platform manufacturer will supply appropriate code used to access the specific hardware.

The presentation layer also deals with various encryption issues that we need to prevent cheating and ensure robustness as well as identify packets and check for out-of-sequence packets. These can also be a good clue as to whether there is some underhanded play going on (see Chapter 8, "Removing the Cheating Elements").

Finally, the application layer deals with how the data is represented by the game. At this level, we are concerned with the various compression and data-decoding standards that we have used for the representation of state information in the game, and so on.

So, we build the data in the application core, then pass it to the code that represents the presentation layer (proprietary). Next we must make a call to the underlying operating system (or equivalent), giving it enough data that it can process the request. Everything else from the session layer down to the physical layer ought to be dealt with by the network library. Part of that responsibility might be in a third-party library, and some will be in the manufacturer's own driver and development kit.

The smallest unit of communication is the socket, and provides the logical bridge between the game world and the real world.

Server-Side Sockets

Generally speaking, these are "listening" sockets. This means that they do nothing until data arrives, at which point the data is decoded, processed, and an answer sent, if one is available. Of course, game servers may also need to broadcast information from time to time, but they can only do this if a connection is available (a TCP stream, or previous UDP connection). Part of the server's responsibilities, therefore, includes processing incoming data and multiplexing to make sure that no incoming updates are missed, whilst not blocking any of the pending communications.

Using a request-response mechanism simplifies things because it allows the client to indicate that it is ready to receive an update, whilst also flagging to the server that it needs to perform some processing. If the game developer chooses to allow broadcast updates over UDP (as opposed to request-response over TCP), then the control algorithms become more difficult to implement. Part of this is being able to match the incoming data with the game state and preparing some kind of response having updated that game state.

There will be times when there is so much going on that this becomes difficult, and the temptation is to allow the clients to present the results of the actions rather than working it out on the server. The networked versions of *Civilization* use this approach. Since the game logic is present in the clients anyway, it seemed logical. However, it does open the doors for cheating, because if the data can be unraveled, fake updates can be passed to the server. These are hard to catch, because the server does not maintain the same level of detail, nor do any of the processing.

So, however hard the implementation seems to be, it is worth making a robust server-side algorithm that can match game states properly *and* simultaneously handle the network connections to prevent the above scenario.

Finally, having worked out the appropriate response, the server has to have a mechanism for sending data—more importantly, sending the right data to the right client, at the right time. This is also something we deal with in this chapter.

Client-Side Sockets

On the face of it, the client side is much easier to appreciate. After all, all it needs to do is open a socket, send the data, and wait for a response. However, it also needs to maintain a hard real-time application and cope with network problems, whilst simultaneously accepting input from the player.

The network-communication programming is therefore the smallest part of the equation, but also has some important challenges of its own to contend with. These include response matching—which is made easier if a strict request-response mechanism is used, and only slightly more tricky if broadcasts are allowed—and inter-client communication.

USING POLLING

Polling is a technique that allows the game client or server to check to see if network data is available while also giving the appearance of continuing to process normal game events. In fact, most game programmers should be well aware of polling techniques, as they are used in real-time systems to prevent them from becoming blocked in a busy waiting loop.

There are many different kinds of polling algorithms, some more sensible and effective than others, and some that have specific significance in game programming. It is important to remember that at the core, any program has to be broken down into a series of sequential steps.

Even if they run in parallel in a multi-threaded, multi-processor environment, the lowest unit of execution is still a step-by-step process. Polling is the mechanism that allows other things to continue, even when the system is also waiting for something to happen in a specific sequence.

Server-Side Polling

In principle, the server is constantly polling to see if it has to do anything. This does not just include the network layer, as it may be polling for a number of reasons:

- Polling for incoming data
- Polling for changes to the game environment
- Polling the status of the system

And polling can happen at many levels—from the system down to the interactions between clients. After all, it is no good for the game server to be able to play out the in-game decisions if the database falls over, so some polling selection needs to take place.

One part of the system should be able to choose (intelligently, we hope) between different things to poll, at a high level. This might need to be weighted according to activity in different areas of the *system* as a whole. Those things can select further children to perform polling for them, eventually winding up at the game-environment level, where polling for specific in-game events takes place. In this model, the game itself is just one part of a much larger system that needs to be maintained in real time. The lowest-level actors in the system then need to poll hardware (for example), connections (such as network sockets), or software event queues. Everything is governed by the need to poll specific areas at specific times.

The polling frequency might change depending on changes in the system as a whole. Intelligently scheduling polling activities and splitting the load according to actual activity is something that might be less important for some games than others. The most complex environment will be clustered servers (such as those used for *Eve Online*), where the communication between servers can be as important as the communication between client and server.

This means, for example, that if the network is not active, the scheduling system might choose to poll it less than another, more urgent, aspect of the system. The polling mechanism itself then needs to be applied across the various system services (i.e., sockets, in this case) to determine whether there is any work to do.

Those, in a nutshell, are the server side–polling challenges. The client side is not nearly so complex an environment.

Client-Side Polling

Client-side polling is really only about the game on the one hand, and the network on the other. Leaving aside the game itself, as the game is beyond this book's scope, we shall concentrate on the polling mechanisms that enable the network and multi-player aspects of the game.

If a request/response architecture that only reacts to the player is used (i.e., a Web game), then a robust polling mechanism might not even be necessary. After all, these tend to be oriented toward the player scheduling the action as opposed to being a flowing gaming experience, due to the nature of the connectionless communications medium. (A side note: AJAX can be used for asynchronous game-environment polling, if that proves to be something that the game developer wants to offer. In addition, games that are played through the browser, such as Adobe Flash games, are grouped together with traditional networked games for the purpose of this discussion, and will definitely need a robust polling mechanism.)

A network game client might poll for one of the following reasons:

- To see if there is a response to a previous request
- To check for game-environment changes
- To check for things like personal messages

At the same time as the network polling is going on (i.e., asking the game server for updates and monitoring the connection for replies), the client also has to continue playing the game. This includes rendering the results of the last round of data that came in in response to polling the server, and polling the player for reactions to that rendering.

So, the scheduling mechanism will also have to deal with the possibility that the client is not polling the game server uniquely—i.e., it will need to poll other, related services in order to manage all the system tasks. These system tasks then process in a sequential fashion, as does the polling mechanism itself.

SEQUENTIAL PROCESSING TECHNIQUES

Programming is often thought of as the act of breaking down a complex problem into a series of steps. Game programming is no different, and computers must have tasks expressed to them in a sequential fashion.

Even if the result is that two processes run side by side, doing different things, because there are two processors available, the decision that spawned those two processes was based on sequential processing, and each process will achieve its goal through sequential processing.

This step-by-step approach means that we cannot poll every possible aspect of the system simultaneously. We can do it very quickly, so that it seems simultaneous, but it will not be simultaneous in the eyes of the processor. And the more activity there is to process, the less simultaneous it becomes, until it is patently obvious that there is a sequence to the way that the services are being polled. For this reason, we need to have a model that predictably polls in a way that makes sure that we never leave something out, and that every aspect of the system gets the attention that it deserves.

Socket Polling Example

As an illustration of polling, we are going to tie it in with the subject of this chapter: network programming. A server, after all, has to have a good way to poll multiple network connections, even if multiplexing is being used.

We will cover the implementation of multiplexing in the next section; for now, you can assume that the result is a list of sockets that have data waiting on them that can be polled to retrieve that data. This actually solves half the problem, as you don't strictly *need* to poll anymore, but just process the data in a logical order.

The basic model that we use is called "round robin," and applies equally to polling as data processing. The model is simplicity itself: Each socket is polled in turn, and data processed in a sequential pattern. Once a socket has been processed, the round-robin model states that control is passed to the next socket, which is then processed, and so on in a circle. When the last socket has been processed, then the processing begins anew with the first socket.

Whether you are polling the sockets for data or processing data that you know is there, the round-robin approach makes sure that

- Each socket gets equal attention.
- None of the sockets are missed.
- Sockets are processed in a predictable fashion.

All of these are good. But the round-robin model has some basic flaws. Chiefly, it is possible to spend an inordinate amount of time processing small amounts of data, while "busier" sockets stack data that never gets processed. This is due to the fact that each socket receives the same level of attention, whilst it might not have the same level of activity. Put another way, assuming that we really are polling in a round-robin fashion, what happens when only one socket has activity, and 99 are dormant?

Clearly, the round-robin approach really only works in a system where all clients require equal attention, which is rarely going to be the case in a gaming system.

Enhancements to Basic Round Robin

By way of an illustration, we are going to look at two possible enhancements to the basic round-robin scheduling model for real-time systems. These are

- Active time slicing
- Most-active polling

Both of these require that we maintain a dynamic list that gives us the order in which we will process the items. This list will change over time as the criteria for activity measurement changes the processing priority and amount of processing power devoted to each item.

Implicitly, the items at the top of the list should receive the most attention, as they are the ones with the most activity. Other than this premise, the processing is identical to the round-robin model described above.

Where the enhancements differ is in how this attention difference is applied. In the case of active time slicing, each item is specifically linked to a number that indicates the number of operations (or pieces of data) that may be processed by the system. More active items get a larger slice of processor time.

The most active–polling enhancement takes a slightly different approach, and simply returns to the most active items more often. This removes the need for an accurate time-slicing algorithm, which can become messy when a thread needs to be interrupted and suspended prematurely.

Both approaches can be fine-tuned to the game's own requirements, and both retain the predictable essence of round-robin scheduling whilst allowing the dynamic flexibility that ensures that the most-deserving items get the most attention.

SOCKET PROGRAMMING

This section puts sockets into practice, and is full of code that can be used in basic socket programming tasks. Of course, the snippets will need to be extended to provide the functionality that is required for a game, but the underlying code provides a solid foundation.

The discussion of socket programming is based on Unix-style calls, but similar functions can be found in most operating systems or development kits. The language that I have chosen for the implementation is C, for speed and portability. C++ variations also exist, and work in much the same way.

Really all that is needed is a handful of functions and data types. These are all well documented in the appropriate programming guides. The following is more of a recipe than it is a guide to every possible network function call available to the programmer. If the recipe is followed, then you will have a working prototype—but as for any good chef, this is only the starting point. You can work with the recipe to make the result your own. Depending on the game being developed, these changes could be quite extensive.

On the client side, the basic steps are as follows:

1. Create a socket of the appropriate type (i.e., TCP or UDP).
2. Bind it to a local socket (for security reasons).
3. Connect to the server (address and protocol).
4. Query the server (using send and receive).
5. Interact with the user (the game).
6. Interrupt to get updates from the server (receive data).
7. Send data to the server (post-interaction).

On the server side, as we have seen, the steps are as follows:

1. Create a socket of the appropriate type (i.e., TCP or UDP).
2. Bind it to a local socket (because that's where the incoming calls will be placed).
3. Listen for incoming calls (from clients).
4. Connect to client calls.
5. Send and receive data whilst updating the game state.
6. Ad infinitum....

Obviously, in both cases, there will be some multiplexing and/or polling required to make sure that, once connected, the correct flow of events for the game system as a whole is maintained. But the network-communication steps are more or less as presented above.

The remainder of this section details the steps required to actually create code that enables the game to follow these processes. We start with a look at the data types provided by most C implementations in the sockets.h library.

Data Types

There are some special data types provided by the sockets.h library that are also duplicated in platform-specific socket application programming interfaces (APIs), such as WinSock. These contain information about the socket type, address, status, and so on. For example, there is a function that returns a socket identifier. In order to create the socket, and hence the identifier that represents it, it is first necessary to tell the network library everything about the nature of the connection.

The standard Unix data type for this information is called sockaddr_in. Other APIs will have something that is identical, or at least very similar. The Unix variant looks like the following:

```
struct sockaddr_in {
    short int          sin_family;    // address family,
                                      //    AF_something
    unsigned short int sin_port;      // the port
    struct in_addr     sin_addr;      // the IP address
    unsigned char      sin_zero[8];   // padding
};
```

Windows also has an equivalent, as do other libraries; they are laid out in more or less the same way.

You will notice that the IP address is inconveniently contained inside a sub-structure called in_addr. The in_addr sub-structure is also defined in a way that makes it hard to access directly. For example, it actually contains one single member, s_addr, which is a four-byte number representing the IP address—not programmer friendly, in the least!

Luckily, however, there are a number of functions that can help us build the data types that we need, so we don't need to become experts in translating numbers between arcane formatting specifications. The first of these functions is used to turn a string of IP numbers (i.e., 12.34.567.89) into an s_addr value, which can be placed in the sockaddr_in structure. The inet_addr function that provides this is used in the following way:

```
struct sockaddr_in my_socket_addr;
my_socket_addr.sin_addr.s_addr = inet_addr(''12.34.567.89'');
```

Again, notice that the actual IP address is assigned to the s_addr member of the sub-structure sin_addr, which is itself a member of the sockaddr_in structure, which is the base type of the variable my_socket_addr. It is all quite confusing at first, but the value of s_addr is the four-byte number mentioned previously.

In addition to the inet_addr function, there are some functions used to ensure that the byte ordering for numerical data types is correct. This is an important point, because the byte ordering (little endian or big endian) is not always the same from one platform to another.

So, the client and the server might run on hardware with different byte ordering, as might the development platform and the deployment platform (i.e., PC versus console). The two byte-ordering schemes are known as "host" and "network." The four worker functions that can be used to translate between them are as follows:

- htons(): host-to-network short
- htonl(): host-to-network long
- ntohs(): network-to-host short
- ntohl(): network-to-host long

So, the line of code from the preceding snippet now becomes:

```
my_socket_addr.sin_addr.s_addr = htonl(inet_addr(''12.34.567.89''));
```

The additional code is presented in bold font. We can also use the hton and ntoh functions with the preceding structure to, for example, set the port number correctly when the socket is created. This is the next step in building the network connection.

Sockets and Ports

When we first start using the network, we need to open a socket that is bound to a specific IP address and port. The actual IP address and port that are used will depend on whether we are looking at the problem from the point of view of the client or server.

If we are writing a server communications layer, we bind the socket to our local IP address. If we are writing from the point of view of a client, we bind to a remote IP address representing the server (or another client). This IP address will probably have been obtained by calling a DNS function to convert a text address (for example www.mygameserver.com) to an IP address.

A socket is created with the `socket()` function, which takes a few key parameters. The first is the protocol family (`PF_INET`), along with the type of socket (`SOCK_STREAM` or `SOCK_DGRAM`). There is also the possibility to select a protocol, but we can set this to 0 to choose it based on the socket type. That way, the function will create a valid socket for stream or datagram communications without us worrying about what the value should be for each one.

The `socket()` call returns a descriptor that can be used to reference the socket. In standard implementations based on the traditional Unix model, this descriptor is just a simple integer number. This clearly limits the amount of available sockets to the size of an `int` at the operating system level.

The next part of the sequence depends on how you want to implement the network layer. It can be bound to a specific port or left unbound. The `bind()` function links the socket descriptor to a specific port. This is the equivalent of the IP:port convention used to connect to MUDs using a Telnet application:

```
telnet xxx.xxx.xxx.xxx:port
```

A socket will be associated with a port in the end, even implicitly, because it's needed at the system level. You should remember that the port that we are talking about here is only *local*, and has no impact on the *remote* port, because that is dealt with when we actually connect to the remote system.

The calls used to bind the two together use the identifier returned by the socket function. What follows is the whole stanza in C code for setting up a socket and associating it with a port (which can then be used for calling or listening for data). Note that for the sake of clarity, we have left out the error-checking code that would normally be present to ensure that the socket has been allocated correctly, that the IP address could be found, and so on.

```
// set up the socket address structure
struct sockaddr_in       my_socket_addr;
my_socket_addr.sin_family = AF_INET;
my_socket_addr.sin_port = htons(PORT_NUMBER); // PORT_NUMBER
#defined somewhere
my_socket_addr.sin_addr.s_addr = inet_addr("12.34.567.89");

// set up the socket itself
int socket_id = socket ( PF_INET, SOCK_STREAM, 0);

// bind the socket, port, and address together
```

```
bind ( socket_id, (struct sockaddr *)&my_socket_addr, sizeof
my_socket_addr);

// put error checking here
```

There is one little trick that can be used with this code. If you want the system to pick a socket and local IP address, then you can specify a 0 for the port and INADDR_ANY as the address. Since these are all local values, it doesn't really matter, unless the *incoming* call will be on a specific port.

Connecting to Remote Machines

On the client side, we can call the connect() function to connect to a remote host, using a socket and socket address set up with code similar to the preceding. For this we need another address information structure, which, this time, will relate to the remote address that we want to call.

So, having set up a socket and stored the identifier, we can now populate another sockaddr_in structure (this time called remote_addr) and call the connect() function:

```
connect ( socket_id, (struct sockaddr *)&remote_addr, sizeof
remote_addr);
```

Note that the connect() call looks rather similar to the bind() call, and that we don't need to call bind(). The remote IP address and port are implicitly bound to the socket by the connect() function.

From the point of view of the client system, that is really all that is necessary. As long as the server has accepted rather than rejected the connect() request, the two machines can exchange data using whatever protocol they have set up (i.e., Telnet, HTTP, FTP, etc.) The server side is a little more involved, because it needs to listen for a connection and then accept the call if it wants to exchange data.

Server-Side Connections

For server-side communications, the bind() operation is not optional because the system will assign a random port if the local port is not bound to the socket. This is a bad idea because the client on the other side will not know the port number to connect to.

Of course, there's no way to tell it, there being no network available, so for server-side network programming, the bind() call becomes extremely important. However, since we are going to be listening on the socket, the IP address can just be set to the local host.

So, we use the same code as before to set up the socket and bind it locally (probably using a known value for sin_port, and INADDR_ANY to pick up the local IP address) before calling the listen function, thus:

```
listen ( socket_id, 10 );
```

The value 10 in this case specifies that we are willing to let 10 calls queue up before we deal with them (by calling the accept() function). This is a reasonable number, and the 11th caller will be automatically rejected to keep the queue clean.

So far, so good. However, a point to remember is that when the program accepts the call, the call will be assigned a new socket ID. This means that the current one can be left in place, listening for more incoming calls. This behavior is the cornerstone for the multiplexing system.

For each client that connects on the port, a new socket is allocated to allow communication with the client. Because we're expecting more than one client connecting, we also need to make sure that we have enough places in memory for as many socket identifiers as the game server is willing and able to deal with.

In addition, the accept() call is a blocking call. In other words, it doesn't return if there's nothing to talk to, and the program will sleep until a connection to accept comes along. This means that there is no point blindly calling accept() as the first operation of the server, because it runs the risk of also being the last.

Luckily, there is another useful multiplexing function, select(), that lets us get around this by monitoring sockets that we have set up to receive connections. The select() call operates on sets of sockets.

Generally speaking, there are three kinds of sets defined in the network library:

- Sets of sockets that we read from
- Sets that we write to
- Exception sets

Since the client is in charge, we usually have a use for the first set only. In addition, just because the socket set is identified as one that we read from, it doesn't mean that we cannot write to it. We can, but the call to select() will return a positive value for only those sockets that have data ready to be read from.

The way the select() function works is that the server software is responsible for managing a master set of current sockets. These are then copied to a set that can be passed to select(), which then removes those that are not ready to be read from. The resulting set can then be processed in a round-robin (or an enhanced variation) fashion.

The master set will always contain the so-called listener (the socket that we give to the listen() function). If there is a new connection to deal with, the master socket will still be in the copied set after we have called the select() function. Naturally, it is best to process the listener socket first, even before the rest are dealt with, as pending connections should be given priority to avoid them stacking up on the queue.

The following code example assumes that we set up the listener socket as per the previous code samples, and then just want to check for incoming connections in an appropriate fashion:

```
// listening_socket is an int, and has been created with a call
to socket()
listen( listening_socket, 10); // wait for a connection
// set up the master socket set
fd_set master_socket_set;
FD_ZERO(&master_socket_set); // remove any existing sockets
FD_SET( listening_socket, &master_socket_set ); //put the
listener in the set
max_socket_id = listening_socket; // need to track the biggest id
for select()

// Off we go!
while (1) {
  // copy the master list and call select
  fd_set tmp_socket_set = master_socket_set;
  select ( max_socket_id+1, &tmp_socket_set, NULL, NULL, NULL);
  // check to see if there are any "new" connections
  if (FD_ISSET (listening_socket, &tmp_socket_set)) // is it set?
  {
    // allocate a new socket id
    struct sockaddr_in remote_socket_addr;
    socklen_t addrlen = sizeof(remote_socket_addr);

    // accept the connection
    int new_socket = accept ( listening_socket,
  (struct sockaddr *)&remote_socket_addr, &addrlen);
    FD_SET(new_socket, &master_socket_set); // add it to the
master set
    if (new_socket > max_socket_id)
      max_socket_id = new_socket; // update the max
  } else { // there is no new connection on the listener
    // check the other sockets in a round-robin fashion
    for ( i = listening_socket+1; i <= max_socket_id; i++) {
      if (FD_ISSET(i, &tmp_socket_set)) // is there any data?
      {
```

```
            // read the data from the socket
        }
      }
    }
  }
```

In the `for` loop that represents the round-robin processing of the sockets, we start from the lowest identifier and then proceed to the highest identifier that has been present in the system. It would also be worth keeping better track of the socket identifiers so that only possible ones are tested. In the preceding code, a lower-order socket, once closed, would still be tested by the `for` loop.

The `NULL` values in the `select()` call represent sets for write and exception sockets and a timeout value, none of which we need in this simple example. The `FD_` macros used are provided by the socket library for dealing with sets of sockets and the `select()` function.

The ones used here are as follows:

- `FD_ZERO`: Remove all sockets from the set.
- `FD_SET`: Set the socket in the set.
- `FD_ISSET`: Test to see if a socket is set in the set.

We also introduced the `accept()` function that allows the client to establish the socket prior to allowing the client to send its data. As you can see, it also provides for capturing the remote address, so that the connection can be terminated if checking is being done on this level for security reasons.

Finally, the one part that we have not put in the above is the code to read data from the socket that we now know (through the `select()` function) has data waiting. Now that we can set up connections, we should look at data-transfer functions.

Sending and Receiving Data

On the client side, we assume that the following tasks have already been carried out:

- Resolve the host to an IP address.
- Open a socket (on a specific port).
- Wait for the acknowledgement that the socket is open.

At this point, the server is listening and ready to receive data from the client. The first burst of data ought to be from the client to identify itself to the server. After this, assuming that the credentials are correct, the game dialog can begin.

Data is sent down a socket with the send() function. This acts rather like file handling, and the function takes a socket identifier (descriptor) as its first parameter and then a pointer to the data, the length, and some flags. To use these flags, it is necessary to look up the definition in the platform's online guide (man page, or documentation provided in a Windows help file). In the following examples, we shall ignore them, and concentrate on making sure that the data is correctly encapsulated.

The easiest example is sending character data. This is no more extravagant than the following:

```
char szData [1024];
strcpy(szData,''Hello TCP/IP'');
send ( sock_id, szData, strlen(szData), 0);
```

The send() function also returns the number of bytes sent. Clearly, this can be less than the actual number that the application needs to send, due to packet-size limitations. It is up to the programmer to send the rest of the data at some point in the future; if the packet length is set to 128 bytes, and there are 270 bytes to be sent, then three attempts will need to be made before all the data is transmitted.

Receiving data is no more complex. The recv() function, which takes the same parameters as send() and returns the number of bytes received, is used. The value of 0 is reserved for cases where the other side has closed the connection. A negative value is used to indicate an error.

On the server side, the server can do nothing until the client or clients connect and identify themselves. At this point, it can send a first update, and wait for further instructions thereafter. The same send() and recv() functions are used to do so.

Any data can be sent, be it character based or binary. However, there is a small problem with sending data such as integers *as integers*. Those who regularly deal with binary files on heterogeneous platforms will attest to this; it is worth taking a small detour here to examine the issue.

We shall assume that you are writing a game that distributes a level file across Unix (Mips/Alpha based) and Windows (Intel based) platforms. Furthermore, let us assume that these level files are created on the Windows platform. To identify blocks of data (records), you decided to use a length indicator of two bytes (classic integer), which will tell the reading application how many bytes are in the block, or record. This is sometimes known as the "record-length indicator."

The following is a fairly simple C rendition of a possible function to write the data to a file, minus the error checking for clarity:

```
void WriteRecord( char * szRecordData, FILE * hFile )
{
  int nLength = strlen(szRecordData);
  fwrite ( &nLength, sizeof(int), 1, hFile); // write the length
     indicator
  fwrite ( szRecordData, sizeof(char), nLength, hFile); // write
     the data
}
```

Now, if you were to run the code on Intel and Motorola architectures, the resulting file would look very different. This is because the byte ordering is different on these two architectures. We saw this briefly above when dealing with IP addresses and port numbers: The network and host architectures may be different.

This means that, in binary, 128 bytes (for example) is represented as the following:

00 80   Intel architecture
80 00   Motorola architecture

So, if you write out the value 00 80 in hexadecimal on the Intel platform and read it in blindly, using the fread() function, on the Motorola platform, then the result will be incorrect. In fact, it will be an integer with the value 32,768, because Motorola platforms expect the least significant byte to arrive first.

Typically, we have a lot of control over level files and where they end up. This might not be the case with network architectures because of the fact that we are likely to try to use a very powerful server, possibly running a different byte-ordering architecture, and we might not know the architectures of all the clients.

Using a similar approach as above, the following might be possible, to stream level data to a client:

```
// THE FOLLOWING IS A BAD IDEA
void SendRecord( char * szRecordData, int nSocket_ID )
{
  int nLength = strlen(szRecordData);
  send ( nSocket_ID, &nLength, sizeof(int), 0 ); // send the
     data length
  send ( nSocket_ID, szRecordData, nLength, 0); // send the data
}
```

This code will only ever work when both systems use the same byte ordering. Luckily, there are many solutions to work around the problem.

You should remember that whenever data is sent as binary information, such as `int` values, this problem will occur. It is much better, if marginally less efficient, to send information as single bytes and do the byte ordering in code, either using the `ntohs` or `ntohl` (and `htons`/`htonl`) functions or through a custom solution.

To send the number 128 using a custom solution, having chosen to use a two-byte scheme, the application would send 00 and then 80 (hexadecimal representation), explicitly in that order. To send a value of 256, the application would then send 01 followed by 00; the recipient would know that it should count the 255 in the least significant byte, add it to the 01, then add the 00 of the least significant byte—the value 00 FF, of course, being equal to 255. In this way, it is possible to replace any byte ordering that is implicit by platform with an explicit one.

There is another option: to tell the receiving system what byte ordering is in use by sending a character 1 or 0. The end result is the same. The receiving system still needs to compensate for an eventual mismatch, so it is probably better just to send explicitly byte by byte (or at least pack the data into a data string, and send the whole lot at once) or use the built-in byte-ordering functions.

Datagram Socket Send/Receive

All of the above relates to stream sockets, which are permanently connected. Datagram sockets work in a slightly different way, and have some functions that specifically support their unconnected nature.

You will remember that datagram sockets (`AF_DGRAM`) are not connected in the same way as the sockets we've been looking at so far. Each packet of data that we want to send has to have an address specified as part of the stanza, and each packet is sent independently of the others.

The way to do this is just to create a local socket in the usual manner, and then populate *another* `struct sockaddr` to contain the destination address, which is passed to a variation of the `send()` function, called `sendto()`, as follows:

```
sendto ( nSocket_ID, szRecordData, nLength, 0,
    &sock_addr_to, sizeof(*sock_addr_to));
```

The last parameter is just the length of the `sockaddr` structure. Putting it in this way makes the code a bit more portable, as we explicitly measure the structure in the function call. The `sendto()` returns an integer that indicates the result, just like the `send()` function.

The companion function to `sendto()` is `recvfrom()`, which is the exact opposite and takes the same parameters. It is used in the opposite direction, and is a blocking call.

If all of this seems a bit tricky, remember that you can still use a datagram socket in a connected way by specifying connect() and using send() and recv() as normal, and specifying _DGRAM instead of _STREAM in the various address and socket-setup structures. However, this will make the socket a connected datagram socket. Any advantages that were being exploited by using a disconnected socket are therefore lost.

Closing the Socket

Once the initial data exchange has been completed, the application can use the shutdown() function to specify that traffic in one direction is no longer allowed. This can be useful in some circumstances, and the following possibilities are offered:

```
shutdown ( nSocket_ID, 0 ); // receives no longer allowed
shutdown ( nSocket_ID, 1 ); // sends no longer allowed
shutdown ( nSocket_ID, 0 ); // sends/receives no longer allowed
```

The last option should be used only if no traffic may be exchanged at all, but the system still needs to reserve the connection. Once the system knows that it no longer needs the nSocket_ID, it can call the close() function (or, on Windows, using WinSock, closesocket()). The close() function takes the socket descriptor, as in:

```
close ( nSocket_ID );
```

Now that we have examined all the worker functions, it is time to look at how these get put together in some examples of how the various snippets can be integrated.

Client Example

The first example is a function to open a socket to a named host on a specific port. We assume that the server is a real name (like www.mygameserver. com), and therefore need to use gethostbyname() to look up the IP address.

This step can be omitted if the game infrastructure uses only a static IP address. This aside, the code is as follows:

```
// returns a socket descriptor, or an error code
int OpenSocket ( char * szHostName, int nPort )
{
  struct hostent *host_entry; // host entry for the lookup
  struct sockaddr_in remote_socket_addr;
  int nSocket_ID; // we'll return this, hopefully
```

```
// look up the IP address
host_entry = gethostbyname( szHostName );
if ( host_entry == NULL ) return -1; // doesn't exist?
// open a socket
nSocket_ID = socket ( PF_INET, SOCK_STREAM, 0 );
if ( nSocket_ID == -1 ) return -2; // can't get a local socket
// create the remote address structure
remote_socket_addr.sin_family = AF_INET;
remote_socket_addr.sin_port = nPort;
// get the IP address that we looked up
remote_socket_addr.sin_addr = *((struct in_addr *)host_entry-
    >h_addr);
// zero out the padding
memset(remote_socket_addr.sin_zero, '\0',
      sizeof(remote_socket_addr.sin_zero));
// connect the socket to the address
if (connect ( nSocket_ID, (struct sockaddr
    *)&remote_socket_addr,
      sizeof(remote_socket_addr)) == -1)
{
  // we don't need the socket anymore
  close ( nSocket_ID );
  return -3; // connect failed
}
// finally, return the socket descriptor
return nSocket_ID;
}
```

You will also note that we have put in some very basic error checking to make sure that everything is correctly assigned and that all the various pieces are in place before returning the socket descriptor.

Once the socket is open, we might want to send a status request and then wait for updated information. It is assumed that the game is going to unfold using a request-response model. You should be aware that there are many other possibilities, however—for example, the server might want to pre-empt by broadcasting information. In addition, some level of probing might still be needed to ensure that all clients are still connected. In our model, however, we assume that this is dealt with elsewhere.

In addition, we are going to use a simple seeded random-number generator to try to add a little security. This is not very robust, and can be cracked, but it shows the principle of encapsulating sensitive data in an encoding scheme. The complete function is as follows:

```
int SendRequest ( int nRequest, int nSocket_ID )
{
  int nSeed;
  // pick a seed at random...
  srand(time(null));
  nSeed = (int) rand();
  // use the seed to encode the request
  int nEncodedRequest = nRequest;
  srand(nSeed);
  nEncodedRequest += rand() % 1000; // keep them numbers low
  // build the data string
  char szData [1024];
  sprintf( szData, ''%d|%d'', nSeed, nEncodedRequest );
  // finally, send...
  int nBytesLeft = strlen (nEncodedRequest);
  int nSentSoFar = 0;
  do {
    int nSent = send ( nSocket_ID, szData+nSentSoFar, nBytesLeft, 0 );
    if ( nSent == -1 ) return -1; // something went wrong!
    nBytesLeft -= nSent;
  } while ( nBytesLeft > 0 );
}
```

The kicker here is that the seed is sent as plain text, along with the encoded request, which makes it easy to crack if the encoding mechanism is known. This makes it much less secure than other possibilities mentioned in Chapter 8.

Also, you will notice that we've put in a little bit of code to make sure that all the data gets sent. A real implementation would probably put this in its own SendAll() function so that it could be reused across other data-sending functions.

Now that we can open a socket to an address and send a request, the next thing we need to be able to do is receive the response, decode it, and return the result. We assume that this result is an integer in this case:

```
int ReceiveResponse ( int nSocket_ID )
{
  char szData[1024];
  int nReceived = recv ( nSocket_ID, szData, 1023, 0 );
  if ( nReceived == 0 ) return 0; // nothing to report
  // get the seed, using strtok, and then the data
  int nSeed, nEncodedResponse;
  char * tok = strtok( szData, ''|'' );
  nSeed = atoi ( tok ); // we need error checking here!!
```

```
    tok = strtok( NULL, ''|'' );
    nEncodedResponse = atoi ( tok ); // we need error checking here!!
    // decode
    srand( nSeed );
    return nEncodedResponse % (rand() % 1000);
}
```

For the sake of simplicity, this code merely grabs a single blob of data. A real-world application will probably need to encapsulate that data such that there is a start and end tag that lets us know when all the data is received. Real-world data exchanges usually extend over several blobs of game-related data.

Server Example

In a sense, the server is just the partner to the client, which has to be able to read the seed, determine the request, and provide the response. For these basic tasks, the preceding code can be re-used, but there are also some additional things that the server needs to be able to do—mainly because it is talking to multiple clients, whereas each client typically only communicates with a single server.

So, all of the preceding code works for the basic communication, but what about a solution for the multiple-client problem? We have seen one, using the select() function that lets us know when there is data pending that needs to be dealt with, but there are many variations on the basic theme, which we shall now put into code.

Selecting Sources

Sometimes it is necessary for the server to be able to "listen" selectively; this may be because it is more efficient to concentrate scheduling on busy connections as per the augmented round robin discussed previously, or maybe for other reasons.

The select() function only tells us, based on a set of sockets, which ones have data waiting to be read. It doesn't tell us which have recently been busy. For example, if a client is doing nothing but monitoring the server, then this is probably going to be dealt with less often than some of the connections to clients involved in (for example) a battle or some other interaction. However, the call to select() reveals that there are multiple connections, and all have data waiting—so what should the server do? There are several solutions to this conundrum.

Randomly Process Sockets

The first is the easiest, and could be seen as the fairest way to try to give as much attention to the sockets as possible. It is also a simple illustration of how to selectively listen to specific sockets upon demand. The approach just requires that we select one of the sockets at random, test to see if it has data, and if it does, process that data:

```
while (1) {
  select ( nMaxSocket+1, &socket_set, NULL, NULL, NULL) // test
      all sockets
  // omitted for brevity :
  //   CHECK THE LISTENER FIRST FOR NEW CONNECTIONS
  // pick one
  int nSocket = rand() % nMaxSocket;
  if (FD_ISSET(nSocket, &socket_set))
  {
    // process the data on nSocket
  }
}
```

We have left out the part of the code where the listener is interrogated for new connections. There are some other issues with this code, too, but it is a *possible* way to proceed. If we know that all connections have equal weight, then it is a fair distribution of processor time. Sometimes, however, we want to do it a bit differently.

Keep an Activity Log

An activity log can be used to specifically weight the application's attention to sockets that have a high activity level. This activity could be measured on a volume or quality basis (some actions have a higher activity quotient than others, regardless of the number of requests made). The only issue is that it also requires that we continually sort the list to be accurate—using, for example the C qsort() function. If this is an acceptable overhead, then the code is really quite simple.

First, we need to put the socket identifiers in an array allocated using the malloc() function. Each entry needs a place for the descriptor and a value that indicates how active it has been relative to the system behavior. This might look something like the following:

```
struct ACTIVITY_ENTRY
{
  int nSocket_ID;
  int nActivityLevel;
};
```

Following this, we need a function to compare two entries so that they can be sorted using the C qsort() function. This code might be akin to the following:

```
int CompareActivity ( struct ACTIVITY_ENTRY sA, struct
     ACTIVITY_ENTRY sB )
{
  if ( sA.nActivityLevel < sB.nActivityLevel ) return -1;
  if ( sA.nActivityLevel > sB.nActivityLevel ) return 1;
  return 0; // they must be equal, in this case
}
```

With the comparison function and data structure in hand, we have the ability to manipulate and sort a list of socket descriptors.

To prevent processor hogging, we also probably need a system to reduce the activity counter as well as increase it. Otherwise, a very busy process (client) will force the system into a loop, only ever dealing with one or two clients roundly ignoring and the rest.

One approach would be to give more attention to high– transaction volume clients by visiting them once for every cycle. So, if there are 100 sockets open, the busiest one gets visited 99 times for every cycle, whereas the middle-ranking ones get visited 49 times, and the end one gets visited just once.

Of course, this can be adjusted according to data volumes and speed of play, but the principle remains the same: We attach more weight and give more attention to those sockets producing most of the interaction. If they have no data left to process, of course, their place in the queue is relinquished, and their activity count reduced accordingly. These principles, when implemented, ought to provide a reasonably well distributed attention model.

Sequentially Process Sockets

The opposite end of the spectrum is to use the list to process sockets sequentially, from top to bottom, having either sorted them at random (for some attempt at attention fairness) or chosen some other criteria.

There is not much else to say about this approach; it is really just mentioned here for completeness sake. The underlying algorithm is just like the FD_ISSET one above, except that the application will need to perform a select() to update the socket set and *then* loop through the socket pool (array), checking FD_ISSET to see if there's any work to do, in a sequential fashion.

One important thing to note with using the array is that the programmer is also responsible for making sure that any sockets that are closed are removed from the array, as well as from the master socket set.

The other side to this is that any new sockets are added (by checking the listener socket, usually socket 0 in the set) both to the master set *and* the array. The game developer has to decide whether the overhead and additional complexity is balanced by the benefits that it brings.

Remember that each layer of network complexity that is added takes away from some other aspect of the system. Sometimes, the additional overhead is just not worth the extra effort.

Use Timeouts and Interrupts

Finally, any of the above can be combined with a system of timeouts or interrupts. A "timeout" occurs when something that has been happening for a while seems to be taking too long, and the system decides to do something else. The option then remains to see if the process can be completed at a later date. On the other hand, an "interrupt" occurs when something happens that has to be dealt with immediately and cannot wait for the next time slice to be allocated. Balancing time in this way is a key function of any hard real-time system (such as aircraft-control systems or a video game), and this complexity is increased due to the multi-user nature of the gaming environment.

There are many potential ways to implement timeouts, but all of them rely on being able to do two things:

- Time the current process that has the system's attention.
- Use criteria to gauge whether to continue processing once the pre-allocated time slice has come to and end.

This technique of time slicing is also very common in real-time systems, and allows a process to have a certain amount of time allocated for processing. As we have already mentioned, there could be fixed time slices or there could be variable ones used by the system.

For example, we might decide to combine the time slice with the socket processing described above such that more active sockets get bigger time slices in which their status is checked several times. If they have no data, their time slice could be ended prematurely, and control returned to the system. This could provide a better solution than simply increasing the frequency by which their sockets are checked.

An interrupt-based system requires more complex programming because every piece of data is initially given the same weight. Subsequently, each socket gets processed by some kind of scheduling daemon in a round-robin fashion until something happens that interrupts the current task. Polling is then used to determine the order by which the sockets will be processed, and might necessitate a system whereby each incoming request for attention requires a response from the server to tell the client that it can go ahead.

Potentially, this adds yet another piece of data to the network exchange. Again, this could have a negative impact on performance. However, it would mean that the most urgent of the requests can be dealt with first, so even a low-activity client can get attention fast if something happens to it that requires immediate attention.

Finally, you should not forget that the server system is in complete control, and has the possibility to equate player data with their network connections. The two pieces of information can be used together to make sure that the socket reading and system updates get done in a way that is best for everyone.

Buffers

One other aspect of server-side programming is that effective network communication will often require the use of buffers. The assumption is that the bottleneck is not the processor, but the network itself. A "buffer" is just a place where information that can be gathered together quickly is stored before it is processed by a more lengthy operation—i.e., a network write (send). Compared to processing speeds and data-transfer rates around a computer system, a network is slow, and buffering is supposed to make sure that it is never the weak link.

To try to help smooth out the latency effects of the network, predictive buffers can also be used to queue up data in advance of receiving confirmation of the prediction. This is helpful, for example, when processing movement commands for an in-game entity that is moving in a direction that is unlikely to diverge. Using prediction and buffers together in this way can help make communication more efficient.

Sessions

Finally, sessions are a very important part of network-game programming for Web games and other varieties of game models. They are the responsibility of the server, which is why they are mentioned here.

Sessions are required to help prevent hacking and cheating, and to protect the player's own account. They might not offer complete protection against all possible attacks, but they do go some way to making attacks more difficult.

The easiest way to demonstrate an unsecure way to test sessions using a Web environment is as follows:

- Have a database that contains the player's username and password, as well as a session identifier, which is set to NULL in case the player is not logged in.

- Upon login, a session identifier is generated and passed back to the Web client as a hidden area in a form (login via username/password by query, *not* by comparing in script).
- The same form also contains the player's own ID, and is used whenever a request is made of the system.
- When the player logs out, the session ID is cancelled (set to NULL).

If the player then tries to perform an action, the session identifier is passed to the system, which validates it against the database. If it fails (as it will if the player is not logged in), then the player is prompted to log in again.

This is the basic session-handling model, and there are many variations. The key points to remember are that the database should never be directly queried for the password, and that these passwords should, wherever possible, be encrypted. Additional protection can then be provided by using a timer to time out sessions, and generating different session identifiers per request/response pair. The underlying mechanism remains the same, however.

OPEN-SOURCE CODE LIBRARIES

The last section of this chapter is designed to encourage you to consider using open-source solutions in your projects. There is simply no need to re-invent the wheel for major platforms where open source is prevalent, and there are many benefits of using the programming skills of others to enhance one's own creations.

Even the Torque engine (not quite open source, but still a very cheap option) supports cutting-edge consoles and takes much of the pain out of network programming. Of course, the game still needs to be correctly designed and implemented, but these frameworks make it much easier.

In addition, commercial frameworks like XNA (from Microsoft) make life even easier, as they encapsulate much of the functionality required and hide the vagaries of the underlying platform from the developer. They do, however, limit the platform to those supported by the framework technology.

Of course, for PCs running Windows and Linux, it is usually possible to get open-source code to run all the parts of the network-game model, including

- Client TCP/IP libraries
- Server TCP/IP libraries
- Full server implementations

So where does one start?

MUD Libraries

Even if you have no interest in MUD development per se, open-source MUD code is worth examining as it touches on all the basic principles of a good network-game design:

- Messaging system: inter-player communication
- User management: username/password and access rights
- Persistent universe: with objects and locations
- Location-driven architecture: with ownership and locations

The point of this list is that even if a MUD is technically text only, if you exchange "data" for "text," quite a robust MMORPG can be built on these very solid foundations. They are well understood, and have been refined over time to take advantage of many different extensions to platform technology.

What's more, you can add data to the text and come up with a hybrid that can be played over the Internet, over the Web, or using some kind of proprietary client without changing the core on the server. The result, if designed correctly, will still allow most, if not all, of the features intended by the initial design.

With this in mind, let's look at each one in more detail.

Messaging System

A messaging system is core to many online games. For example, at the core of a MUD is usually a very robust chat-style communication layer capable of

- Receiving incoming messages
- Posting messages privately
- Posting messages to everyone
- Etc.

This is exactly what is needed if a game is being created, and the heart of the messaging system could be reused in other communication environments to create different kinds of games. The key is how the result of each request is displayed on the screen.

Under the hood, it is just text flying around, and the representation is what will differentiate a MUD from an MMORPG, as well as things like hit points, possessions, etc. that are key to role-playing games in general.

There are even MUDs (MUCKs, MUSHes and MOOs) that can offer a graphical front-end and that interpret the data that is exchanged in the messaging system in a certain way. Those of you who are familiar with MUDs will also remember that one had to make a choice before using the system between teletype (vt100) terminals and ANSI terminals. This was because even in the early- to mid-1990s, the Internet was robust enough to allow MUD clients to display colored text or plain black and white. Moving from this to graphics is just a small step in terms of the model used to transport the data.

As long as the communications layer and messaging system is robust, it can be reused (the techniques, at least, if not the source code itself). It is worth pointing those of you who want to copy code chunks from open-source projects to the upcoming section on licensing.

User Management

Each user exists in his or her own piece of the game environment—meaning that there has to be some user management beyond the afore-mentioned messaging system. This goes alongside the mechanisms for storing user data, as well as the session handling that allows for logging in and out. Of course, there is also the personalization of each user, and other aspects that are common to all kinds of online games. Again, open-source solutions can be very instructive in the implementation of these aspects of network game programming.

Persistent-Environment and Location-Driven Architecture

MUDs also have a game environment that contains pieces that are persistent. This means that they continue to exist even when there is nobody logged in, and that they are predictably in the place that the player left them unless someone else has moved them. Hand in hand with this, the messaging system, and user management is the fact that the MUD is built on a location-driven architecture. This is very useful in creating network games, which tend also to be built around a sense of location.

Action Games

Networking code is also part of some major games that have been released into open source (*Quake*, for example). Much of the issues that they had to deal with when the first networked version was released are still prevalent today.

The code might not be cutting edge in terms of graphics, but the network communications haven't changed that much. The problems of latency, jitter, and lag still exist, and the solutions are largely the same. There might be some advances in intelligent prediction (*Street Fighter IV*, for example, uses combat prediction), but many of the solutions remain the same.

Much can be learned from these pieces of code that are more or less implementations of techniques that have grown up from action games. It is also fair to say that most MMORPGs, including ones like *Second Life*, are less graphically accomplished than games like *Eve Online* or *Unreal Tournament*. It is almost like they feel they don't need it—the point is that an online game can be great fun without the high-end graphics.

However, in the same way that a single-player non-networked game with networking bolted on is not a network game, a great MUD with a terrible front-end will not win any fans beyond a hard-core set who believe in the environment even without the bells, whistles, and high-realism graphics.

Bearing these thoughts in mind, there are still some great lessons to be learned from using the source.

Level/Map Management

Action games, more than most, seem to be delivered as maps, or levels. You might compare this approach with a MUD, where the game environment is delivered as it is encountered, usually as text snippets. It is a question of the volume of data that needs to be exchanged in order to describe the game environment.

Clearly, given the required quality of action game environment rendering, it is not usually possible to stream *everything* because too much data would be required to render the screen. However, there may be a happy halfway house such as that used in other environments, based on the placement of predefined and downloadable objects. In fact, this could even be based on a system like Google Earth, where content is refined as the viewer zooms in. Anything that can help to reduce the in-flight data will make this more achievable, including downloadable asset packs.

At the end of the day, however, nothing beats a level file, even if it does have to be downloaded before the player can get into the game. Action games use them very well, and much can be learned from their approach.

One reason that level files are so big and complex is that there is usually a very competent 3D engine under the hood that can deal with very complex environments.

On the network side, these games show exactly how to maintain congruence between the map and the clients by exchanging data. Again, these are valuable lessons that the budding network game developer will need to learn to be successful.

Attention-Based Updates

In addition to the rendering aspect, action games need some way to maintain the data-transfer rate at times when many clients might be involved in some in-game action. In Chapter 7, "Improving Network Communications," we saw some of the causes of lag and jitter, as well as how to eliminate them. Using attention-based updates is one way to try to get the optimum performance from the system. The key is that those items that have the attention of the player must be updated first, and that things that do not can be rendered later, differently, or not at all, depending on the quality of the network connections.

Advanced Rendering

Some aspects of the rendering system for network games can get quite advanced, especially since these games usually need to be more adaptive than a locally played version of the game. These include, for example, line-of-sight rendering based on downloaded information from the game server. This is important because these may actually not even include details beyond the local area. For security reasons, it is better only to deliver to the client the data that it needs to prevent possibly rendering things that ought to remain hidden. This will serve to reduce network traffic, but also will increase server-side processing, which must be borne in mind when deciding how rendering details will be exchanged with clients.

Split Network Models

Finally, many action and strategy games also use a network model that splits the responsibility between clients and the server. This results in farming out work, which can also help increase overall system efficiency.

There is a risk, of course, associated with this. Part of the problem is that if the decision making is farmed out to the client, and a hacker is sitting on the other side of the man-machine interface, then he or she may choose to interfere with the local decision-making process. The result is passing data back to the server that is inherently wrong. Worse than this is the interception of data, so that it can be modified before it is returned to the server, thereby giving a false view of the game environment.

There are plenty of ways that this can be countered, but the question of efficiency still remains to be answered. After all the cross checking, encryption, error correction, and processing, the solution still has to be more efficient than processing everything on the server in order for it to be worthwhile. Sadly, we might not know this until it is too late: during implementation.

Web Gaming

As you are reading this, there are probably more open-source Web-gaming projects to consult than any other kind because the Web is a cheap and easy platform to develop for. The accessibility, as well as the low expense of setting up a virtual server, makes it a great starting point for many projects.

Under the hood, Web games are great because they rely on existing networking standards for communication, display, and update, and offer a split-responsibility scripting model. These key points make it a very attractive platform to develop for.

The split-scripting model means that the client and server can both be scripted to the point that the workload can be distributed between them. This can be true for game-logic as well as rendering and data-exchange scripting.

Ultimately, this can mean that there is a lot of logic in the client. As long as this does not affect gameplay, and is only used to render the effect of that gameplay to the players, then there will be no problem in adopting this model.

Perhaps the most attractive feature of Web-game programming is that the network communication is hidden behind the existing platform architecture of the World Wide Web. In addition, open-source solutions exist for practically every aspect, from user management to content delivery and secure session management. This leaves the programmer free to concentrate on implementing the best possible game, given the limitations imposed by the Web-page environment.

FINAL THOUGHTS

This chapter has dealt with three very important areas:

- The theory of network communication
- Implementing network communication
- The practice of network communication

Hopefully, it has given you enough ammunition to create something special in the networked-game arena. There is certainly enough for any aspiring network-game developer to cut his or her teeth, even if he or she does not have the skills to make the next *Burnout: Paradise* or *Halo 3*.

However fast networks become, and however reliable connections appear, there are several areas of network programming that will always remain more or less the same:

- There will be more content than bandwidth.
- Client systems will be unpredictable.
- Hackers, cheaters, and bots are a fact of life.

People who design games will be constantly surprised when they are told that the idea they have will cause unnecessary data exchange that cannot be catered to with current networking technology. By the same token, they will be surprised at the amount of time that programmers claim the system needs to spend error checking and correcting. That is processing time that could be used for other things, and they're right to be a little put out, but it is vital to making sure that every player gets a consistent experience. One thing that everyone should be able to agree on, though, is the necessity to try to identify and mitigate the effects of hackers, cheaters, and those who seek to use bots to further their in-game career.

Some of this awareness can tie in with the algorithms used to counter the unpredictability of client systems. The key here is that the algorithms we use for tracking in-game activity in the hope that we can optimize the scheduling give us a hook into the data that is being exchanged. If we can spy on that data, we can analyze it and try to ensure that nothing under-handed is going on.

A simple example might be that a developer decides to use an opti-mized algorithm for monitoring sockets for incoming data that takes account of their activity. He then analyzes, in real time, the activity levels and decides that, above a given threshold, he will start to take interest in sockets representing clients with an unusually high activity level. He can then single them out for further analysis, such as shot accuracy, and other giveaway signals that someone is using a proxy system to play the game (see Chapter 8 for a discussion of proxy systems). Hopefully, nine times out of 10, the game will catch and penalize the culprit. Although the end decision rests with the developer, it is worthwhile to strike a bal-ance between overzealous rat-catching and letting people get on with it.

Finally, never underestimate the workload that programming the network layer requires. Yes, there is one chapter out of 10 in this book dedicated to programming, but that is not a reflection of the amount of resources a developer must dedicate to it.

Testing is important, too—not just *more* testing, but *smarter* testing, which will inevitably mean that the network layer has to be tested as it is developed. This means that, like the AI, which goes hand in hand with network programming and testing in a multiplayer environment, it can never be left until the last minute as a bolt-on for a single-player game. The two models are just too different. A multi-player game has to be so from the ground up.

REFERENCES

[FRI01] "The Effect of Latency and Network Limitations on MMORPGs." Tobias Fritsch, Hartmut Ritter, and Jochen Schiller (Freie Universität Berlin), *NetGames '05*, October 10–11 2005, Hawthorne, New York, USA.

INDEX

A

accept( ) function, 281, 283

accessibility, 144

action games, 297–299

action-event chains, 124

active time slicing, 275

activity logs, 291–292

activity threshold model, 123

adaptive pipeline (AP) proto-col, 220

Adobe Flash platform, 52

advanced information pack-ages, 210

advanced rendering, 299

advertising, 155

advertising networks, 133–135

Age of Empire games, 49

AI. *See* artificial intelligence (AI)

AIR technology, 69

AJAX. *See* Asynchronous JavaScript And XML (AJAX)

algorithms, time-slicing, 172

alpha testing, 239–240, 261–262

alternate reality games, 28, 50, 53

ANSI screen control, 37

AP protocol. *See* adaptive pipeline (AP) protocol

API. *See* application programming interface (API)

applets, 68–69

application layer, 270

application programming interface (API), 72, 78

application software, 67–68

arcade games

See also real-time action games

action, 142–143

data exchange, 45–47

defined, 28

gaming models, 43–44

security, 44–45

arcade-style combat, 129

artifact prediction, 185

artifact-by-artifact updates, 180

artificial intelligence (AI)

code re-use in testing, 261–262

predictions, 185

simulated play testing, 233

artificially constricted games, 97

asset synchronization, 39, 43–44

Asynchronous JavaScript And XML (AJAX), 68

attention-based updates, 298–299

augmentation, 196, 212–214

authoritative clients, 212, 214

authorization data, 192

auto-aim proxies, 216

auto fire–style buttons, 210

auto-recovery, 192

automated detection approaches, 202

automated playing, 37, 41, 202, 210, 215–216

automated software packages, 199